Greenhill Books

Guns of the Elite Forces

Guns of the Elite Forces

John Walter

Greenhill Books, London
Stackpole Books, Pennsylvania

Guns of the Elite Forces

This new, completely revised edition published in 2005 by
Greenhill Books, Lionel Leventhal Limited, Park House,
1 Russell Gardens, London NW11 9NN
www.greenhillbooks.com
and
Stackpole Books, 5067 Ritter Road,
Mechanicsburg, PA 17055, USA

British Library Cataloguing-in Publication Data
Walter, John, 1951–
Guns of the elite
1. Firearms – History – 20th century
2. Firearms – History – 21st century
3. Special forces (Military science) – Equipment and supplies
I. Title
623.4'42

ISBN 1-85367-637-3

Library of Congress Cataloging-in Publication Data available

For more information on our books, please visit
www.greenhillbooks.com, email sales@greenhillbooks.com,
or telephone us within the UK on 020 8458 6314.
You can also write to us at the above London address.

Typeset and edited by Donald Sommerville

Printed and bound in Great Britain by
MPG Books Ltd, Bodmin, Cornwall

To Alison and Adam,
for getting me through the bad times

Contents

Illustrations

Abbreviations

AA	Anti-aircraft
AAI	Aircraft Armament, Inc. (US manufacturer)
AAT	Arme Automatique Transformable (French machine-gun)
ABL	Armée–Belge–Leger ('Belgian Army' in French, *Armée Belge*, and Flemish, *Belge Leger*), usually associated with the FN Mle 49 rifle
ACOG	Advanced Combat Optical Gunsight (USA)
ACP	Automatic Colt Pistol (cartridge designator)
ACR	Advanced Combat Rifle (USA)
AK	Avtomat Kalashnikova (USSR/Russia)
AKM	Avtomat Kalashnikova Modernizirovaniy ('modernised Kalashnikov', USSR/Russia)
AKMS	AKM with folding stock, 'skladyvayushimsya prikladom' (USSR/Russia)
AKS	AK with folding stock (USSR/Russia)
AMR	Anti-matériel rifle
AN	Avtomat Nikonova (Russia)
APB	(i) Silenced Stechkin pistol (USSR)
	(ii) Simonov underwater submachine-gun (USSR/Russia)
API	Armour-piercing-incendiary (bullet)
APS	Avtomaticheskaya pistolet Stechkina (USSR)
ART	Adjustable Ranging telescope (USA)
ARWEN	An acronym of 'Army Weapons [Research] Establishment' and 'Enfield' (UK)
ASAI	Advanced Small Arms Industries (Switzerland, manufacturer)
ASN	Avtomat Skorostrel'nya Nikonova ('high speed' assault rifle, Russia)
ASS	Silenced assault rifle (USSR/Russia)
AUG	Armee-Universal-Gewehr (Austrian assault rifle)
AVF	Avtomatischeskaya Vintovka Fedorova (Russia/USSR, assault rifle)
AVS	Avtomaticheskaya Vintovka Simonova (USSR, automatic rifle)
AVT	Avtomaticheskaya Vintovka Tokareva (USSR, automatic rifle)
BAR	Browning Automatic Rifle

BATF	Bureau of Alcohol, Tobacco and Firearms (USA)
BBSP	Blowback shifted pulse [operation], applied to the Russian Nikonov assault rifle
BDA	Browning Double Action (FN pistol)
BDM	Browning Double Mode (FN pistol)
BGS	Bundesgrenzschutz (West German/German border guards)
Bren	An acronym of Brno and Enfield
BSA	BSA Guns Ltd (British manufacturer)
CAL	Carabine Automatique Légère (FN automatic carbine)
CAW	Close Assault Weapon (USA)
CAWS	Close Assault Weapon System (USA)
CCO	Close Combat Optic (US weapons sight)
CETME	Centro de Estudios Técnicos y Materiales Especiales (arms manufacturer, Spain)
CIA	Central Intelligence Agency (USA)
CIDG	Civilian Irregular Defense Group (formed by the US special Forces in Vietnam from local tribesmen)
CIS	Chartered Industries of Singapore (manufacturer, now STK)
CLRR	Convertible Long Range Rifle (USA)
COIN	Counter-insurgency
COIN-OPS	Counter-insurgency operations
COPP	Combined Operations Pilotage Party (UK)
CQB	Close-quarters battle (UK)
CRW	Counter-revolutionary warfare
CRWW	Counter-Revolutionary Warfare Wing (SAS, UK)
CTW	Counter-terrorist warfare
CWS	Crew-served Weapons Sight
ČZ	Československá Zbrojovka AS (Czechoslovakian manufacturer)
DA	Double-action
DAO	Double-action only
DA/SA	Double or single action
DEA	Drugs Enforcement Agency (USA)
DGL	Disposable Grenade Launcher
DK	Degtyareva Kruptokaliberniy (USSR, large-calibre machine-gun)
EBO	Elleniki Biomekanica Oplon (Greek manufacturer)
ESI	Escadron Spéciale d'Intervention 'Diane' (Belgian police CTW unit)
FAL	Fusil Automatique Léger (FN automatic rifle)

FALO	Fusil Automatique Lourd (heavy-barrel FAL)
FAL Para	Folding-butt 'paratroop' version of the FAL
FAMAE	Fabricaciones Militares do Arsenal de Ejercito, Santiago (Chilean manufacturer)
FA MAS	Fusil Automatique Manufacture [d'Armes de] Saint-Étienne (French manufacturer)
FAP	Fusil Automatico Pesado – the Spanish-language equivalent of FALO (q.v.)
FBI	Federal Bureau of Investigation (USA)
FCR	Future Combat Rifle (USA)
FEG, FÉG	Fegyver é Gázkészülékgyár (Hungarian manufacturer)
FFV	Forsvarets Fabriksverken AS (Swedish manufacturer)
FG	Fallschirmjägergewehr (paratroops' rifle, Germany)
FN	FN Herstal SA (Belgian manufacturer, formerly Fabrique Nationale d'Armes de Guerre)
FNA	Fàbrica National de Armas (Spanish manufacturer)
FNC	Fabrique Nationale Carabine (successor to the CAL)
FSB	Federalnaya Sluzhba Bezopasnosti ('Federal Security Service', Russia)
FSO	Federal Bodyguard Service (Russia)
GEO	Grupo Especial de Operaciónes (Spanish CTW unit)
GIAT	Groupement Industriel d'Armaments Terrestres (French government agency)
GIGN	Groupement d'Intervention de la Gendarmerie Nationale (French CTW group), colloquially known as 'Gigène'
GIS	Gruppo Intervenzione Speciale (Italian Carabinieri unit)
GMG	Granate-Maschinen-Gewehr (Heckler & Koch grenade launcher)
GMW	Granate-Maschinen-Werfer (Heckler & Koch grenade launcher)
GP	[Pistole Browning à] Grande Puissance
GPM	German Police Model (Heckler & Koch pistol)
GPMG	General-purpose machine-gun
GSG-9	Grenzschutzgruppe-9 (West German/German CTW unit)
HEAB	High-explosive, air burst
HK, H&K	Heckler & Koch, Oberndorf/Neckar (German manufacturer)
HOE	Holographic Optical Element
HRT	Hostage Rescue Team (USA, FBI groups)
HSP	Hahn-Selbstspanner-Polizei[pistole]
HWaA	Heereswaffensamt ('Army Weapons Office', Germany)

IIT	Image-intensifier tube
IMI	Israeli Military Industries (manufacturer)
INSAS	Indian Small Arms System
IPSC	International Pistol Shooting Club
ITM	International Technology & Machines (Swiss manufacturer)
IW	Individual Weapon (UK)
IWS	Individual Weapon Sight (UK)
JHP	Jacketed hollow point (bullet)
JSOR	Joint Services Operational Requirement (USA)
JSCS	Joint Services Chiefs of Staff (USA)
JSSAP	Joint Services Small Arms Program (USA)
KGB	Komitet Gosudarstvennoy Bezopastony (secret police, USSR)
LAM	Laser aiming module
LAW	Light Automatic Weapon (light machine-gun)
LMCS	Lightweight Modular Carbine System (USA)
LMG	Light machine-gun
LRDG	Long Range Desert Group (UK)
LRRS	Long Range Rifle System (USA)
LRS	Laser Rifle Scope
LRSR	Long Range Sniper Rifle (USA)
LSW	Light support weapon
MAB	(i) Marine Amphibious Brigade (USA)
	(ii) Manufacture d'Armes de Bayonne, Hendaye (French arms manufacturer)
MAC	(i) Manufacture Nationale d'Armes, Châtellerault (French arms manufacturer)
	(ii) Military Armament Corporation (USA, manufacturer)
MAG	Mitrailleuse à Gaz ('gas-operated machine-gun', Belgian FN design), now known as 'Mitrailleuse d'Appui General'
MBT	Main Battle Tank
MCP	Micro-channel plate (used in intensifier sights)
MG	(i) Machine-gun
	(ii) Maschinengewehr (Germany)
MILSPEC	Military Specification
MKb	Maschinenkarabiner ('machine carbine', Germany)
MP, MPi.	Maschinenpistole ('machine pistol', Germany)
MVD	Ministerstvo Vnutrenniki Del ('Ministry of Internal Affairs', USSR)

NAHAL	Fighting Pioneer Youth (Israel)
NATO	North Atlantic Treaty Organization
NM	National Match (USA)
NOCS	Nucleo Operativo Centrale di Sicurezza (Italian CTW unit)
NRA	National Rifle Association (Britain, USA)
NSV	[Pulemet] Nikitina-Solkova-Volkova (USSR, machine-gun)
NTK	Nittoku Metal Industries (Japanese manufacturer)
NVA	North Vietnamese Army (US abbreviation)
NWM	Nederlandsche Wapen- en Munitiefabriek (Dutch manufacturer)
OCIW	Objective Combat Infantry Weapon (USA)
OCSW	Objective Company Support Weapon (USA)
OES	Occluded Eye Sight
OHWS	Offensive Handgun Weapons System (USA)
OSS	Office of Strategic Services (USA)
PB	Silenced Makarov pistol (USSR)
PDSS	Underwater anti-sabotage team (USSR/Russia)
PDW	Personal Defence Weapon
PFLP	Popular Front for the Liberation of Palestine
PMT	Photomultiplier tube
Pi.	Pistole (Germany)
PK	Pulemet Kalashnikova (machine-gun, USSR)
PKM	Modernised Kalashnikov machine-gun (USSR/Russia)
PLO	Palestine Liberation Organization
PM	Pistolet Makarova (USSR/Russia)
PMM	Modernised Makarov pistol (USSR/Russia)
PMT	Photo-multiplier plate
PPS	Pistolet-Pulemet Sudaeva (submachine-gun, USSR)
PPSh	Pistolet-Pulemet Shpagina (submachine-gun, USSR)
PSG	Präzisions-Scharfschützen-Gewehr (sniper rifle, Heckler & Koch)
PSM	Pistolet Samozaryadniy Malogabaritniy ('small-calibre pistol', USSR/Russia)
PSP	Polizei-Selbstlade-Pistole (Heckler & Koch)
PSS	Simonov silent pistol (USSR/Russia)
PTRD	Protitotankovoye ruzhe Degtyareva (single-shot anti-tank rifle, USSR)
PTRS	Protitotankovoye ruzhe Simonova (auto-loading anti-tank rifle, USSR)
RCMP	Royal Canadian Mounted Police
RIS	Rail Interface System (USA)

RMR	Revolver Manurhin-Ruger (France)
RMSBS	Royal Marines Special Boat Squadron (UK)
RPD	Ruchnoi Pulemet Degtyareva (light machine-gun, USSR)
RPG	Rocket-propelled grenade
RPK	Ruchnoi Pulemet Kalashnikova (light machine-gun, USSR)
RSAF	Royal Small Arms Factory, Enfield (British arms manufacturer)
RSS	Repeatable Secure Striker (FN trigger system)
RWS	Rheinisch-Westfälische Sprengstoff AG (German manufacturer)
S&W	Smith & Wesson (US manufacturer)
SA	Single-action
SAFN	Semi-Automatic, FN (FN Mle 49 rifle)
SAS	Special Air Service (UK)
SAW	Squad Automatic Weapon (light machine-gun)
SAWS	Small Arms Weapon System
SBS	Special Boat Service (UK)
SD	Schalldämpfer, 'silencer' (Germany)
SDP	Steyr-Daimler-Puch (Austrian arms manufacturer)
SEAL	Sea-Air-Land Teams (US Navy)
SG	(i) Sayeret Golani ('Golani Infantry', Israel)
	(ii) Scharfschützengewehr (German for 'sniper rifle'; *see also* SSG)
	(iii) Stankoviy [Pulemet] Goryunova (machine-gun, USSR)
SFM	Société Française des Munitions (French manufacturer)
SGM	Stankoviy [Pulemet] Goryunova Modernizirovaniy (machine-gun, USSR)
SIG	Schweizerische-Industrie-Gesellschaft (Swiss arms manufacturer)
SKS	Samozariadniya Karabina Simonova (semi-automatic carbine, USSR)
SLEM	Self Loading, Experimental Model (UK)
SMG	Submachine-gun
SMLE	[Rifle,] Short, Magazine Lee-Enfield (UK)
SNT	Snayperskaya Vintovka Tokareva (sniper rifle, USSR)
SOCOM	Special Operations Command (USA)
SOE	Special Operations Executive (UK)
SOG	Special Operations Group (USA)
SOPMOD	Special Operations Modification (USA)
SPAS	Special Purpose Automatic Shotgun (Franchi, Italy)
Spetsnaz	Diversionary Troops (USSR)
SPIW	Special Purpose Infantry Weapon (USA)

SPS	Samozariadniya Pistolet Serdyukova (automatic pistol, Russia)
sS	schwere Spitzgeschoss ('heavy ball', Germany)
SSB	Special Service Brigade (UK, Second World War)
SSG	Scharfschützengewehr ('sniper rifle' in German; *see also* SG [ii])
STANAG	NATO standardised fitting
Sten	An acronym of Shepherd, Turpin and Enfield
StG, Stgw	Sturmgewehr, 'assault rifle'
STK	Singapore Technologies, Kinetics Division (manufacturer, formerly CIS)
SUIT	Sight, Unit, Infantry, Trilux (British weapon sight, formerly 'SUSAT')
SUSAT	Sight, Universal, Small Arms, Trilux (British weapon sight, now 'SUIT')
SVD	Snayperskaya Vintovka Dragunova (sniper rifle, USSR/Russia)
SVT	Samozariadniya Vintovka Tokareva (semi-automatic rifle, USSR)
SWAT	Special Weapons and Taclics
SWD	Special Weapons Development (manufacturer, USA)
TGS	'Total-Granate-Systeme', Heckler & Koch grenade-launcher
THV	Très haute velocité (French 'very high-speed' ammunition)
UDT	Underwater Demolition Team (USA)
UMP	Universal Machine-Pistol (Heckler & Koch, Germany)
USAF	United States Air Force
USCG	United States Coast Guard
USMC	United States Marine Corps
USN	United States Navy
USP	Universal-Selbstlade-Pistole (Heckler & Koch)
UTL	Universal Tactical Light
VC	Vietcong (guerrilla force in Vietnam)
VSS	Simonov silent sniper rifle (USSR/Russia)
WLAR	Winchester Light Automatic Rifle
WP	Warsaw Pact

Preface and Acknowledgements

The replacement of the traditional means of making war with terrorism – not, of course, a modern concept – has brought the activities of security services into ever-sharper focus. The successes and failures of police and military anti-terrorist operations have been scrutinised, and interest in their equipment has undoubtedly grown correspondingly in a climate of increasing (if sometimes irrational) fear. Consequently, where once there were comparatively few books on firearms, there are now rows of books and videos dealing specifically with the arms and equipment of Special Forces.

Even though the primary goal remains the same as it was when I started work in the mid-1980s – to provide an accessible and authoritative overview of the firearms used by Special Forces throughout the world – it is now almost two decades since the original *Guns of the Elite* was published and technological development makes wholesale changes essential. I hope that the present book, like many of the latest guns, combines the strengths of its predecessor with the improvements suggested by experience.

Though I take full responsibility for my opinions, and for errors that may have escaped scrutiny, I am keen to acknowledge a debt to the many people who have contributed to the project. The principal manufacturers have always been keen to supply details, which was particularly valuable in the days before websites could be accessed at will and digital cameras eased the task of obtaining illustrations. I have always enjoyed an excellent relationship with Pietro Beretta SpA of Gardone Val Trompia, Italy, in particular; but Heckler & Koch of Oberndorf, Germany; FN Herstal SA of Herstal-lèz-Liège in Belgium; Carl Walther

GmbH of Ulm/Donau, Germany; and SIG of Neuhausen/ Rheinfalls, Switzerland, have always provided support. Glock GmbH of Deutsch-Wagram, Austria; Oy Sako Ab and Sako-Valmet of Jyväskylä, Finland; Luigi Franchi SpA of Fornaci/ Brescia, Italy; Accuracy International of Portsmouth, UK; Steyr-Mannlicher GmbH of Steyr/Oberdonau, Austria; and PGM-Précision of Les Chavannes have also responded when asked. In North America, Colt in its many guises; Kahr Arms; Para-Ordnance, Inc.; Smith & Wesson; the Savage Arms Company; and Springfield Armory (now Springfield, Inc.) were among the first to provide help. Chartered Industries of Singapore, now Singapore Technologies, also contributed invaluable details of its products. The British Ministry of Defence and the US Department of the Army provided photographs and information, and the assistance of David Penn, Keeper, Department of Exhibits, Imperial War Museum, is gratefully acknowledged.

I have also valued the help given by individuals, ranging from friends of long-standing to 'one off' correspondents who, perhaps unknowingly, provided vital parts of the jigsaw. I greatly miss the co-operation of Ian Hogg, who died in 2002, soon after supplying me a wealth of information, and only now realise how much I had depended on his cheerful assistance when the original book was being prepared. I must also belatedly acknowledge contributions made to the earlier editions by Herbert Woodend MBE, Custodian of the Pattern Room Collection (first in Enfield, then in Nottingham and now part of the Royal Armouries in Leeds) who died in 2003.

I must thank Terry Gander, editor of *Jane's Infantry Weapons*, for eliminating errors at the draft stage and ensuring that my opinions did not always run unchecked, and Lionel Leventhal of Greenhill Books – not only for proposing the original book back in 1985, but also for keeping faith with the project for twenty years.

John Walter
Hove, England, 2005

Chapter 1

In the Beginning

In the summer of 1940, facing up to the invasion threat posed by German troops in the Pas de Calais and haunted by bittersweet memories of the Dunkirk evacuation – 'victory snatched from the jaws of defeat' – the British people badly needed a morale-booster. Though penned in the home islands, the British were keen to find ways of retaliating. Finding better ways to defend the British coast was vital, if defensive, but many of Britain's leaders (especially Prime Minister Winston Churchill) placed greater faith in the maxim that attack is the best form of defence.

While the RAF was battling the Luftwaffe in the skies of southern England, therefore, the first true 'Special Forces' units were formed.

There was nothing particularly revolutionary about the concept. While walking home from the War Office in Whitehall, Lieutenant-Colonel Dudley Clarke, mindful of historical lessons, considered the value of controlled aggressive action by small well-trained bands acting independently of centralised command. Searching for a name for his irregulars, he seized on 'commando', after the military units used by the Boers that had plagued the British Army forty years earlier in the South African War. Dudley Clarke's superior was Field Marshal Sir John Dill, Chief of the Imperial General Staff, who could realistically have been expected to oppose the idea of an 'army within the army', but Dill was also worried by rock-bottom army morale after the withdrawal from Dunkirk and understood the need for achievement. He explained the matter to Churchill, and within a day the Commandos were born.

Their role was to disrupt the communications, efficiency and nerve of the Wehrmacht in 'shoot and scoot' missions, seeking to cause as much trouble in the shortest time possible, then retire in the confusion. If the defenders reinforced the position, the next strike could be made in the area from which the reinforcements had been drawn. And so operations continued throughout occupied Europe, North Africa, the Mediterranean and the Aegean, the Commandos in time spawning a dozen or more offshoots such as the US Rangers and the ANZAC Independent Companies.

Many early raids were fiascos, confirming the worst fears of some in the military hierarchy, but morale improved once Admiral Sir Roger Keyes (hero of the legendary Zeebrugge Raid in the First World War) was appointed to direct the Commando operations. By October 1940, some 2,000 men had been recruited into the 'Special Service Brigade' and divided into commandos numbered 1–12. Unbelievably rigorous training programmes began in the surf and on the beaches of the Western Highlands.

The Combined Training Centre in Achnacarry trained not only the British Commandos, but also US Rangers and the Royal Marine Commando detachment formed in 1942. Training was often very dangerous, often undertaken with live ammunition – forty men were killed at Achnacarry during the war. In terms of the successes achieved by the Commandos, the price was small. But the deaths, and mock gravestones in the camp, punched the message home: brains as well as brawn were required for Special Service.

After the initial reverses, the Commandos' fortunes improved on the strength of spectacularly successful raids on the Lofoten Islands, in March 1941, and Vågsøy and Måløy in December, by which time Keyes had been replaced by Captain Lord Louis Mountbatten. The best was yet to come. A suspicious building had been spotted during a routine sweep over the village of Bruneval, near Le Havre, and a photo-reconnaissance Spitfire ultimately brought back one of the classic air-reconnaissance photographs of the war, a perfect oblique view of a cliff-top villa and the dish antenna of a German *Würzburg* radar. In a daunting, unbelievably ambitious raid in February 1942 the Commandos not only silenced the defences, but also stole the entire radar dish – an exploit matched in its daring only in 1969, when Israeli NAHAL parachute troops seized a Russian-made radar station from Ras Gharib.

Large-scale clandestine activities are never guaranteed successes, as was proved by the loss of 600 highly trained Commandos covering the British withdrawal from Crete in May 1941. By the end of the year, something was needed to restore flagging spirits and a spectacular coup was planned: the assassination of Erwin Rommel, officer commanding the *Afrika Korps*, in his headquarters at Beda Littoria in Libya.

Proposed by Lieutenant-Colonel Geoffrey Keyes, son of the former Director of Combined Operations, its chances of success were adjudged to be practically nil. Keyes persisted, however, and the scheme was eventually approved for the night of 17 November 1941 – the day before a British offensive seeking to relieve Tobruk was to begin.

A small party was detached from the main force on the perimeter of Beda Littoria to cut communications between the headquarters and Cyrene, while the remaining twenty-two men, their faces blacked, proceeded stealthily into the deserted market place a mere hundred yards from a large house which, they were told, served as Rommel's headquarters. The building would be stormed by six men led by Keyes, while the remainder were to guard the approaches to the building.

Keyes led his party around the building to begin the assault at the main door. Then the problems started. The German sentry seized the muzzle of Keyes's Colt revolver, trying to wrest it away, and retreated against a wall using Keyes as a shield before being shot. A burst from a Thompson submachine-gun discouraged a soldier about to descend the stairs. Keyes pointed to light shining under the guardroom door, which opened to reveal eleven dumbstruck German soldiers. Captain Campbell lobbed a No. 36 grenade into the centre of the room as Keyes opened the door for a second time. A rake of submachine-gun fire prevented most of the Germans replying, but a single shot felled Keyes as the British soldiers closed the door. After the grenade had done its job, and a fruitless search of the house had been made, Campbell forgetfully emerged from the back door and was promptly shot by one of the Commando sentries. And there had been no sign of Rommel at all. He was elsewhere.

The Beda Littoria raid, a heroic failure, gained Keyes a posthumous Victoria Cross but achieved little else. Yet its lightning attack with grenades, light firearms and explosives was typical of the many independent operations carried out during the Second World War.

Initially, the British Special Forces had to make do with standard firearms and grenades. This was not in itself disastrous, because the basic small-arms, if somewhat unadventurous, were reasonably effective. Though the bolt-action SMLE was not ideal in a firefight, it could be operated quickly and carried twice as many cartridges as most rival designs. The Bren Gun was portable, extremely accurate and well liked, and could be used to pick off key targets with single shots while providing appreciable extra firepower when required. Handguns varied; the standard 0.38in Enfield (Webley) revolver, the 0.38/200 Smith & Wesson and various Colts including the US Government M1911A1 pistol all saw use early in the war. However, none of the small-arms initially provided what the Special Forces sought most: the ideal combination of handiness and firepower which, though it had not necessarily defeated inventors prior to 1939, had certainly failed to persuade military authorities (and their government paymasters) that investment would be justified by the returns.

An early favourite was the Thompson submachine-gun, made by Colt for the Auto-Ordnance Corporation and revered by police and mobsters alike during the Roaring Twenties. The Thompson fired the 0.45in ACP pistol cartridge, widely recognised as a good man-stopper, but was particularly cumbersome – with its loaded 50-round magazine, it weighed 15lb (6.8kg) – and many doubted the efficiency of its locking mechanism. Ordinarily quite reliable, the Thompson was prone to jamming when poorly lubricated . . . and this predictably proved to be a liability in North Africa.

Supplies of the improved blowback Thompson M1, with a 30-round box magazine, appeared in 1942. The M1 was greatly appreciated by the British Commandos and the US Rangers, who preferred it to the later M3 'Grease Gun'. But the basic Thompson design remained too complicated and too expensive to produce in great quantity. The British developed the Lanchester instead, simply by copying the German MP. 28 (Bergmann), but then graduated to the Sten Gun.

Credited to Major Richard Shepherd and Harold Turpin, pilot models of the Sten were made in 1941. A whole new BSA factory was erected at Tyseley, on the outskirts of Birmingham, and volume production began that summer. As the Lanchester production line had also been completed, supplies of this otherwise obsolescent design were diverted to the Royal Navy and the RAF so that the Stens could be supplied to the Army.

By the end of the war, millions of Stens had been made in a variety of Marks. The unbelievably basic 'Woolworth Wonder' or 'Stench Gun' eventually cost no more than 7s 6d (37½p) for what were reputedly its main components – a pipe and a bedspring. Yet the Sten Gun worked surprisingly well. Lubrication was practically unnecessary and, as accuracy was not prerequisite in an essentially short-range weapon, bullets could be sprayed far and wide with impunity.

The Sten supplemented the Thompson in the hands of the Special Forces, its dreadful finish coming as something of a shock after the good manufacturing quality of its predecessor. Efforts were eventually made to improve the Sten, and a special compact gun was developed experimentally in 1943–4 for commando and paratroop units. The final Mk 5, with a wood butt, a handgrip and a bayonet lug, was developed in time for Operation 'Market Garden' – the ill-fated airborne operation at

Arnhem in September 1944. The Sten Mk 2S had a special Maxim-pattern silencer surrounding the barrel, giving it a peculiarly bulky appearance compared with the standard gun; but it was very effective as long as only single shots were fired, and inspired the current L34A1 silenced Sterling.

A particularly interesting copy of the Mk 2 Sten was the Gerät Potsdam, made in Germany towards the end of the Second World War and complete down to the last detail of its markings. These guns were designed for clandestine pro-German resistance elements operating behind Allied lines, which would be betrayed immediately by the presence of too many examples of the MP. 40.

During 1941, the Commandos had been joined by the Long Range Desert Group (LRDG), a mobile reconnaissance group drawing inspiration from the Arab nomads living in the trackless sands of the North African desert, and David Stirling's L Detachment that was effectively the precursor of the Special Air Service (SAS). Tony Geraghty, in *Who Dares Wins*, explained that:

> Stirling drafted a long memorandum . . . wherein he argued that strategic raids – that is, deep penetration behind enemy lines – did not require the ponderous naval back-up of full-blown Commando assaults . . . Instead, Stirling proposed using parachutist saboteurs to inflict a level of damage on enemy airfields equivalent to that of a Commando force twenty times greater.

Stirling had been injured in a parachuting accident and was confined to a hospital bed. He realised that his submission would not get past the junior officers at Army headquarters in Cairo, and decided upon action in keeping not only with his ideas but also with the subsequent exploits of the Special Air Service. Said Geraghty:

> A high wire fence surrounded the headquarters area . . . Leaving his crutches outside the fence, Stirling hauled himself painfully over, and dropped into the compound. He then walked gingerly into the main administrative

> block, bumping into various offices and their occupants, before discovering that Auchinleck was out. By now, the internal security staff had been alerted to his presence. Stirling found the Deputy C-in-C, Lieutenant-General Neil Ritchie, just before they found him . . . Ritchie scanned the paper and subsequently recalled Stirling for a discussion of the scheme with Auchinleck. Soon afterwards, in his new rank of captain, Stirling was given permission to recruit 66 men from the remains of Layforce Commando.

The SAS was largely confined to North Africa during this period, successfully sabotaging Axis airfields at comparatively little cost. Success bred success; the Commandos, the LRDG and SAS were soon joined by the Special Boat Service (SBS), the Royal Marines Boom Patrol Detachment, the Combined Operation Pilotage Parties (COPPs, specialising in beach reconnaissance) and a host of other special-purpose forces.

As the war ran its course, more units appeared. Popski's Private Army was formed by a Belgian businessman of Russian origin, Vladimir Peniakoff, whose company-size reconnaissance and raiding force was active in North Africa and later in Italy. Merrill's Marauders, officially the 5037th Composite Unit of the US Army, was organized in October 1943 under Brigadier General Frank Merrill and trained specifically in jungle fighting for service in Burma. The Chindits, alias the Long-Range Penetration Group or 77th Indian Infantry Brigade, were raised by Orde Wingate in the summer of 1942 and successfully harried the Japanese for two years.

The *Encyclopedia of World War Two* (1978, ed. Thomas Parrish) aptly summed up a popular opinion of these units by saying of the Chindits, '[they] were as controversial as their tactics. Many staff officers regarded them as eccentric and undependable. But despite their detractors' claims, they played an important role . . .' in the conduct of the Second World War.

The Germans were less interested in creating Special Forces, though their paramilitary units, particularly the SS, ran efficient assassination squads. A covert-operations unit known as the

Brandenburgers specialised in infiltration, but ultimately fell foul of politics and served largely to pave the way for Otto Skorzeny and his commando unit. Skorzeny's men achieved some remarkable successes, including the rescue of the deposed Italian leader Benito Mussolini in seemingly impossible circumstances, but their choice of weaponry was largely conventional. However, specialist equipment often had to be acquired outside Germany . . . sometimes with the aid of forged British banknotes. Thesemay have been printed inside a sealed compound within the Sachsenhausen concentration camp.*

During the Winter War against the Finns, in 1939/40, the Russians had learned from bitter experience the value of well-trained snipers. One thorn in their flesh was Simo Hähyä, a farmer who had won many pre-war marksmanship trophies. Attached to a unit on the Karelia Front, Häyhä, firing an open-sighted Model 1928 Mosin-Nagant rifle, was claimed to have killed more than 500 Russian soldiers in fifteen weeks. As a result of experience in Finland, the Russians selected the most accurate of their Tokarev SNT40 rifles for snipers' use, fitting them with telescope sights, but the SNT40 proved appreciably less reliable than the bolt-action 1891/30-type Mosin-Nagant. The latter was ordered back into production in 1942 and remained the standard Eastern Bloc sniping rifle until 1963.

The best of the Russian snipers preferred the 1891/30 to the semi-automatic for reasons that are as relevant today as in 1941: the manually operated rifle was more reliable, less prone to structural failure and had no mechanical noise in the action. This was particularly important when silence was essential – the ejection/reloading cycle of the SNT was accompanied by considerable clatter. Vasiliy Zaitsev, one of the best-known Soviet snipers, almost always fired Mosin-Nagants, and left-handers, such as Lyuba Makarova, found that the SNT ejected fired cases too close to their faces for comfort.

---

* The existence of this operation, run by SS-Sturmbahnführer Bernhard Kruger and staffed by highly-skilled Jewish internees, only became common knowledge years after the war had ended.

Despite the troubles originating from the disruption of manufacture after the German invasion of Russia in June 1941, the Tokarev was by no means a failure. Poor equipment would not have been tolerated by the Soviet snipers, who were rightly respected by their opponents and exacted a terrible price for the German invasion. Provided it was kept reasonably clean – a stricture still applying to automatic weapons – the Tokarev functioned satisfactorily enough in the hands of good-quality troops such as the Russian marines.

> The Russians backed out of their trench. Anxious to put the German sniper in a maximum amount of blinding sunlight, they followed the irregularly curving front line until they found a spot where the afternoon sun would be at their backs . . . Aware that the sun would reflect on their scopes, they waited patiently for it to go down behind them. By late afternoon, now wrapped in shade, they had Konings at a disadvantage. Zaitsev focused his telescopic sight on the German's hiding-place. A piece of glass suddenly glinted at the edge of the sheet. Zaitsev motioned to Kulikov, who slowly raised his helmet over the top of the parapet. Konings fired once and Kulikov rose, screaming convincingly. Sensing triumph, the German lifted his head slightly to see his victim. Vassiliy Zaitsev shot him between the eyes . . .*

Snipers also made their presence felt in the Pacific, where the Japanese not only became past masters in the art of concealment, but also had a degree of fanaticism sufficient to persist long after most Western marksmen would have prudently 'withdrawn'. The lessons were not lost on the Americans, while, even at Arnhem, the Germans feared British snipers largely because the latter were taught to aim at the head (and thus be more likely to kill) whenever circumstances permitted.

* William Craig: *Enemy at the Gates – The Battle for Stalingrad.* Zaitsev was credited with killing 242 Germans during the battle for Stalingrad before being seriously injured by a landmine. However, many stories such as this have now been discredited as Soviet propaganda.

The successful German paratroop invasion of Crete in 1941 was accompanied by such an excessive casualty rate that the Wehrmacht never again undertook airborne attacks on such a large scale. Many survivors of the drop believed that the Schmeisser submachine-gun and Mauser bolt-action rifle could not provide sufficient firepower to overcome tenacious defenders, and also that the standard light-support weapon, the MG. 34, performed much better on its complicated buffered quadrupedal mount (an unnecessary encumbrance for paratroops) than on its bipod.

This conflict between the need for adequate fire-support and the penalties of weight and size led to the development of the Fallschirmjägergewehr 42 or FG. 42, which, as its name 'paratroop rifle' suggests, was produced specifically to provide German airborne forces with a portable selective-fire weapon firing the standard full-power rifle cartridge to maximize effective range.

Prototypes were submitted by Krieghoff, Mauser and Rheinmetall, the successful design being credited to Rheinmetall engineer Louis Stange, but most guns were made by Krieghoff (code 'fzs'). The earliest guns were just 37in (940mm) long and weighed 9.93lb (4.5kg) empty. The FG. 42 had an integral bipod, a detachable 20-round box magazine protruding laterally from the left side of the receiver, and a 'spike'-type bayonet in a tube beneath the muzzle. The gun locked with a rotary bolt and had a straight-line layout to minimize climb in automatic fire, though this required sights raised well above the gun. Many stampings and pressings were used in an attempt to simplify production, but very few rifles were made because of production problems and the restriction of manganese steel to more vital projects.

Despite being used by Otto Skorzeny's men during the highly successful release of the deposed Italian leader Benito Mussolini (September 1943), the early version of the FG. 42 was insufficiently robust; the later variant was longer and heavier, with a laminated wood butt and the bipod moved to the muzzle from around the gas-port assembly. It also had a different muzzle brake, an adjustable four-position regulator and various detail differences. FG. 42s were allegedly used with great success at Monte Cassino (finally taken by British and Polish units on 18 May 1944), impressing Hitler so greatly that he decreed that they be distributed to the elite troops of the Wehrmacht to replace the ageing bolt-action Karabiner 98k. Unfortunately, production never matched demand – by no means an unusual event in German small-arms circles.*

Hindsight is a wonderful, if retrospective tool. Consequently, it is easy to see why some guns failed to find the niche that is so clearly obvious to today's observer. One of the best examples of this process is the US 0.30in-calibre M1 Carbine, which deserves to be considered as a landmark in military weaponry, even though its true value passed largely unnoticed at the time simply because it had been created to arm non-combatants and units that were serving in largely administrative roles or away from the front lines.

Its origins are traceable to an experimental Winchester rifle unsuccessfully tested by the US Marine Corps in 1940, competing against the Garand and the Johnson. The Winchester was prematurely adjudged a failure; but it embodied an excellent short-stroke gas piston system, designed by David M. 'Carbine' Williams, and could have been developed to rival the Garand had it not appeared at an inopportune moment in history.

Three years previously, in 1937, US Army Chief of Infantry, Major-General George Lynch, had highlighted a need for a light semi-automatic personal weapon more powerful than the 0.45in ACP M1911A1 Colt-Browning with an effective range at least ten times the 25 yards of this particular pistol. Strident opposition came from the Ordnance Department, and the

---

* It seems unlikely that they could have been used at Monte Cassino in large numbers. HWaA inventories indicate that only 524 guns were accepted in 1944 and 3,873 early in 1945. It is not clear whether others had been sent directly to the Luftwaffe (which controlled Germany's paratroops), but by 1944, theoretically at least, all small-arms procurement should have been channelled through the Army authorities.

project seemed set to founder until a draft specification was circulated to interested parties in October 1940 calling for a gun weighing less than 5lb (empty) that could fire fully automatically when required to do so and could accept a detachable box magazine holding fifty rounds.

The conflicting demands, for light weight, enough power to give an effective range of 250 yards, and a high-capacity magazine, prevented the existing service-pattern cartridges being used. Winchester developed a new straight-side 0.30in cartridge, adapted from the commercial 0.32in WSL ('Winchester Self Loading'), and nine carbines were sent to the army for trials. The incompatibility of the fully-automatic capability and the excessively large magazine with a gun weighing merely 5lb was soon noted, and these features were dropped.

Winchester then entered the gun competition by adapting the Williams short-stroke piston system and scaling down the USMC trials rifle, producing the first prototype in an incredible thirteen days. After a successful demonstration at Aberdeen Proving Ground, the entire trials were postponed while a second Winchester carbine was made. A mere 34 days later, the gun was dispatched to Aberdeen. Amazingly, the Winchester defeated the Garand and Hyde guns, victors of previous trials, and was ordered straight into production as the 'Carbine, Caliber .30, M1'.

Its combat debut was eagerly awaited, but anticipation was soured when the first reports filtered back from the Ordnance Department 'experts'. The carbine had many attractive features: it was reliable, handled well and was quite accurate at short range, but the 0.30in bullet was, rather stupidly, adjudged a poor man-stopper by the criteria of the standard M2 Ball used in the Garand. Most armchair soldiers conveniently forgot that the carbine was specifically designed to be effective *only to a distance of 300 yards*, but their lack of enthusiasm was rarely shared in the field and the eventual production of more than six million guns made the point. The Special Forces, British and American alike, relied greatly on M1 (semi-automatic) and M2 (fully automatic) Carbines in jungle theatres where their handiness, light weight and good rate of fire were advantageous.

Had the M1 Carbine chambered a more effective round, it might have been an even greater success. The post-war commercial version chambering the 5.7mm Johnson Spitfire cartridge – not unlike the current 5.56mm M193 in terms of power – showed what could have been done in 1941, pre-empting the AR15/M16 by sixteen years. It is ironic that the so-called Pig and Goat Boards, appointed to investigate the lethality of cartridges under consideration for the Garand in the 1930s, had shown what was necessary: a long and relatively unstable projectile which tumbled or 'set-up' on striking the target to cause serious wounds. The most lethal performer in these trials at short-range had been the Japanese 6.5mm pattern.

The German Maschinenkarabiner arose out of a requirement similar to that which had created the M1 Carbine in the USA, seeking to replace the Schmeisser machine-pistol with a more powerful semi- or fully-automatic weapon without sacrificing high fire-rate. After protracted experiments, beginning in the mid-1930s, the German ammunition technologists had settled on the 7.9mm Kurz cartridge. This combined a short cartridge case with a lightweight bullet, weighing 125 grains compared with 198 grains for the standard sS ball, but was appreciably more powerful than either the 9mm Pist. Patr. 08 and the US M1 Carbine round. It was, however, markedly less hard-hitting than the standard German 7.9mm service rifle cartridge beyond 400 metres and was ideally suited to the light automatic 'machine carbines'.

Mindful of the billions of full-power 7.9mm cartridges that had been stockpiled by 1939, Hitler was initially firmly opposed to the light automatic. Once the Wehrmacht had advanced into Russia, however, the situation changed. The German infantry still relied heavily on the bolt-action infantry rifle, and the Russian PPSh submachine-gun, though crude by German standards, left an indelible impression on the invaders. Issued on a tremendous scale, the PPSh was accompanied by a 71-round drum magazine that gave awesome firepower.

Although the Führer was insisting that production of the obsolescent Kararabiner 98k should be accelerated even as late as March 1943, an experimental Maschinenkarabiner (MKb) had been submitted a year previously and the Heereswaffenamt (HWaA) had accepted the Haenel prototype at the expense of its Walther rival. Encouraging field trials were undertaken by SS Division 'Wiking' in the spring of 1943, more than half the troops reporting that the machine-carbine was a suitable replacement for the Schmeisser submachine-gun and Mauser infantry rifle. One man in ten had even opined that the Maschinenkarabiner could replace all the infantry weapons up to the MG. 34 and MG. 42.

The MKb. 42 (H) became the MP. 43 and limited production began.* By the autumn of 1943, discouraged by accuracy/ reliability problems with the new Gewehr 43 and troubled by the reverses in Russia, Hitler finally accepted that the MP. 43 should replace the MP. 40. However, production problems prevented the MP. 43 achieving the anticipated universal distribution, and production of the Karabiner 98k and Gewehr 43 continued until the end of the war.

The use of an intermediate cartridge should have permitted a reduction in the weight of key components, yet the MP. 43 was surprisingly heavy; at over 13lb (5.9kg) with a loaded 30-round magazine, it was heavier than the full-power FG. 42. This was largely due to the use of stampings, pressings and other advanced sheet-metal forming techniques that were still in their

* It has often been claimed that assault rifles enabled Kampfgruppe Scherer to fight its way out of the Kholm Pocket on the Eastern Front in early 1942. The story originally appeared in 'Das Sturmgewehre' in *Wehrkunde* early in 1953, was repeated in Eckardt & Morawietz's *Die Handwaffen des brandenburgisch-preussisch-deutschen Heeres 1640–1945* (Verlag Helmut Gerhard Schulz, Hamburg, 1957), and then so often that it has become accepted as 'fact'. However, when the defenders of the Kholm Pocket were breaking out of encirclement in February 1942, only a few Haenel prototypes had reached the HWaA. It seems most unlikely that valuable test-pieces would be dropped into an obscure part of Russia; the guns concerned are much more likely to have been Gewehr 41 (M) or Gewehr 41 (W).

infancy. The German designers erred towards caution, subsequent experience indicating that weight could be reduced appreciably. However, the excessive weight and straight-line configuration made the gun controllable in burst-firing and its combat debut was encouraging. The MP. 43 became the MP. 44, with purely minor revisions, and the MP. 44 was then renamed Sturmgewehr 44 (StG. 44) at Hitler's insistence. The term *Sturmgewehr*, in its English translation 'assault rifle', has since been adopted as a generic term.

Whether either the FG. 42 or the MP. 43 owes its modern reputation to anything more than luck, however, is debatable. Each has been hailed as a masterpiece, but questions remain unanswered. The layout of the FG. 42 clearly owes something to the Solothurn MG. 30 – the predecessor of the MG. 34 – but had the designers seen the Johnson light machine-gun of 1941?

There seems little evidence that the Wehrmacht high command ever seriously considered the MP. 43 as a universal replacement for the full-power rifle, even though the HWaA enthusiastically promoted it. Had Hitler had his way, the MP. 43 might simply have remained the German equivalent of the M1 Carbine – with the Gewehr 43 as the standard infantry rifle and the FG. 42 for the paratroops.

By the end of the war, however, sufficient examples of the MP. 43 and StG. 44 had been captured to cause the Allies to consider their future armament requirements; and the Germans, realising that the StG. 44 fell short of perfection, had issued specifications for the lightened 'StG. 45'. Designs had been submitted by Mauser, Gustloff Werke and others, but were still under examination when hostilities ceased. The promising Mauser StG. 45 prototype, also known as Gerät 06, ultimately provided the basis for the modern CETME and Heckler & Koch systems.

Apart from the appearance of the Sten and the Rifle No. 5 (a 'jungle carbine' variant of the SMLE), and increasing enthusiasm for the US Carbine M1 as the war progressed, few basic changes were made in the small-arms issued to the SAS and other British

Special Forces, though the Canadian-made Pistol GP Browning No. 2 Mk I ('FN-Browning GP-35') gradually achieved wider distribution. Colt-Browning pistols were also purchased from Bonifacio Echeverria in Spain ('Star' brand) and from Hispano Argentino Fábrica de Armas SA ('HAFDASA', 'Ballester-Molina') in Argentina.

The much-appreciated predecessor of the pistol adopted by the British Army in 1957, the FN-Browning, had the unique distinction of being manufactured for both sides' special forces concurrently – German paratroops favoured the guns being made in the occupied Fabrique Nationale factory in Herstal while Anglo-Canadian guns were made by Inglis in Toronto.

Various special-purpose guns appeared, including the Welrod and the Projector, Arm Mk 1 (and the silenced High Standard Model B pistol procured for the American OSS), but their distribution was rarely significant. However, the Second World War did provide an ideal proving ground for the new machine-guns. Among the great successes were the Bren Gun (which was still in limited front-line service when the Gulf War began in 1991) and the Browning; disasters included many Italian and most Japanese designs. The German MG. 34, though excellent in some respects, merely paved the way for the roller-locked MG. 42, and the crude, but otherwise efficient Russian Degtyarev was not perpetuated after 1945.

Several promising designs failed because resources were diverted to support existing production weapons, or where development was curtailed. For instance, the US Marine Raiders, Rangers, the 1st Marine Parachute Battalion and other elite US airborne forces used small numbers of Johnson light machine-guns, the perfected version Model 1944 weighing only 14.7lb (6.67kg) with its monopod. The Johnson had some excellent features, including unusually low weight and quick-change barrel. Its advertising literature made much of these, claiming that 'official reports ... tell of its efficiency under battle conditions and, above all, its flexibility. It has been used for single-shot sniping at ranges up to a thousand yards and has been fired full automatic from the hip at advancing groups of Japanese at ranges of a few feet.'

The Johnson was denied the opportunity of wider recognition by the understandable reluctance of the US authorities to divert production resources from existing well-tried designs such as the Springfield and Garand rifles, the M1 Carbine, the Browning Automatic Rifle (BAR) and the Browning machine-guns. As a result of the lack of support, which prevented continuous product-development being undertaken, the Johnson guns were more prone to jamming and somewhat less robust than some of their rivals. But if the German FG. 42 is seen as a milestone in small-arms history, a genuinely controllable rifle-size full-automatic, then at least a thought should be spared for the Johnson, which was doomed in the manner of the later Stoner Mk 23 Mod. 0 light-machine gun in Vietnam.

Chapter 2

Warfare Since 1945

No sooner had hostilities ceased than Allied intelligence experts took the chance to investigate not only the weapons that had been used by their enemies but also those which were being developed. The haphazard affairs of the Japanese ordnance departments had comparatively little to offer the Western Powers, but Germany was a different matter entirely. Secretly, many Anglo-American specialists were prepared to admit that there was much to learn. In addition to the FG. 42 and the MP. 43/MP. 44/StG. 44 series, not forgetting the incomplete StG. 45 and the highly-rated MG. 45V, there were countless projects to examine, ranging from ultra-high-speed salvo-firing guns to the Zippermeyer sound cannon!

The Russians were the first to act. They have claimed that their experiments with 'intermediate' cartridges began before the Second World War, which is undeniably true; the Fedorov rifle introduced during the First World War had been deliberately chambered for the rimless 6.5mm Japanese rifle cartridge instead of the 7.62mm rimmed Russian pattern, and additional experimentation had been undertaken in the 1920s. Though most of the pre-1941 Soviet efforts had concentrated on pistol-type cartridges, it has been claimed that a 5.45mm round had been developed before the Winter War with Finland began in 1939. However, the carbine submitted by Simonov in 1941 still chambered the 7.62 x 54R cartridge and was revised for the M43 intermediate round only in 1944, after the German MP. 43 had shown the Russians that their policy of mass attack, based around the crudely effective PPSh-41 submachine-gun, would be improved greatly by an assault rifle.

The first assault rifle to be tested, submitted in 1944 by Aleksey Sudaev, eventually proved to be unacceptable, clearing the way for promising gas-operated Simonov and Kalashnikov prototypes. Simonov's semi-automatic carbine (SKS) and the more radical Kalashnikov assault rifle (AK) both entered general service in 1949. Experience soon showed that the Kalashnikov was a far better combat weapon, and the SKS was discontinued in the early 1950s. It is still used in Russia for ceremonial duties, but no longer has any military significance.

Simonov-type carbines proved to be very successful outside the USSR, however. Enormous numbers were made in the People's Republic of China, apparently to arm the militia at a time when the army was struggling to re-equip with AK copies, and the design was still being made in Yugoslavia in the 1980s. The Yugoslavian guns were often fitted with refinements such as grenade launchers.

The Kalashnikov remains most people's concept of an assault rifle. In excess of 70 million have been made, in several countries, receiving so much media exposure in the hands of guerrillas, urban terrorists and 'freedom fighters' that their silhouette is easily recognizable. The guns have also appeared on a variety of flags and banners (the flag of Mozambique, for example), which is a tribute to their success.

The original AK was a short and rather clumsy gun: comparatively heavy at 10.5lb (4.75kg) with a loaded 30-round magazine, but its efficiency belied its apparently crude construction and slapdash finish. The Kalashnikov is simply the latest in a long line of small-arms embodying the post-1917 Russian development philosophy that subtleties of construction and high-polish finish are irrelevant if the gun is sufficiently sturdy and fires reliably.

The gas-operated AK, locked by a turning bolt, fires its 122-grain bullet from the M43 intermediate cartridge at about 2,460ft/sec. It is acceptably accurate and, particularly when fitted with the perfected compensator, surprisingly stable in the automatic mode. Not surprisingly, changes have been made to the Kalashnikov since its inception more than fifty years ago: the improved AKM, introduced in 1959, was much lighter, and the reductions in calibre in the mid-1970s (to 5.45mm) have flattened the looping trajectory of the original 7.62mm cartridge.

Though the Russians were therefore quick to follow the German assault-rifle lead, the remaining Allies were much more sceptical. Once again, the old problem of maximum effective range took precedence. Though analysis of the German 7.9mm Kurz cartridge, the MP. 43 and the other experimental *Sturmgewehre* showed their merits, the US Army, particularly, refused to countenance cartridges whose maximum effective engagement range was only 400–500 yards. Immediately after the Second World War had ended, amalgamating German, Polish emigré and indigenous research, the British produced the EM-1 (Thorpe) and EM-2 (Janson) rifles around a special 0.280in cartridge firing a 140-grain bullet at a muzzle velocity of 2,535ft/sec, less powerful than the US 0.30-06, but better than the lighter German 7.9mm Kurz.

The roller-locked EM-1 was soon discontinued in favour of the EM-2, which had a modified Kjellman flap-lock, and the British government optimistically entered the EM-2 in the NATO trials of 1951–2. The rifle had several obvious advantages: its 'bullpup' design, with the magazine behind the pistol grip, permitted a standard-length barrel in an otherwise compact design. Minor, but by no means insoluble problems appeared during the trials – the gun was not particularly accurate, and had an assortment of teething troubles – but the US Army was implacably opposed to the EM-2, and the project foundered amid recriminations and allegations of national self-interest. Even though some later EM-2 rifles were adapted to chamber the 7.62mm T65 (the precursor of the 7.62 x 51mm NATO) and even the US 0.30-06, the design had soon disappeared into history.

The US Army decided to adopt the experimental T44 rifle, which became the M14, but was little more than an updated

Garand with a detachable box magazine. Most remaining NATO powers took variants of the FN-designed Fusil Automatique Leger (FAL); even the British accepted the Belgian gun in the interests of standardisation, production of the Rifle L1A1 beginning in the Royal Small Arms Factory, Enfield, and the Shirley factory of BSA Guns in 1956.

The Korean War of 1950–3 was fought on comparatively conventional lines, with the small-arms that had served since the Second World War. Most of the Special Forces that had performed so well prior to 1945 had been disbanded by this time. After Korea, however, a perceptible change in warfare occurred. Gone was the classic large-scale confrontation between major powers; instead, the dissolution of the great colonial empires promoted the 'freedom fighter' – a guerrilla, often but not inevitably Communist-motivated, determined to overthrow the existing order and then impose his ideology to bring order from the resultant chaos. Nowhere was this more obvious than in the fragmenting empires, especially where little attempt had been made to educate the population, or where national borders had been drawn with little regard for ethnic demarcation.

Though small-scale 'traditional wars' arose in the Middle East and the India-Pakistan sub-continent, the involvement of the Great Powers in the period between the end of the Korean War in 1953 and the Gulf War of 1991 was comparatively limited; most of the conflicts were between opposing guerrillas, guerrillas and local authorities, or guerrillas and supposedly powerful Western nations. One outcome of the change in warfare has been the erosion of traditional industrial supremacy, which is rarely capable of defeating guerrillas who can carry the sympathy of the people with them.

Confrontations between the French and the Viet Minh in the First Indo-China War (1946–54), for example, showed that Western strategists often underestimated their comparatively weakly armed opponents, hastening the ignominious French withdrawal. Many of the lessons were lost on the Americans,

whose embroilment in Vietnam (1961–73) never wholly
subdued the Vietcong and North Vietnamese Army (NVA) in
fighting that was brutal and bloody in the extreme.

Yet not all the subtleties were lost. The US Special Forces –
the 'Green Berets' – strove hard to form teams of local irregulars
(CIDG) to help repel the advances of the Vietcong. Worried by
the success of the 'Hearts and Minds' campaigns, even on a
limited basis among anti-Communist tribesmen, the North
Vietnamese gave priority to attacks on SF/CIDG bases such as
Lang Vei, near Khe Sanh. In February 1968, this numerically
insignificant base was attacked by regular units of the NVA
supported by PT-76 light tanks. Though some of the tanks were
knocked out, the remainder penetrated the camp perimeter and
the NVA poured through the breach. Encircled, the CIDG
fought back desperately for the remainder of the day; and, after
darkness had fallen, the survivors broke out to reach the haven
of Khe Sanh. More than half their number were dead, wounded
or in the hands of the North Vietnamese, but they had made the
point that the guerrilla fears nothing so much as a rival guerrilla.

For all the millions of tons of bombs, defoliant chemicals,
shells and small-arms ammunition expended during the conflict
– and the loss of more than 50,000 American lives – the
Communists eventually gained not only Vietnam and
neighbouring Cambodia, but also laid the seeds of a sea-change
in US public opinion that could countenance involvement in
wars only if the body-count was minimal. This has, in turn,
increased an over-reliance on technology; and, it could be
argued, has given encouragement to fanatical groups who regard
conciliatory moves as demonstrations of weakness.

The Portuguese could not halt the march of nationalism in
Angola or Mozambique, and the Belgians were panicked into
withdrawing from the Congo. Experience in the Yemen, Central
America and Afghanistan makes the point over and over again:
guerrillas are rarely conclusively defeated solely by the non-
nuclear military might of even the most powerful industrialised
nations (whose politicians are perpetually wary of all-out war).

Among the few highlights in what is otherwise a catalogue of misfortune are the British exploits in Malaya (1948–60) and the rebuttal of Indonesian infiltration in Borneo (1963–6), where emphasis was put on fighting irregulars on their own terms – but with all the sophisticated back-up available to a modern soldier.

The initially inauspicious reactivation of the SAS during the Malayan Emergency heralded the re-emergence of the classic Special Forces soldier. The British campaigns in Borneo placed a premium on skills more suited to a hunter: the art of concealment, endurance, determination, a tracker's skill, local knowledge and perfect confidence in issue weapons.

> Turnbull . . . achieved an eye for spoor as accurate as [his native tracker's] . . . reading the splayed toe-prints of an aborigine for what they were; the terrorist's footprint, which invariably revealed cramped toes that had once known shoes; and spotting a fine human footprint imposed by the more canny walker on an elephant footmark in an attempt to blur the trace. Turnbull once followed the tracks of four men for five days, until he spotted the hut they were occupying. He then waited for an impending rainstorm to arrive, correctly guessing that the sentries would take shelter, and drew to within five yards of the hut before killing the four guerrillas . . . According to one officer who served with him, Turnbull used a repeater shotgun with such speed and accuracy that it would "fill a man with holes like a Gruyere cheese"*

The increase in the type of fighting encountered in Malaya and Borneo gradually changed attitudes to small-arms. During the 1950s, most NATO-aligned armies had adopted the comparatively cumbersome FN rifle, the FAL, which weighed about 11lb (5kg) loaded and measured 44in (1,120mm) overall. Despite its undoubted power, impeccable reputation and suitability for long-range fire, the FAL was no more appropriate for jungle warfare than the equally large US Rifle M14.

---

* Tony Geraghty: *Who Dares Wins*. The exploits are those of Sergeant Bob Turnbull of 22 SAS.

Then, in the mid-1950s, the US Army – a strong advocate of long-range power in the trials that saw the demise of the British EM-2 rifle – suddenly decided to seek a smaller gun firing a lighter, handier cartridge. As the wood of the M14 stocks rotted in the tropics, the new gun was also to feature a synthetic butt and fore-end.

After protracted testing, and a lengthy battle against 'big bore' champions in the Army hierarchy, the Armalite rifle designed by Eugene Stoner became the Rifle M16. Built around an adaptation of the commercial 0.222in Remington sporting-rifle cartridge, which had proved itself against thin-skinned game, the M16 represented a great reduction in gun weight and allowed the soldier to carry more of the appreciably lighter cartridges (182 grains compared with 396 for the standard 0.30in Ball M2 round). The finalised M16, with a loaded 30-round magazine, weighed a mere 8.7lb (3.95kg)!

The M16/M16A1 series has been purchased for military use throughout the world, and remains popular for SWAT operations. This is particularly true of the modified compact close-range and heavy-barrel sniping variants of the M16 that are now being made in the USA by Armalite, of Geneseo, Illinois, and independent gunsmithing businesses such as Bushmaster Firearms, Eagle Arms or Olympic Arms. Guns have also been acquired in quantity by the British Army, initially for 'Limited Theatre' purposes, and were particularly popular in Borneo. They were also greatly in evidence during the Gulf War and the current operations in Iraq, where they replaced the less desirable L85A2 in the hands of the Royal Marines and the Special Forces.

Apart from the positioning of the recoil spring in the butt, which can cause problems if the butt breaks (and effectively prevents the M16 being used as a club), the worst problem has concerned the American 5.56mm M193 bullet. Undeniably destructive at short range, the projectile is not especially effective beyond 400 metres and soon proved to be easily deflected by branches and obstructions. This was solved in Europe with the issue of the SS109 bullet, heavier and slower than the M193, allied with a faster rifling twist to improve stability. However, although this compromise improved carrying properties appreciably, lethality was reduced.

After an inauspicious beginning, experience in Vietnam showed that the intermediate cartridge and (ultimately) the small-diameter bullet were suitable for combat use, indirectly confirming the advocacy of the Germans during the Second World War and the Russians thereafter. However, most of the 'traditional' wars contested prior to the early 1980s by industrialised nations were still undertaken with infantry weapons that chambered full-power ammunition. These included the conflict between Iraq and Iran, and the brief confrontation between Britain and Argentina in the South Atlantic in 1982. Ironically, both the British and Argentine armies were equipped with FN-designed infantry rifles, general-purpose machine-guns and pistols. The principal difference lay in the light machine-guns, where the Argentine heavy-barrelled FAL proved to be inferior to the L4 Bren Gun (even though the Brens were apparently confined to the Royal Navy), and in support weapons. British troops were particularly keen to capture the Argentine 0.50in-calibre Brownings, which were speedily turned against their former owners.

Yet it cannot be denied that the open treeless expanse of the Falkland Islands proved to be more suited to the traditional concepts of infantry confrontation than, for example, the all-enveloping jungles and rain forests of Malaya, Vietnam or Borneo. The fighting also reflected a traditional role:

> Corporal Hunt, a section commander in Z Company, was scanning through his IWS, as were all who were equipped with them, and spotted enemy movement on the skyline above them . . . 8 Troop skirmished forward again, taking a newly acquired [ex-Argentinian] .50 inch heavy machine-gun with them. Clearing enemy positions as they went, they arrived at the limit of their objective . . . Dytor [Troop Commander, Z Company], reorganizing on his Company

objective, could clearly see the enemy fire which was coming from positions immediately to his front and about 200 metres away. He at once started the Troop forward with their .50 heavy machine-gun, three GPMGs and three Bren LMGs to engage this fresh target.*

Apart from the reference to the Individual Weapon Sight (IWS) and the substitution of the GPMG for the Vickers Gun, this could have described an action during the Second World War. The 'Sight, Infantry Weapon, L1A2' (Rank Pullin SS20) was a cumbersome first-generation image-intensifying sight issued in conjunction with the L1 infantry rifle or the GPMG. Many of the photographs taken in the Falklands show these sights to good advantage. Interestingly, despite the relative industrial strengths of the participants (and the parlous state of the contemporary Argentine economy), the defenders had second-generation French Sopelem and American Varo AN/PVS-4 StarLight image-intensifiers and excellent night-vision systems. Improved night vision was particularly useful in the Falklands, where dusk fell shortly after four o'clock local time.

Photographs taken in the Falklands reveal that the US M16 rifle was popular with many Commando officers and the men drawn from the Mountain and Arctic Warfare Cadre, who usually trained the Commandos but served in the Falklands as 3 Commando Brigade Reconnaissance Troop. Lee-Enfield type L42A1 sniper rifles were also in evidence.

Since the Falklands campaign, however, comparatively few wars have been fought in the traditional manner. Indeed, as this method involves a potential for large-scale casualties, the trend can be seen, in many Western states at least, towards removing the human element from conflict. This is, of course, a political issue; the effect on electorates of scenes of body bags being brought out of combat is feared by governments – the US

* Brigadier Julian Thompson, Officer Commanding 3 Commando Brigade, describing events during the night attack on Mount Longdon and Two Sisters, 11/12 June 1982; from *No Picnic: 3 Commando Brigade in the South Atlantic, 1982*.

authorities recently tried unsuccessfully to sanitise media coverage of the Iraq war, trying to hide images of flag-draped coffins being flown back to the USA, and it takes little imagination to see the same happening in Britain, German, Italy or France if death-rolls rise . . . even on peacekeeping duties.

Attempts to remove vulnerable personnel from the battlefield, which in some agencies is now taken to be *any* personnel, have resulted in the development of a wide range of sophisticated weaponry. Increasing reliance is placed on electronic eavesdropping, made possible by satellite technology; pilotless drones to undertake battlefield surveillance; and weapons such as cruise missiles and laser-guided bombs that can be delivered from long range.

Among the most recent public demonstrations of this trend, which was in itself unusual, has been a 'race' held in the USA for Autonomous Ground Vehicles (AGVs) – robotised vehicles that are designed to fulfil tasks that often expose non-combatants to risks that are now perceived to be unreasonable. The project is said to have been accelerated by the high-profile story of US Army Private Jessica Lynch, captured in the early days of the war with Iraq and then rescued by US Special Forces in circumstances that are still touched with controversy.

The 'winner' of the AGV race only managed to complete a little over seven miles of the intended 142-mile route through the California desert, but this is now merely seen as a stepping-stone to the ultimate goal.

But the technology that allows the creation of an AGV, a cruise missile or a smart bomb sometimes creates a myth – that technological might alone is right, and that 'Shock and Awe' will somehow provide a result without the casualties (at least, in this case, on the Allied side). This can be true in the short term, but customarily sidesteps the question of aftermath. One of the lessons of history is that force alone can never work unless there is sufficient justification, and unless there is a long-term 'hearts and minds' strategy of the sort that has been conspicuously absent in many of the current zones of conflict: Iraq, Sudan, parts of central Africa, and the long-lasting disputes between the Israelis and the Palestinians.

Consequently, though conventional armed forces will often win the opening round of a one-sided war with ease, they are not so well equipped to undertake the roles of policemen. Nor can armies deal easily with terrorism. It has often been argued that the recent incursions into Afghanistan and Iraq have made the world a more dangerous place, partly by raising the profile of Osama Bin Laden and Al-Qaeda (in particular) and partly by polarising disaffected societies into camps of a fanaticism unseen since the mediaeval Crusades.

Short-term political solutions are usually difficult to find and each individual situation is likely to deteriorate as the 'terrorists' – and the adage that one man's terrorist is another man's hope for freedom should be remembered – acquire increasingly sophisticated means of delivering their messages. Audacious attacks, such as that on the World Trade Center in New York or the Madrid rapid-transit railway system, may be high-profile, but they represent only the visible tip of a largely hidden pyramid of small cells. It is these cells that Special Forces and counter-terrorist groups must often detect and destroy, and it is here that small-arms design is likely to make the most progress.

Since the original *Guns of the Elite* was published, in 1987, there has been comparatively little change in the design of the weapons of the rank-and-file in most armies. The US Army still issues a variant of the M16, the British have the A2 version of the L85, and the French continue to use the FA MAS. The Germans, after abandoning the potentially revolutionary caseless-cartridge G11 (a casualty of the burgeoning costs of German reunification), have accepted the Heckler & Koch G36; and the Italians have finally taken the Beretta AR 70-90 in quantity. Yet these guns are all still conventional in design and performance.

Military industries undoubtedly have a vested interest in encouraging the arms trade, but, at least as far as infantry small-arms are concerned, the effort being put into research and development has yet to alter the traditionalist view. Attempts are still being made to provide multi-role firearms, combining the ability to fire grenades or shotgun ammunition alongside the conventional high-velocity rifle firing ultra-high-speed flechette rounds, but combination weapons await a major change in policy before they can make headway. All that can be seen at present is a trend towards large-scale issue of conventional infantry rifles, such as the M16A2 or the AK-74M, but fitted with grenade launchers, image-intensifying sights and designators.

Perhaps the most interesting of the current generation of projects is the FN 'Personal Weapon' or P-90, which was originally intended to arm second-rank or non-combatant personnel but is being taken very seriously as an ideal solution to the age-old problem of balancing the need for adequate firepower (which rules out guns firing pistol ammunition) with restrictions of size and weight (which in turn limit the power of the ammunition that can be fired comfortably). This is an interesting throwback to the M1 Carbine, though the FN rifle chambers what is effectively little more than a highly developed high-velocity handgun round instead of a purpose-built intermediate cartridge. Early impressions of its combat potential have not been entirely favourable.

Another trend that can be discerned is the widespread issue of special sights. The example set by the British and the Austrians, who have issued the L85 and AUG with optical sights, has been followed elsewhere. It is now commonplace to see US Army troops carrying M16A2 rifles fitted with optical sights, or M4 carbines fitted with optical sights and designators (laser or light beam) beneath the muzzle. Improvements in manufacturing technology and increases in production capacity have now reduced the cost of image-intensifying systems to a point where mass issues are permissible, and there can be little argument that enhanced marksmanship has resulted.

A third trend may be seen in the increasing incorporation of synthetic parts in small-arms design. Though guns such as the

AUG, introduced in the late 1970s, have always been renowned for a 'Space Age' appearance and the Glock was (and indeed, still is) often misleadingly regarded as the 'undetectable gun', the infantry weapons of most large-scale armies still rely not only on old designs – fifty years old, in some cases – but also on traditional metal-based manufacturing techniques. Even though these sometimes prove to be derived from pressing, welding and other fabrication systems pioneered in Germany during the Second World War, they are nonetheless expensive in terms of capital investment and unit-cost unless production runs into hundreds of thousands. However, the use of sophisticated injection moulding allows parts to be designed with more regard for ergonomics than was once the case; the ease of decontamination after a nuclear, chemical or biological attack is also often enhanced.

Few commercial enterprises can take financial risks of this magnitude, and, in the last decades, the manufacture of such weaponry has become increasingly concentrated in the hands of a few large and powerful businesses. These in turn have been swallowed up by even larger conglomerates . . . or have failed, often because they have been unable to replace obsolescent product-ranges that have come to the end of their natural life. FN Herstal, Colt, Smith & Wesson, Walther and even Heckler & Koch have fallen victim to this trend in recent years, whereas Glock is still on an ascendant that could cease just as soon as another handgun grabs the headlines.

Currently, the application of synthetic components is seen to best effect with handguns. This is partly because they are comparatively small, and structural rigidity is easier to obtain in a small envelope; it is also partly because the use of sophisticated (and by inference expensive) raw material is less critical than in a rifle, and also because the pistols chamber low-power ammunition. There is still a tendency to substitute a metal frame – now often stainless steel – for a synthetic frame if the chamberings become too powerful, but this problem will undoubtedly be solved in a few years time.

Chapter 3

The Terrorist Threat

Fighting guerrillas on their own terms and dealing with urban terrorism in a politically acceptable way have brought the greatest changes in the guns of the elite. Virtually any weapon needed to fulfil a specific task will now simply be brought in. SAS personnel, for example, have been seen carrying M16/M16A1 rifles, Ruger Mini-14, Steyr AUG, Heckler & Koch G3 and G41 rifles, and a wide variety of sniping equipment, including Finnish Tikka and Accuracy International PM (L96A1) rifles. Infra-red, laser-assisted and image-intensifying sights have all been used to good effect, particularly after dusk when traditional open sights are useless.

Submachine-guns, too, have found increasing favour for short-range work, but their use is not without hazard. The massacre of Israeli Olympic athletes at the Munich Games in 1972, and the subsequent reaction by the West German authorities, highlighted the continual dichotomy between assault and dialogue. The terrorists initially seized eleven hostages, killing two; during the subsequent counter-attack, unfortunately, fifteen more died – all the surviving athletes, five terrorists and a policeman. The West German government was shocked into forming a specialist CTW unit under Ulrich Wegener, to prevent further occurrences on the Munich scale. Owing to an understandable reluctance to form an elite unit from the ranks of the German Army, GSG-9 was attached to the Bundesgrenzschutz, the Federal Border Guard, and based at St Augustin near Bonn.

One positive result was the anti-terrorist operation mounted at Mogadishu airport, in the Somali Republic, by Major Alastair Morrison and Sergeant Barry Davies of the SAS together with nearly thirty GSG-9 representatives led by Wegener himself. The aim was to free the crew and nearly eighty terrified passengers on a Lufthansa jet seized by four hijackers intent on bartering for the release of the notorious Baader-Meinhof gang, but all hopes of a peaceful solution vanished when the hijackers murdered the pilot.

On 17 October 1977, therefore, the main SAS/GSG-9 assault team hit the plane from both sides, entering through the emergency exits above each wing to the accompaniment of 'flash-bang' concussion/blinding grenades. Eight minutes later, it was all over; three of the four terrorists (two male, one female) lay dead and the surviving woman terrorist had no fewer than nine bullet wounds. None of the assault team had been seriously hurt, and the passengers had escaped virtually unscathed.

But none could deny an element of good fortune. The terrorists had chosen to fight on their feet, so the seated passengers had been below the line of fire; neither of the grenades that the terrorist leader had thrown had done anything other than damage the substantially-constructed aircraft seats; and there had been no fire, despite the proximity of aviation fuel and a liberal sousing of duty-free alcohol. After the event, much concern was voiced about the suitability of the Smith & Wesson Model 36 revolvers, chambering the ineffectual 0.38in Special round. Hollow-point ammunition had not been used and the attackers had failed to stop the grenades being thrown, despite hitting the thrower at least four times. The man had been finished off with a 9mm Parabellum HK54 (the original designation of the MP5) submachine-gun.

The concern was justifiable; lessons were plain for all to learn. However, not all future operations were to be so fortunate – not least being the assault by Egyptian Force 777 commandos on a hijacked airliner at Valletta airport in September 1985, which cost the lives of nearly sixty people. Though many of the luckless hostages died from smoke inhalation, some had gunshot wounds and a few were shot accidentally after emerging from the aeroplane; clearly, the tactics were very poor.

Another misjudgement occurred in September 1986, when a Pan-Am Boeing 747 was hijacked to Karachi airport. The Pakistani special services group elected to shoot the Palestinian terrorist leader, who had been observed spending much time in the cockpit, as a prelude to an all-out assault. Unfortunately, the chosen sniper, expert marksman though he may have been, was expected to hit a head-size target at a range of about 400 yards with a Finnish-made 7.62 x 51mm Tikka bolt-action rifle. Though this was judged to be possible – albeit at the limits of what could be expected – no allowance was made for the strength or angle of an aircraft windscreen built to withstand the impact of large birds and tested, as Boeing subsequently confirmed, by hitting it with ten pounds of hamburgers travelling at 290mph. Two 7.62mm bullets struck the cockpit glass, but failed to penetrate; and the sound of the impact so unnerved the hijackers that they opened fire on the passengers, killing more than twenty.

Among the greatest successes in the history of counter-terrorist operations was the Israeli Operation 'Thunderball'. In June 1976, a combined PLO and Baader-Meinhof force had seized an Air France Tel Aviv–Paris flight and redirected it to Entebbe airport in Uganda. The resulting murder of one of the hostages persuaded the Israeli government to act decisively and members of the crack '269' Commando, drawn from Sayeret Golani and 35 Parachute Brigade, hit Entebbe on the night of 3/4 July 1976. The raid was a stunning success, 103 people being released for the loss of only Lieutenant-Colonel Yonatan Netanyahu, the Israeli commander. One elderly hostage had been murdered previously and two were killed during the raid, one having mistakenly attacked his rescuer, but the minimal cost in lives had justified the risk.

The restricted space in the four C-130 Hercules transports dictated the choice of the Ingram submachine-gun, rather than the Uzi, and night-sighted Kalashnikov assault rifles were used in a search for an ideal combination of firepower in a small package. Identifying these 'Kalashnikovs' has proved difficult; some sources aver that they were Valmets supplied from Finland – as the Israeli Galil rifle (itself a modification of the basic Russian design) was still in its developmental phase. However, photographs of the Israelis' triumphant return show that some of the rifles, at least, once had folding bayonets under the muzzle; the mounting blocks are usually visible ahead of the auxiliary grip, added to facilitate holding the muzzle down in automatic fire. As only the Chinese Type 56 Kalashnikov variant has a folding bayonet, some (if not all) of the guns used at Entebbe must have been captured from the Egyptians or the PLO.

Operation 'Nimrod', the successful storming of the Iranian Embassy in Palace Gate, London, in May 1980, was another victory for special forces in an urban environment. The British SAS Counter-Revolutionary Warfare (CRW) team was called in to rescue the 'survivors' of twenty hostages being held in the embassy by seven terrorists, who had commenced an unacceptable series of executions by killing the Iranian press attaché and dumping his body on the steps.

The operation was awkward and very risky, the hostages being kept in separate groups inside a building containing more than fifty rooms. The only way into the front of the embassy was to abseil down the façade and blow out an armoured-glass window, trusting to luck and the superior training of the SAS CRW squad. A simultaneous attack on the rear would, it was hoped, divide (and thereby conquer) the terrorists' efforts.

The embassy assault was the first in which the SAS, wary of the inaccuracy of their Ingram submachine-guns, turned to the 'Hockler' (the Heckler & Koch HK54/MP5) as a result of witnessing the events at Mogadishu in 1977. Clothed in black, wearing gas masks and flak vests, armed with the submachine-guns and Browning GP pistols, the attackers descended the ropes and began the assault confident in their 'Killing Room' training, which taught them to hit the target unerringly with a 'tap-tap' – two shots in the head or chest – even if they were tumbling, or if visibility was poor.

Unfortunately, a flailing boot broke one of the windows during the abseil down the back of the building and the element of surprise was largely lost. One SAS man was trapped on the rope, preventing the forcible removal of the armoured glass with the explosive charge, and the glass was hacked and kicked-in to the accompaniment of 'flash-bangs', concussion grenades liberally laced with magnesium powder to give a brilliant blinding flash.

Inside the building, the terrorist leader, attempting to shoot the leading SAS man as he entered the back of the embassy, was brought down by PC Trevor Lock, one of the hostages, and eliminated with a burst from an SAS man's submachine-gun during the ensuing struggle. A hundred seconds after the first team had begun the descent, the second team blasted the armoured glass out of the front of the building and the 'front men' darted into the building under cover of concussion grenades (and a CS gas grenade calculated to disable the sixth terrorist hiding in an upstairs room).

The SAS man stuck on his rope, and in danger of burning every time he swung towards the offending window at the back of the building, was unceremoniously cut down. On running into the embassy, he came face to face with a terrorist and instinctively shot him dead.

On the second floor, in room ten, the telex room, the SAS had taken no chances, shooting three terrorists heedless of their attempts to hide among the hostages. One hostage lay dead, executed by the terrorists, and another had been seriously wounded. In Room Nine, the terrorist guarding the five women hostages had surrendered, been uncompromisingly hurled down the stairs and dragged out into the street. Upstairs, the seventh man had also met his fate; eleven minutes had passed, six terrorists and two Iranian Embassy officials were dead. But the remaining hostages were free, and the CRW operation had been a great success.

The submachine-gun is ideally suited to use in situations where the maximum rate of fire must be combined with an ability to place single shots with extreme accuracy at short range – not forgetting total reliability and lethality only sufficient to halt the intended target. Conventional high-power military rifle cartridges (even the intermediate 5.56mm M193 and 7.62mm M43) fire jacketed bullets that will almost certainly tear through an animate target at short range, risking the deaths of other, possibly innocent participants.

Though the same stricture was once applied to the traditional metal-jacketed 9mm Parabellum bullet, the development of many soft- and hollow-point rounds, together with ultra-high penetrators, has invalidated such criticism. Among the most lethal of the new breed is the Glaser Safety Slug, a concoction of Teflon-encased shot inside a copper case specifically designed to penetrate and fragment. The Glaser Slug is especially effective.

Owing to the progress made with the projectiles, 9 x 19mm has made a comeback in special forces' use. However, the use of the more arcane projectiles is often frowned upon by military and police authorities as being against the spirit of their operations and, more realistically, embarrassing to their political masters. The dilemma is not new; the use of Dum-Dum bullets was prevented by the Hague Convention of 1907 and, even during the First World War, the Germans switched from flat- to round-nose 9mm Parabellum bullets, allegedly to prevent the Allies making capital out of atrocity stories; more recently, many individuals have discovered that a small coin or a piece of barbed wire embedded in the nose of a baton round increases its effectiveness significantly, but also causes an appreciable nuisance politically.

There can be no justification for using 'doctored' rounds – plastic bullets or otherwise – for crowd control when less radical solutions can be found. However, terrorists abide by no code other than their own and any attempt to impose 'political' strictures on airport defence, for example, inevitably hamstrings the defenders.

Despite the outcry over the issue of 9mm Heckler & Koch MP5s to British police or airport patrols from the mid-1980s onward, the submachine-gun has tremendous advantages over large-calibre pistols; it is large enough to take the intensifier sight needed to repel night attacks, has a sighting radius that is long enough to promote accurate shooting, and an automatic-fire capability that can be held in reserve.

Although the pistol is handier and can be got into action very quickly, it is appreciably more difficult to shoot: recoil is greater owing to the low gun weight, inhibiting accurately placed follow-up shots, and the short sight radius magnifies aiming errors. The pistol is undoubtedly indispensable for rapid-fire at less than twenty yards, but of much less use to repel a night attack from a co-ordinated force.

Some armies rejected the pistol entirely in the 1960s, while others attempted to combine the functions of an infantry rifle and a submachine-gun in an assault rifle. Those who rejected the pistol soon found the bulk of the submachine-gun awkward in circumstances where concealment was paramount, while the assault weapons were never as effective at long range as the large-calibre infantry rifles.

Special forces have done much to re-establish the reputation of the submachine-gun in counter-terrorist operations, largely owing to a continual reassessment of the balance between firepower and handiness. The emergence of the current generation of submachine-guns is entirely coincidental, rather than a major contributory factor; although the Uzi, Beretta Mo. 12S and Ingram were undeniably very efficient, the publicity accorded them overlooked that the world's best distributed design in the 1980s was the British Sterling – simple and reliable, but designed prior to 1945! The Heckler & Koch MP5 was not even a submachine-gun in the classic sense, but rather a diminutive automatic rifle.

The tactical use of the submachine-gun by CTW squads differs little, fundamentally, from the use made by the German *Sturmtruppen* of the First World War. The goal remains the same: maximum effect with the greatest possible surprise. Just as the early storm troops trained in mock trenches before mounting an assault, so the modern CTW specialist trains in 'Battle Houses' or 'Killing Rooms', where each corner may hide a pop-up terrorist. Some targets are partly obscured, many hold hostages, others need friend-or-foe identification before firing; the whole course is designed to simulate the conditions encountered in action, even to the extent of smoke, gas and concussion grenades, though the psychological strain of the real thing cannot be readily duplicated.

Modern training is geared to the totality of fighting in a modern urban environment, with the perfection of 'non-gun' techniques such as abseiling, unarmed combat and room-clearance. A greater premium is placed on marksmanship than previously, with one-shot or (particularly with the pistol or submachine-gun) a 'tap-tap' rapid two-shot kill being all but obligatory. In the confines of a small room, there can be no second chance.

Combat shotguns and sniper rifles were also to the fore in the embassy sieges and anti-hijack operations, and have become a regular feature of combat teams. In each team of four or six men, at least one will have a specialised firearm. Shotguns are useful to blow locks from doors (helping to minimise aiming errors) and are also a great deterrent; sniper rifles permit accurate placement of shots at long range – even if the rifles are little more than standard weapons with telescope sights. For example, optically sighted Heckler & Koch HK33 rifles were carried by some members of C13, Scotland Yard's anti-terrorist squad, and D11 (the elite Metropolitan Police marksmen) during the Libyan Embassy siege.

Continued improvement in optical sights, together with the widespread distribution of passive infra-red and image-intensifying sights, has enabled the sniper to double as an intelligence gatherer. Consequently, a marksman may have to observe his target for hours before deciding whether to shoot or await a better chance. However, modern sniper rifles – particularly those used for counter-terrorist warfare – are often very much heavier than the army-inspired service patterns used during the Second World War and Korea, and even in Vietnam. Fitting bipods, which to many seem anachronistic on a rifle, allows marksmen to observe for long periods with a minimum of fatigue.

One of the very best examples of sniping occurred in Djibouti in 1976, when Somali revolutionaries kidnapped a busload of French schoolchildren. The danger of the situation was such that only simultaneous elimination of the terrorists would ensure the survival of the children. The task fell to the French national CTW unit Groupement d'Intervention de la Gendarmerie Nationale (GIGN), led by Lieutenant Marcel Prouteau. His plan was to position his superbly trained snipers so that each man could be allocated to an individual target. A radio ring-link was established between the men and Prouteau so that firing could be ordered only when the snipers had a clear shot. When the command was given five of the six terrorists were killed instantaneously with single shots from ranges of up to 200 metres. Though one child was murdered before the GIGN squad could reach the bus to eliminate the sixth and final terrorist, the operation was adjudged a great success.

The last decade of the twentieth century brought no notable slackening in international tension. Though some of the major areas of conflict were stabilised – most notably, South Africa – countless new flashpoints emerged to replace them. Especially worrying was the fragmentation of what was once Yugoslavia into an ugly territorial war in which lines of demarcation were constantly being drawn and re-drawn. The situation was sometimes simplistically considered to be Catholic Croat against Russian Orthodox Serb against Bosnian Muslim, but the issues were far more complex. They encompassed the settlement of long-held grudges, long-suppressed desires for territorial expansion, and deep-rooted demands for religious freedom.

Elsewhere, though the Iran-Iraq war ceased, the invasion of Kuwait by Iraq caused a war in which leading Western powers became embroiled on a large scale. Trouble between Jew and Arab still raged in the Middle East, and though strides towards a lasting peace have been made from time to time, extremist factions on both sides have been reluctant to embrace them. The massacre of Palestinians by a supporter of the right-wing Israeli Meir Kahane, the violence perpetrated on Jewish settlers in the Gaza Strip by the Fatah Hawks (extremists on the fringe of the PLO) and the cycle of Palestinian suicide bombings and Israeli retaliation all underscore that problems can never be solved overnight. The spectre of sectarian violence in Northern Ireland still haunts the British Government. Hutu has killed Tutsi in Rwanda; Tamils still kill Singhalese in Sri Lanka. The list is endless.

On one day in July 1994 – a quiet one – *The Times* reported the bombing of the Israeli Mutual Association in Buenos Aires, with the loss of nearly a hundred lives; the apparent victory of the Rwanda Popular Front in its bloody struggle against pro-government forces; clashes between resistance forces and Indonesian troops in East Timor; and all against the backcloth of the continuing struggle in Bosnia.

A decade later, on 27 May 2004 (another quiet day!), the same newspaper was reporting the threat of an Al-Qaeda attack 'on an international summit or political convention within the next few months'; the political aftermath of the enforced removal of more than 100,000 Christian refugees into neighbouring Chad (and the slaughter of thousands more) by the Islamic government of Sudan; heavy fighting between American troops and al-Mahdi militants in the Iraqi holy city of Najaf; the arrest of radical Islamic suspects in Tokyo; a bomb attack on an English-language school in Karachi, in Pakistan, blamed on extremists of Harkat-ul Mujahidin al-Alami; and the discovery of a mass grave of Muslim civilians in Bratunac, in Bosnia-Herzogovina, that had lain undetected since Bosnian Serbs had murdered them in May 1992.

A particularly worrying long-term problem has been posed by the fragmentation of the Soviet Union and its many satellites into disparate states of uncertain political stability. Many observers rejoiced in the end of the Cold War, but the problems may only now be beginning. Though the political complexion of the Warsaw Pact was diametrically opposed to that of NATO, the confrontation between the two super-power blocs was essentially a stalemate. Each knew that the other possessed weapons of devastating capability, and that any pre-emptive strike would be followed by retaliation in kind before results could be achieved.

The bloody conflict between pro-Yeltsin and pro-Rutskoi forces in Russia in the autumn of 1993 ended in a violent attack on the White House – Moscow's parliamentary building – by units loyal to Yeltsin, supported by armoured vehicles, tanks and artillery. The human cost was difficult to ascertain, though reports were filed of more than 400 dead.

The ensuing democratisation of former Communist-led states has created its own share of uneasy alliances and flashpoints, whilst simultaneously heightening the internal tension that the Soviets had almost always managed to suppress. Countries such as Poland, Hungary, the Baltic States, the Czech Republic and Slovakia, with traditions of self-determination, have remained stable. So, too, have Bulgaria and Romania, though the latter benefited only after the fall of Caeaucescu. Albania is mired in the Balkans conflict, protective of the persecuted Albanian minority in Kosovo, but newly-formed political groupings and rediscovered religious convictions jostle uneasily in one-time constituents of the USSR such as Azerbaizhan, Tazhikistan and Georgia.

There can be no doubt that one of the most dangerous flashpoints is provided by Chechnya, regarded by the Russians as an integral part of the Russian state and by many Chechens as a separate entity. The results of the conflict have been bloody in the extreme, with the brutality of the Russian forces in Chechnya – much of which is devastated ruins – being matched only by the ruthlessness of the Chechen separatists.

The ability of the modern guerrilla to acquire sophisticated explosives, anti-aircraft missiles and even bioterrorism agents is well known. Atrocities carried out in the name of Al-Qaeda have escalated to a point where co-ordinated action in the USA on 11 September 2002 led to the destruction of the twin towers of the

World Trade Center in New York and a death roll approaching 3,000. There was little that CTW forces could do to prevent the attack, and, even in the aftermath, opinions differ over what would constitute a justifiable response in similar circumstances. Even if the airliners had been shot down, could not collateral damage on the ground have been as bad as the actual event?

The Chechen separatists have made devastating attacks on residential areas in major Russian cities and on the underground railway in Moscow, and, most recently, assassinated the pro-Russian Chechen premier during a military review. Another public atrocity, which is now remembered principally because of the deaths of many hostages, was made when 800 theatre-goers in the Palace of Culture in Moscow were imprisoned by 60 Chechens – 42 men and 18 women – on 23 October 2002. Led by Movsar Barayev, the attackers immediately planted explosive devices and, as each of the women wore a bomb-belt, forced the authorities to consider their response carefully. Two people had been killed during the initial attack and eventually, when shots were heard from inside the building on the morning of 26 October, the Alpha Unit of Spetsnaz (the Russian special forces) was given permission to attempt to rescue the hostages.

A conventional 'all-out' assault was ruled-out by the large open spaces of the auditorium, which provided very little cover; it was obvious that the Chechen women would detonate their belts long before they could be eliminated, and that the civilian casualties would probably be unacceptably high. Consequently, the decision was taken to pump a strong sedative – apparently an opiate known as fentanyl – into the air-conditioning system in an attempt to reduce the alertness of the terrorists.

Shortly after dawn, the Russians stormed the building in classic style, using explosive charges to blast through walls and relying on snipers to eliminate the Chechen guards in the foyer.* When the Alpha Unit men entered the auditorium, hostages and terrorists alike had been completely overcome by the gas. The unconscious female bomb-carriers were summarily executed, and the male terrorists were killed either in the theatre itself or during a brief firefight in the corridors.

When the operation had been completed, all but one of the women had been killed (an injured survivor was subsequently found in hospital) and all of the men of the group had been killed excepting for two captives and possibly a few escapees. The Russians had lost one man, and two hostages had been killed by gunfire.

The operation would have been regarded as a great success – one of the greatest of all CTW feats – but for the condition of the hostages, many of whom died from the effects of gas that had clearly been too strong. Returns made on 28 October revealed that 115 had died, and that 150 of the 646 people who were still being treated in hospital were in intensive care. Ultimately, the death roll was to be placed at 129 and Russian public opinion hardened. This was not helped by President Putin's reluctance to accept that the blame lay at least partially with the use of gas, justifiable though the tactic must have seemed in the prelude to the assault. Blaming the deaths on the susceptibility of the individual hostages to breathing difficulties and heart attacks – undoubtedly true in some individual cases – merely inflamed the situation, particularly when the Russian authorities refused to release details of the gas so that medical treatment could be improved.

The attack on the Palace of Culture reminded anti-terrorist services that large-scale CTW operations are difficult to co-ordinate, and entail a very real risk to the lives of hostages if the opponents are determined enough. There is a tendency to label 'terrorists' as insane, but the reality is simply that they often have a dedication to their cause that – for reasons of belief or indoctrination – transcends death. This concept is now so alien to Western society that it poses a potentially unbridgeable gap to understanding the suicide bombers' mind set.

---

* This they did with efficiency, firing from positions on rooftops and from the balconies of flats standing about 200 metres distant. However, it is believed that only two shots were fired to kill the only two terrorists who had remained in place.

With exceptions such as the Entebbe Raid, successful CTW operations tend to be small-scale and the task that faced the men of the Russian Alpha Unit was particularly onerous. It is probably fair to observe that the Russians made mistakes, but also that there was little precedent to guide them. Not all situations unfold so publicly.

Russian Special Forces were also involved in the Beslan school siege in North Ossetia in September 2004. Details are still sketchy, and the published casualty figures (331 civilians, 13 police and officials, 11 Russian military personnel) may be a sham. Among the operational mistakes seem to have been a lack of communication and a failure to impose an exclusion zone. Consequently, armed civilians are said to have begun the attack.

Far more successful were the covert attacks made by US Special Forces and Grom ('Thunder'), an SAS-trained Polish counter-terrorist unit, on oil rigs near Umm Qasr in the Gulf of Basra immediately prior to the invasion of Iraq in 2003. Intelligence suggested that charges had been rigged to explode immediately any Allied advance was recognised, with the intention of creating a 'flaming sea' to bar the Allied advance into the strategically-important Iraqi port of Basra, and the decision was taken to neutralise the threat. The plans were interesting for the way in which they combined different elements of attack. The Polish squad, for example, relied on frogmen to approach the platform unseen to disarm any explosive devices that had been attached to the legs of the rig, and commandos to climb the superstructure to disable any charges that lay above the water before confronting the oil-rig crew. The attack was to be at night, when only a handful of armed guards would be patrolling the rig-deck. But it was also to be made from a circling helicopter, and asked a lot of the snipers to dispatch the guards efficiently.

In the event, 25 Poles commanded by Colonel Roman Połko took just three minutes to eliminate the armed guards, which was a tribute not only to the skills of the marksmen but also to those of the helicopter pilots. The men are said to have carried

Glock pistols, Uzi submachine-guns and KA-90 Tantal (Kalashnikov-type) assault rifles fitted with 40mm Pallad grenade launchers. Grom snipers have often favoured bolt-action Hecate rifles, but Heckler & Koch PSG-1 rifles were used on this occasion; their auto-loading action was better suited to rapid fire in the close confines of a helicopter body.

Though many Western countries are using the so-called Peace Dividend to cut deeply into their armed forces, an obvious way of reducing financial burden, they may be doing so much too soon and much too greatly. Probably two decades will pass before the political squabbling in the fragmented ex-Soviet territory finally abates.

Neither does the need for weapons show signs of declining. Indeed, with the demise of the USSR, military-surplus guns have become available not only in great quantity but also at very low prices. This has guaranteed that, instead of supply contracting, Kalashnikov rifles have found their way onto the international market in large quantities. This has forced their price down, and thus facilitated distribution in a way that was difficult (if not impossible) under the old regimes. Russian mobsters are already armed with automatic weapons on such a grandiose scale that compared with 1992, according to *Izvestia*, the crime-rate in Moscow in 1993 had tripled and the murder rate doubled. By 2002 the crime-rate was nearly ten times 1992 levels. Large quantities of ex-Soviet equipment have been exported by way of Baltic ports, particularly Tallinn. In Kaliningrad, when Soviet troops were withdrawing in the spring of 1993, it was possible to buy an AK-74 for a mere $50 and floods of ex-Soviet small-arms have entered the underworld in many Western European countries. In Britain, for example, there was a sudden spate of crimes in Manchester and Liverpool in the late 1990s that involved ex-Soviet 9mm Makarov (PM) pistols.

The continuing need for policing duties, burgeoning terrorist activity, and the occasional small-scale war still assures continuing employment not only for the elite but also, by implication, for the guns of the elite.

Chapter 4

Handguns

Wars continue, and civil strife shows no real signs of lessening, merely changing the focus of attention periodically. Both the Gulf War (1991) and the current conflict in Iraq have reaffirmed that the handgun still has an important military role in Western armed forces, even if this is simply to back up more powerful weapons.

The adoption of the Beretta auto-loader by the US Army, together with the 9mm Parabellum cartridge, led to a wholesale reassessment of police weaponry in the USA. Faced with the ever increasing use of large-calibre pistols, submachine-guns, auto-loading carbines, and even assault rifles by the criminal fraternities, the police have been forced to accept similar weapons.

The 0.32in Smith & Wesson or Colt holster revolver, so familiar to older generations of American policemen, holds comparatively little threat for members of the drug-trafficking rings, who are likely to be carrying an Ingram, an Uzi or a Kalashnikov as a handgun. Yet the problem of arming public servants appropriately is not new; in the 1930s, for example, Clyde Barrow (of Bonnie & Clyde) often used a 0.30in Browning Automatic Rifle – with three 20-round magazines welded together – against policemen and even Federal agents armed with nothing more potent than a Thompson submachine-gun.

The American police forces, long-time bastions of firearms conservatism, were seduced in the 1980s by the lure of the auto-loading pistol. Many patriotically bought the excellent Smith & Wessons; some have followed the military lead and taken the Beretta 92F; and others, more recently, have opted for the Glock.

The advantages are clear to see. Not least are the prodigious cartridge capacities (even though the additional thickness of the grip may not suit everyone) and the ease with which an empty box magazine can be replaced. In this context, despite greater reliability in adverse conditions, the five-or six-shot revolver is no longer as attractive a proposition as it was twenty years ago. The pistols are also generally more powerful, often shoot more accurately, and are undeniably less tiring to shoot – though it should be remembered that most speed-shooting records have been set with revolvers.

Military pistols have undergone little real change, which is largely due to the long-term view with which official adoption is usually taken. Excepting the special forces, which are allowed appreciably more freedom of choice than the regulars, most armies retain conventional weapons such as the Browning GP-35, perfected prior to the Second World War, or the post-war Beretta that is based on the pre-war Walther P. 38. Apart from the Glock, which has been an outstanding success with sales that now exceed two million, the 'hi-tech' genre has yet to convince the world's leading armies of its long-term benefits. Sales of the Czech ČZ 100 have not been inspiring, and the new police-issue ČZ P-01 is little more than a modernised form of the traditionally-made ČZ 85. The Smith & Wesson 'Enhanced Sigma' series has been supplemented by the SW99, a variant of the Walther P99, but neither this nor the German prototype has yet been adopted for military service.

The US armed forces, perhaps acknowledging criticism of the Beretta M9, began another programme of tests in the late 1990s. It will be interesting to see how these ultimately resolve. After the Joint Services Small Arms Program (JSSAP) series, SIG and Smith & Wesson both alleged unfair treatment, and many commentators were prepared to champion the then-unproven Ruger P-85 as a better alternative to the M9. It may be fair to say that the Ruger, in spite of its good qualities, has never encountered large-scale commercial success – even though the series has now proceeded to the KP97.

Excepting the Glock, the only European pistol to have achieved major market penetration in recent years is the ČZ 75/ČZ 85 pattern, which is actually a very traditional design in modern clothing. This gun has been copied in several countries – a certain sign of high quality – and regularly won IPSC Practical Pistol competitions in the 1980s and 1990s with a minimum of fine-tuning. It once seemed that the ČZ had appeared in the wrong place and at the wrong time to gain significant military acceptance, even though a contract to supply 50,000 to the Turkish state police was signed in 1993. But the ČZ pistols remain fitting inheritors of the traditions of a Czech firearms industry that, even during the period of Soviet domination, was always willing to pursue an independent line of thought. Guns of this type are being made in Italy by Tanfoglio, in Switzerland by ASAI (part of the Oerlikon Group), successor to ITM and Sphinx, and, in a modified form, by Israeli Military Industries.

Among significant recent developments in pistol design, apart from the near-universal acceptance of large-capacity magazines, has been the insistence on ambidextrous magazine catches, safety levers and slide-release systems. There has also been a much-touted move to 'double-action-only' ('DAO') trigger systems, which are designed partly for simplicity and partly to enhance safety. They echo the school of thought that considers the provision of too many safety features as an inhibition in combat, and can be considered as the pistol equivalent of a double-action revolver with a transfer-bar system. The guns can only be fired with a deliberate pull through of the trigger, and remain safe at all other times. They can be dropped and thrown about, and will not fire.

The 'old guard' semi-automatics have gradually been replaced by adaptations meeting these criteria. Yet the basic actions are rarely new, and only a handful of the many new pistol systems touted in the last twenty years have achieved service status.

What features should be incorporated in a combat handgun?

It is one thing to win prizes on a Practical Pistol range, where the cartridges have already been sized through the chamber, but quite another for the same gun to function efficiently in desert sand in the hands of an inexperienced army conscript to whom ammunition of mixed parentage has been issued. During the Gulf War, Americans complained that sand and dust jammed their Berettas, while British troops complained that dust and sand jammed their Brownings.

History is littered with instances of men with marksman status on the firing-range freezing in the terror of combat, whilst mediocre shots with ice-cool nerves have often performed far beyond expectations. Much has been made of a survey, compiled immediately after the end of the Second World War, which suggested that only fifteen per cent of frontline US Army soldiers wanted to fire their guns at all and only two per cent were deliberately shooting at the enemy. This has recently been extrapolated to show that soldiers are not prepared to kill, and thus that armies are intrinsically ineffectual. This is quite wrong; the original figures refer to men fresh from harrowing campaigns in Europe and the Pacific, and cannot be compared with today's forces. Other studies purport to show that 95 per cent of today's soldiers will shoot to kill when necessary, the inference being that innate resistance to killing has somehow weakened in the intervening period. The truth is probably much simpler: the men of today are simply much more professional than the conscripts serving in 1945.

Assassinations have failed even though several hits from a weapon of 'the right type' were made on the intended target; others have succeeded when one shot from a theoretically inferior handgun has proved lethal. Once again, the arbiter has often been simply the nerve of the assassin. And, perhaps, luck.

It could be argued that much of the protracted quest for the ideal handgun has been irrelevant, and that character and training are the vital factors. There are many psychologists who would agree. Virtually any handgun that meets basic criteria of calibre and lethality could be deemed acceptable. Questions of long-term maintenance, spare parts and availability of ammunition are obviously inseparable from the decision-making process when the armament of entire armies is concerned. For the average Special Forces member, however, it is often any gun in which an individual is happy to place his trust. That these are usually restricted to service calibres presents no particular problem, as 9mm Parabellum or 0.45in ACP cartridges – now joined by the 0.40in S&W, thanks largely to its use by the FBI – are as good as any when loaded with the appropriate bullets.

Experience has shown that, when it matters most, a submachine-gun or riot shotgun is often a better weapon than a handgun in all but the most confined circumstances. Even the fashionable two-hand grip on a handgun will not better the shooting of guns such as the Heckler & Koch MP5, which have a longer sight radius and greater weight.

Although handguns are unsuitable for most infra-red sights and image intensifiers (many of which weigh several times as much as the gun), battery-powered laser or light projectors are becoming popular. These can be 'visible', using white light, or 'invisible' – operating in the near infra-red spectrum with the assistance of binocular-type night-vision goggles. The projector, aligned with the bore of the pistol, provides an aiming-point; the mark is simply superimposed on the intended target and the gun fired in the normal way, greatly increasing the chances of a hit under dusk or night conditions.

Equipment of this type has been used to great effect, though the 'visible' designators can be seen by the target – who may be quick enough to fire first. The infra-red system is also vulnerable to observation, but only if the viewer has a suitable detector, and goggles can leave the user vulnerable to lateral counter-attack by restricting peripheral vision.

Special-service guns are usually large-calibre locked-breech patterns, though small-calibre blowback types have often been carried for covert use or personal defence. However, some 9mm Parabellum or 0.45in ACP pistols (such as the Kahr P9 and some of the small-frame/short-slide derivatives of the M1911A1) are small enough to compare with the blowback designs, and offer much better hitting power.

Variations on the Browning-link action are virtually universal for military and paramilitary purposes, having proved their worth millions of times – for example in the Colt M1911A1, the FN-Browning GP-35, the SIG-Sauers, the Smith & Wessons and the Glocks. Of the most recent crop of full-bore military pistols, only the Walther P1/P5 series and the Beretta 92 group can offer something radically different. There is little to choose between the best of the modern pistols, and the competitions held during the last thirty years have often given contradictory results. Choice then becomes largely a matter of individual preference.

The West German police trials of 1972–5 arose from the outrages perpetrated by the Baader-Meinhof Gang and the disaster of the 1972 Munich Olympic Games. In addition to wholesale revision of German federal firearms laws, 9 x 19mm was standardised as the military/police cartridge to replace the motley collection of 7.65mm Short, 9mm Short, 9mm Police and 9mm Parabellum-chambered guns in service. Criteria were laid down for service pistols: maximum dimensions of 180mm x 130mm x 34mm, a maximum empty weight of 1kg, and magazines containing at least 8 rounds. Safe holstering with a live cartridge in the chamber was sought, yet the guns had to be ready for firing without any additional manipulation of safety catches or de-cocking levers. A high degree of ambidexterity was specified, and service life was to be at least 10,000 rounds.

Four manufacturers accepted these stringent requirements, and the Heckler & Koch PSP, the Mauser HSP, the SIG-Sauer P225 and the Walther P5 duly appeared. After initial trials, the Mauser HSP was withdrawn, but – surprisingly – the remaining guns all passed with flying colours. As the German state police authorities were allowed to choose what they liked, the diversity of subsequent issues merely reflected the inconclusiveness of the trials. The Pistole 5 (Walther P5) was issued to the state police of Baden and the Palatinate; the Pistole 6 (SIG-Sauer P225) was issued to the Bundesgrenzschutz (Federal Border Guard), the

Bereitschaftpolizei ('Stand-by' Police, called for duty when needed), the Bundeszolldienst (Customs Service), and to police units in Bremen, Hamburg, Hessen, Nordrhein-Westfalen and Schleswig-Holstein; and the Pistole 7 (Heckler & Koch PSP) was issued to the state police of Baden, Bayern and Niedersachsen. The anti-terrorist unit Grenzschutzgruppe 9 (GSG9) also took the P7. Saarland accepted the Heckler & Koch P9S, but West Berlin, owing to long-standing agreements with the Soviet Union, retained the Walther P1 until reunification in 1989.*

The search for a new US military service pistol, undertaken in 1977–83, began as part of the Joint Services Small Arms Program (JSSAP), seeking a replacement for the venerable M1911A1 Colt-Browning pistol.

Among the new criteria were demands for a calibre of 9 x 19mm, double-action lock-work, ambidexterity, and a magazine capacity greater than 13 rounds. Leading European gunmakers participated, anxious to obtain a lucrative contract even though the terms of contract demanded the establishment of manufacturing facilities in the United States. Submissions included the German Heckler & Koch P9S and VP70; the Belgian FN GP, DA and FA pistols; the Spanish Echeverria Star Mo. 28 DA; the US Colt SSP and Smith & Wesson Model 459; and the Italian Beretta Mo. 92S. The 0.45in ACP Colt M1911A1 used in the US Army and the 0.38in-calibre Smith & Wesson Model 15 revolver used by the USAF were included as control weapons.

The trials were spread over several years, during which many well-known handguns were conclusively rejected. Some results were shocking. However, cartridges supplied through the normal military channels were so unsuitable that commercial 9 x 19mm ammunition was substituted. Analysing the failures suggests that this did not suit some of the submissions.

* Owing to these restrictions, the West Berlin guns were supplied by Manurhin – or, at least, they were marked 'Manurhin'. It is suspected that most of the parts were simply sent from Ulm to Mulhouse to be assembled, proved and inspected.

The Beretta 92S was placed first, having passed the accuracy trials (fixed and freehand) and the environment test. There were 14 failures in 28,000 rounds, which gave a 'mean rounds between stoppage' (MRBS) figure of 2,000. This comfortably bettered not only its rivals, but also the 1,500 rounds desired by the JSSAP. There had been three feed, two chambering, two ignition, six extraction and one 'other' failures; outstanding by any standards.* It would be interesting to compare the performance of a revolver with cartridges of similar quality. Some failures would probably be expected, due to irregularities in the ammunition – but there would have been no feed problems or failures to extract, and a 'miss' would simply be rotated out of the hammer-path to allow another shot.

In contrast, at the bottom of the scale, the Star 28 DA had a disastrous time. After marginally passing the accuracy trials and failing the environment test, the pistol recorded 1,142 failures in 5,526 rounds – a MRBS of only 5. There had been 54 feed, 516 chambering, 430 firing, 137 extraction and five miscellaneous stoppages. The Stars might have given a better account of themselves had better cartridges been available, though this did not appear to inhibit the Beretta, the Smith & Wesson M459 (MRBS 952) or the Colt M1911A1 (MRBS 748); unfortunately, fortunes have often been won or lost over a single trial series.

The JSSAP commission recommended the adoption of the Beretta 92S, but the US Army, mindful of developments made during the protracted trial period, demanded that a second series be undertaken with the Beretta 92SB, the SIG-Sauer P226, the Smith & Wesson 459A and the Heckler & Koch P7M13. Despite a reduction of the desirable MRBS figure to 800, and the removal of the more stringent environmental requirements, the Beretta was still declared the winner.

The US Army formally adopted the Beretta 92SB-F in January 1992 as the 'Pistol, Semiautomatic, 9mm M9 (1005-01118-

---

* Trials of a prototype ČZ P-01, undertaken by the Czech police in 2001, gave seven failures in 15,000 rounds, an MRBS of 2,143.

2640)', much to the chagrin of Smith & Wesson. The first five-year contract called for the manufacture of nearly 316,000 guns.

Procurement of the M9 continued against a background of allegations that the decision to adopt the Beretta had been taken before the JSSAP trials had even begun. Court cases questioned the conduct of the trials, and Smith & Wesson, remaining convinced that their perfected pistol actually out-performed the Beretta, successfully persuaded many traditionally revolver-orientated American police forces to accept the Smith & Wesson auto-loader instead of the M9. The 0.45in ACP S&W Model 645 and the 10mm Auto or 0.40in-calibre guns have been favoured, though the fascination with the Glock has eroded this monopoly.

The subsequent Joint Services Operation Requirement (JSOR) demanded that handguns 'should be of 45 caliber'. Heckler & Koch, Colt and other manufacturers responded, and the whole question of the US service handgun was investigated once again. The result favoured the Heckler & Koch USP (*see below*).

Browning Type Guns
Colt Type

The 1911-pattern Colt-Browning pistol, in its improved 1926-vintage M1911A1 form, is possibly the best-known auto-loading handgun of all time and steadfastly refuses to die a natural death – even though it was rejected by the US Army in 1982 in favour of the Beretta 92SB-F. Copies of the M1911A1 (some facsimiles, others radically altered) are still being made in North America by gunmakers such as Auto-Ordnance Corporation, Les Baer Custom, Entréprise Arms, Kimber Manufacturing, Para-Ordnance, Springfield, Dan Wesson, and Wilson Combat. Copies are also being made in the Philippines and the People's Republic of China.

In the Browning mechanism, recoil of the slide/barrel unit is used to drop the breech out of engagement with locking recesses, allowing the slide to recoil alone and return to strip a new round into the chamber. Towards the end of the return stroke, the slide picks up the barrel and locks it back into engagement – strong, simple and efficient. The original Colt-Browning, the US Pistol 0.45in M1911, used a closed-path link; many of the newer guns, often based on the 1923–5 patents leading to the GP Modèle 35, use a cam-finger or simply raise the squared chamber-top into a recess in the slide.

The great advantages of the traditional M1911A1 are its ruggedness and proven stopping power. To its debit are inadequate safety features by today's standards, and recoil strong enough to make it difficult to shoot. In addition, the grip may be a little too square to the axis of the bore. But these arguments do not impress champions of the Colt-Browning, who see simplicity as a virtue and multiplicity of safety devices as evidence that the guns so equipped are designed more to protect inexperienced rookies than help a highly-trained user disable an opponent with the first shot.

Merit can probably be found in each argument, considered individually, but the lure of the big Colt-Browning has often been dismissed simply as an irrelevant historical curiosity. However, Colt has obtained a lucrative return from Government Model clones, chambering the Delta Elite of 1987 for the fashionable 10mm Auto cartridge, and has now proceeded to the XSE series. At the other end of the scale, Colt is also seeking to reintroduce a facsimile of the *original* M1911!

If the special-purpose role of the full-size Government Model is questionable, there is little doubt that good use has been made of compact derivatives – for example the Colt Defender, the Kimber CDP II or the Para-Ordnance C5 45 LDA – in addition to high-power guns that can deliver a potent punch at long range.

FN Type

Derived from the M1911A1, the GP Mle 35, designed by John Browning shortly before his sudden death in 1926 and subsequently perfected by Fabrique Nationale, has been accepted in more than sixty countries for army and paramilitary use. In addition to the guns made by Inglis during the Second World War, GP copies have also been made in countries as disparate as Hungary, Cambodia and the Philpines.

In view of the perceived obsolescence of the GP-35, FN developed the interesting, but complicated and ultimately unsuccessful GP Fast Action during the 1970s to overcome criticism of the conventional 'double-action' trigger system. Trigger systems of this type have been popular in semi-automatics for many years, allowing the first cartridge to be fired merely by pulling through on the trigger, but the effort required for the first shot is appreciably greater than for the second and subsequent shots owing to the automatic cocking action. Consequently, the first shot fired from a traditional double-action automatic almost always goes low, the greater trigger pull tending to pivot the muzzle down. The Fast Action eliminated the problem, but was insufficiently durable; rejected in the US JSSAP trials, it was replaced by the conventional double-action BDA, also known as the GP DA.

The BDA was made in three guises: full-size (BDA9S, 200mm overall, with a 14-round magazine), medium (BDA9M, 178mm, 14 rounds) and compact (BDA9C, 178mm, 7 rounds). Each shared the conventional Browning cam-finger lock, the differences concerning dimensions and cartridge capacity.

As even the BDA was incapable of challenging guns such as the Glock, so Fabrique Nationale progressed to the BDM ('Browning Double Mode'), introduced in 1991. Though the BDM shares the basic GP mechanism, the trigger system has been altered to give the firer a choice, through a rotary selector, of conventional single-action 'pistol mode' or double-action-only 'revolver mode'.

If single action is selected, the hammer returns to the down position once the action has been cycled to load the chamber and the de-cocking lever has been pressed; when the gun fires, the slide returns to leave the hammer at full cock. In the double action mode, the hammer is dropped to an intermediate position by the de-cocking lever. When the gun fires, the slide returns to leave the hammer in the intermediate position, subsequent shots being fired by pressing through on the trigger.

The advantages of the revolver mode are partly a perceived improvement in safety but also a constant trigger pressure for all shots. In pistol mode, the single-action shots require far less pressure on the trigger lever than the initial double-action pull. Whether the complexity is worthwhile, however, must be in dispute. FN Herstal may agree, as all but the original GP (now apparently being made in Portugal) have been dropped in favour of the new Five-seveN and the Model Forty-Nine.

The Five-seveN appeared in 1995, chambered for the innovative 5.7mm cartridge, with formidable armour-piercing performance, that had been developed for the P-90 'Personal Defense Weapon' some years previously. It is not a Browning design, and is described in greater detail below.

The Forty-Nine, with a much more conventional Browning-type breech system, was originally designed to fire the 0.40in S&W cartridge, then modified to chamber the ubiquitous 9mm Parabellum cartridge instead. The trigger system mechanism embodies what FN calls the 'Repeatable Secure Striker' (RSS).

SIG Type

Schweizerische Industrie Gesellschaft (SIG) is another of the world's best-established gunmakers, with an unbroken pedigree stretching back to the 1850s. In 1949, the Swiss Army adopted the Ordonnanzpistole 49 SIG, which was a military version of the SP 47/8 (or P210) developed from the French Petter of the 1930s. The SIG pistol was beautifully made and soon attracted an enviable reputation for accuracy, which was widely ascribed to the length of the bearing surfaces between the slide and the frame – and to the care with which the tipping barrel was fitted in its muzzle bushing.

Quality came at a high price. In the 1960s, therefore, SIG modernised the P210 in an attempt to win a share of the international mass-market. The major changes concerned a new double-action trigger system and simpler construction, for example the locking ribs were replaced by a large block that rose into the ejection port cutaway. The result was the P220, adopted in the mid-1970s as the Swiss Army's Pistole 75. By the summer of 1988, more than 100,000 of these 9mm Parabellum pistols had been sold.

SIG had already entered into agreement with J. P. Sauer & Sohn of Eckenförde, in West Germany, to circumvent restrictive Swiss arms-export laws. To satisfy the German police, a compact variant of the P220 was produced: the P225 (later known in Germany as the P6). Its de-cocking system was essentially similar to that of the Walther P5, but locked the safety pin into the breech-block – strangely, practically identical with the system used on the Walther P1.

The P225 inspired an assortment of successors, including the P226 (9mm Parabellum, 15-round magazine), P228 (9mm Parabellum, 13 rounds) and P229 (0.40in S&W, 12 rounds). A slightly modified version of the P226 ran an extremely close second to the Beretta 92 in the US Army trials, apparently losing more on politico-economic grounds than performance.

The P228, which was introduced commercially in the spring of 1989, was little more than a P225 with a 13-round magazine. Three guns were submitted to the US Army XM11 Compact Pistol trials in 1991, at a time when SIG handguns were already serving with the Drugs Enforcement Agency (DEA), the Bureau of Alcohol, Tax and Firearms (BATF), the Federal Aviation Administration (FAA), and the Federal Bureau of Investigation (FBI). The SIGs passed the preliminary technical examination with ease, including a 15,000-round endurance trial undertaken in the US Army Military Police School. Each of the three guns fired 5,000 rounds and, though seventeen 'chargeable malfunctions' were permissible according to the competition rules, the P228 pistols recorded just one between them – giving an MRBS of 15,000.

In April 1992, it was announced that the 9mm M11 Compact Pistol would be the P228 with special non-corroding finish, and that deliveries were to commence in September that year.

The P229 was simply a P228 chambered for the 0.40in Smith & Wesson cartridge, though a 9mm Parabellum option appeared in 1996. The standard model had a blacked stainless-steel slide, an alloy frame, and a 12-round magazine. Introduced in 1996, the P239 was simply the P229 altered to accept the new 0.357in SIG round, derived from the rimmed 0.357in Magnum revolver round. No changes were needed in the breech face or magazine, though the magazine capacity was reduced to 7 rounds to give a slim grip that was better suited to 'concealed carry' than the wide-bodied P229.

The P245 of 1999 was a variant chambering the 0.45in ACP cartridge, with a single-column magazine holding 6 rounds. The SIG-PRO series (made from 1998 to the present day) has blued-steel slides, matte-finish polymer frames, improved grips, and an accessory rail under the front of the frame ahead of the trigger guard. Fitted with 10-round magazines, the M2009 SIG-PRO and M2340 SIG-PRO chambered the 9mm Parabellum and 0.40in S&W cartridges respectively.

Smith & Wesson Type

The work of the company's chief designer, Joseph Norman, this was the first large-calibre double-action design to be made in the USA. The prototype was finished in October 1948, but very little progress had been made when the US Army suddenly intervened in 1953. The first double-action guns were assembled in December 1954, followed by a pair of single-action alternatives. When the numerical designation system was adopted, these became the M39 and M44 respectively.

The locking mechanism relied on a shaped cam beneath the chamber pulling the barrel down far enough to disengage a single lug above the chamber from the inside of the slide, and there was a Walther-style safety catch/de-cocking lever on the rear left side of the slide. The M39 soon caught the attention of the US armed forces, but only the US Navy and the Special Forces purchased guns of this type in quantity.

Chambered for the 9mm Parabellum round, with an 8-round

single-column magazine, the M39 had a 4-inch barrel. But it was followed by a vast range of derivatives. First made experimentally in the summer of 1964, the Model 59 was not accorded priority until the US Navy ordered some for trials in 1969, and series production did not start until 1971. The gun was an enlarged M39, with a 14-round double-column magazine and a straight backstrap.

The Model 459 of 1979 was an improved form of the Model 59, with a new adjustable back sight protected by prominent lateral wings, ambidextrous controls, and a trigger-actuated firing-pin lock. Introduced in 1983, the M469 was a specially shortened version of the M459, developed for the US Air Force. It had a curved backstrap, a recurved 'two-hand' trigger guard, and a spurless hammer. The lightweight alloy frame and the steel slide had a matte sand-blasted blue finish. The magazine held twelve 9mm Parabellum rounds in double columns.

After the infamous 1986 'Miami Massacre' (*see below*), the Director of the FBI decided in September 1989 to replace revolvers with semi-automatic pistols. A contract placed with Smith & Wesson in January 1990 led to the M1076NS pistol, chambering the 10mm Auto Pistol cartridge, with the de-cocking lever on the left side of the frame instead of the slide. A thousand guns were delivered towards the end of 1990, but the cartridge gave excessive recoil and a sharp muzzle blast, and reports were soon being made of malfunctions. These were serious enough to persuade the FBI to order the withdrawal of the 10mm Smith & Wesson pistols on 31 May 1991, replacing them with 9mm SIG-Sauer P226 pistols ordered on 17 June and delivered some time prior to 3 July, when the re-arming of the Field Special Agents of the FBI had been completed.*

The problem was eventually traced to a most unexpected source. The components of all guns have specific dimensional

* The SIG-Sauer P226 had won a procurement competition held by the FBI in 1988, and 1,500 had been delivered in 1988–9. Though it is claimed that 2,000 P228s were acquired in June 1991, the FBI press-release notes the quantity as *1,000* with a thousand-gun option.

tolerances within which they are deemed acceptable. But it took field service to reveal that a tiny proportion of the new FBI pistols incorporated a series of parts whose dimensions – though acceptable when judged individually – were sufficiently critical to lock the firing system when acting in concert. The replacement of only a single component usually unlocked the 'tolerance jam' and returned the gun to perfect order.

The powerful 10mm Smith & Wessons were ultimately returned to service after modifications had been made, and minor adjustments in the manufacturing specifications have ensured that the problem has never recurred.

The Glocks

One of the greatest successes of the last few decades has been the Glock, developed in Austria. Glock of Deutsch-Wagram entered a prototype in the Austrian handgun trials of 1977–9, but few commentators expected it to compete effectively against weapons submitted by gunmakers with far longer pedigrees. Though the Steyr Pi-18 was generally reckoned as the favourite, Heckler & Koch, Walther, SIG-Sauer, Beretta, Smith & Wesson and others provided a real threat – yet, when the final trials were concluded in 1983, to general amazement, the Glock was adopted as the Pistole 80. Performance had been at least as good as the best of its rivals, so the scales had been tipped by the perennial 'home ground' advantage: the gun was an Austrian design, made in Austria.

Once the surprise had receded, the Glock was inspected critically. Excepting the unique trigger-within-a-trigger safety system, the design was not particularly innovative – but the way in which it was constructed, with a sizeable proportion of synthetic parts, was most unusual. It was so unusual, indeed, that the synthetic frame and grip inspired a campaign of scare-mongering in newspapers and magazines throughout the world; the Glock was damned as the gun that could not be detected by X-rays, and was thus certain to be misused.

The panic stories were soon followed by more realistic

assessments, but it was the colourful untruth that entered popular mythology. Even today, three decades after adoption in Austria, the legend persists. Yet the Glock has a metal barrel, a metal slide, metal springs, metal pins, two metal strips set into the frame to accept the slide, and a magazine containing metal cartridges loaded with metal bullets; consequently, no successful evasion of an X-ray machine – even the comparatively primitive machines current in the 1980s – has ever been made.

Owing to good handling characteristics, simple-but-effectual safety features and an unusually large magazine capacity, the Glock 17 quickly became popular worldwide. Norway's became the first NATO army to adopt the Glock, in 1984, forcing the company to recruit sub-contractors until the Deutsch-Wagram facilities could be suitably enlarged. Subsidiaries have since been opened in the United States (Smyrna, Georgia, 1985), Hong Kong (1988) and Uruguay (Montevideo, 1990). A new factory was opened in 1988 in Ferlach to cope with demand and, by 1995, more than 4,000 police and protection agencies in the USA alone, together with the special forces of at least ten armies, had acquired Glock pistols. The two millionth gun was exhibited at the SHOT Show in the USA at the beginning of 1999.

Gradually, the original 9mm gun has been joined by a series of modifications, including one of the few selective-fire pistols available on today's market. There have been several standard-size guns, including the Glock 17 (9mm Parabellum, 17 rounds), the Glock 20 (10mm Auto, 15 rounds); the 0.45in ACP Glock 21, with a 13-round magazine; the 0.40in S&W Glock 22 (15 rounds); the 0.380in Auto/9mm Short Glock 25, a blowback derivative of the locked-breech design with a 15-round magazine; the Glock 31, little more than a Glock 17 chambering the 0.357in SIG round (15-round two-column magazine); and the Glock 37, with a 10-round magazine for the 0.45in Glock cartridge.

The short-barrelled compact guns include include the Glock 19 (9mm Parabellum, 15-rounds); the Glock 23 (0.40in S&W, 13 rounds); the Glock 29 (10mm Auto , 10 rounds); the Glock 30

(0.45in ACP, 10 rounds); and the Glock 32 (0.357in SIG, 13 rounds).

The ultra-short or 'sub-compact' guns, which have an abbreviated grip as well as a short barrel, have included the Glock 26 (9mm Parabellum, 10-rounds), which is 6.3 inches long and weighs 20 oz; the Glock 27 (0.40in S&W, 9 rounds); the Glock 28, a 0.380in/9mm Short blowback design with a 10-round magazine; the Glock 33 (0.357in SIG, 9 rounds); and the Glock 36 (0.45in ACP) with a 6-round single-column magazine.

Long-barrel/long slide guns have been made for competition shooting (0.40in S&W Glock 24, 9mm Parabellum Glock 34 and 0.40in S&W Glock 35); and the Glock 17T (introduced in 1997) was a training pistol chambered for 9mm FX ammunition, loaded with color-marking or rubber bullets.

Czech Types

The ČZ 75 and its newer derivative, the ČZ 85, also attracted attention in the 1980s. The basic design borrowed many features promoted originally by the SIG SP 47/8 (P-210), including a Browning-type locking system and an unusually lengthy slide-guide cut on the inner face of the frame. The ČZ also had a good double-action trigger and a high-capacity magazine, handled well and, in its '85' form in particular, also offered easily mastered safety/magazine controls.

Like the Beretta M92, but totally unlike the Glock, the ČZ pistols were conventional designs made in largely traditional fashion. They have been very successful, and may have been even more popular had not their Soviet-bloc origins attracted hostile propaganda. A better indicator of potential was that they were extensively copied in the West, by companies such as Tanfoglio in Italy and ITM in Switzerland.* Even the IMI 941

---

* ITM subsequently became part of Sphinx Industries in 1989, after the AT-84 and AT-88 derivatives of the original ČZ-inspired pistol had been introduced and Sphinx was eventually bought by Oerlikon in 2001. Guns are now marked 'ASAI – Advanced Small Arms Industries'.

Jericho pistol is little more than a cosmetically altered ČZ 85 with a polygonally rifled Israeli-made barrel.

It has been suggested that guns such as the ČZ 75/ČZ 85 series succeed because traditional construction impresses those who take the final procurement decisions – high-ranking officers, leading politicians – much more than guns that are made at the forefront of technology from synthetic parts. Whatever the reason, the Czech design is currently acknowledged as one of the world leaders, and the newer (but largely synthetic) ČZ 100 has been unable to replicate its popularity.

There have been many ČZ-made derivatives of the basic designs, ranging from the ČZ 75 Automatic, with a cyclic rate of about 1,000 rds/min and the frame adapted ahead of the trigger-guard to accept a laser-spot projector or an inverted loaded magazine (doubling as a forward grip), to the ČZ 75BD – with a de-cocking system – and the 0.45in ACP ČZ 97B, introduced commercially in 1999 with a 10-round magazine. A compact, squared-contour 9mm Parabellum variant known as the P-01 was standardised by the Czech state police in 2001.

Heckler & Koch Patterns

The Universal-Selbstlade-Pistole (USP) was introduced in 1993 to replace the P7 series, incorporating a Browning-cam breech lock and a recoil-reduction system forming part of the recoil spring/buffer assembly. The frame and the magazine are made of fibreglass-reinforced polymer, the trigger/safety mechanism is a modular design (SA/DA, DAO, with or without de-cocking capability), and the metal components have a corrosion-resistant finish. Accuracy is enhanced by a barrel/slide bearing in the form of a synthetic O-ring, which is claimed to ensure that lock-up is consistent shot-after-shot.

The USP was originally designed and made for the 0.40in S&W cartridge, but 9mm Parabellum (USP9) and 0.45in ACP (USP45) versions soon followed. The first of a sub-series of compact guns appeared in 1996, with a 3.6in barrel. Guns have been offered in 0.357in SIG in addition to 9mm Parabellum,

0.40in S&W and 0.45in ACP. The 0.45in-calibre gun is larger than the others, as it has a 4.1in barrel and a 10-round magazine.

In 1990, the US Special Operations Command (SOCOM) asked for a 0.45in-caliber pistol that not only gave better accuracy than the M1911A1 but could also accept a silencer and a laser aiming projector. The H&K design was declared to be superior to the Colt alternative, prototypes were tested in 1992/3 and a 1,380-gun contract was awarded to Heckler & Koch in 1994. These were to be accompanied by a similar number of silencers purchased from Knight's Armament Company and 650 laser aiming projectors.

The Mark 23 Model 0 SOCOM pistol is generally similar to the USP, but an additional buffer is incorporated in the buffer-spring assembly to reduce the sensation of recoil and thus improve accuracy. The muzzle protrudes from the slide to accept a silencer (or 'sound suppressor'), and a slide-lock allows the pistol to be fired without the action opening – preventing mechanical noise or an ejected cartridge-case compromising the silence of a shot. The front of the frame is grooved to accept the aiming projector, and the fixed sights have Tritium dots to improve performance in poor light. The Mark 23 Special Operations Pistol is a commercial version, with black polymer grips that are integral with the frame, three-dot combat sights, and a conventional double-action trigger.

The most recent version of the USP is the P-2000 or GPM (German Police Model), which is a compact 9mm Parabellum gun with a hammer mechanism that is partially pre-cocked by the slide and then released by pulling through on the trigger. Like the abortive FN 'Fast Action' system, this is intended to allow a consistent, but comparatively light trigger stroke.

Walther/Beretta System

Walther Type
The reconstituted Walther gunmaking business relied for many years on variants of the Polizei-Pistole and the Pistole 38 (PP and

P. 38), originally introduced in 1929 and 1940 respectively. By the 1970s, however, both were found wanting for special purposes. The Polizei-Pistole was too expensive, and had come to be regarded as not powerful enough to fulfil personal defence tasks efficiently; the P. 38, despite its double-action lock-work, was too bulky and too expensive to be considered for large-scale issue.

After toying with half-measures such as the PP Super and the P4, Walther progressed to the P5, an adaptation of the P. 38 that performed quite acceptably in German police trials. The P5 relied on the well-proven P. 38-type locking system, but incorporated a new fail-safe trigger. When the action was at rest with the hammer down, the firing pin matched a hole bored into the hammer, which, resting on the face of the breech-block, could not move the pin. When the trigger was pulled, the hammer was rotated backwards and an arm lifted the firing pin. When the hammer was released, it flew forward to strike the pin-head and fire the chambered round. However, when the de-cocking lever released a cocked hammer, the firing pin was still in its lowered position; thus, not even the rapidly descending hammer could drive it forward. As there was no safety in the traditional Walther manner, the gun could be fired simply by squeezing the trigger.

Though the P5 was moderately successful, the advent of rival designs suggested that it clung too firmly to old technology. Though the guns generally shot very well, proving to be durable, the 8-round magazine and a lack of truly ambidextrous controls were criticised. Consequently, Walther abandoned the proven Barthelmes locking system in favour of an adaptation of the Browning cam-finger system pioneered in the FN-Browning GP-35. This resulted in the P88, offered in standard or compact forms, but this was still recognisably the product of a long-established gunmaker clinging to traditional means of fabrication and failed to halt Walther's slide into near-bankruptcy. This was arrested only when Umarex acquired a majority shareholding, but the P88 was subsequently seen as nothing other than a *Sportpistole* and the P99 (with a modified Browning-type locking system) was introduced to compete on the military-police market.

Beretta Type

The Beretta Model 92 is an interesting gun with a lengthy pedigree, embodying a locking system derived from that of the Walther P. 38. The prototypes were made in 1951, but problems with the original alloy frame took some time to resolve; not until 1955 was the Brigadier, as it was named commercially, destined to achieve any real success. The perfected version of the M951, was introduced in 1976. A double-action trigger mechanism and a 15-round staggered-row magazine were fitted, and the Model 92 was adopted by the Italian forces in the late 1970s.

The guns have since been made in made in five patterns. Guns in the S series have the safety catch on the slide instead of the frame, acting additionally as de-cocking lever. The standard D guns, introduced in 1992, were self-cocking DAO patterns, entirely lacking manual safety and de-cocking devices. They had plain-sided slides and a hammer that lay flush with the rear face of the slide; DS guns were similar, but had an ambidextrous safety catch on the slide.

The FS group contained traditional double-action/single-action patterns with an ambidextrous dual purpose safety/de-cocking lever, a firing-pin lock, a trigger-bar disconnector, and an external hammer. G guns were similar to the FS type, but the lever on the slide lacked the auxiliary safety feature, functioned solely as a de-cocker, and sprang back to the upper position after the de-cocking motion was completed.

Individual variants ranged from the standard Model 92F to the Model 92F-M – a compact gun with an 8-round magazine – and the Model 96, a minor variant chambering the 0.40in S&W cartridge instead of 9mm Parabellum. The greatest success has been the adoption of the Beretta 92F in the USA, as the Pistol M9, and the acceptance of the Beretta 92G by the French as the PA-MAS-G1. It has been suggested that the US trials were not impartial, implying that the decision to adopt the Beretta was influenced by factors including the billions of dollars-worth of US military equipment that had been (and would continue to be) purchased by Italy. However, this has never been proved.

The lock strength of the Beretta is generally reckoned to be less than the Walther, but the P5 did not appear in the US trials and no accurate comparison is available. Once the new M9 pistols were widely distributed in the US Army, reports of failures began to arise; most were due to frames cracking, necessitating the recall of many guns for inspection after firing only a thousand rounds. The Model 92FS appeared in 1990 in response to these complaints, fitted with an extended hammer axis pin and grooves cut along most of the length of the slide. The slide is usually blacked steel, the frame being sandblasted aluminium alloy. Guns made after 2001 have their extractors adapted so that a red-painted head projects laterally from the slide when a round is in the chamber.

The so-called Brigadier slide, which appeared in 1996, has noticeably different contours beneath the ejection port, where a weakness had been discovered. Among these heavy-frame guns has been the Model 92G Elite of 1999, with a stainless-steel barrel and a 'de-cock only' trigger system. The retraction grips were duplicated behind the muzzle, the magazine well was bevelled, the hammer was a skeleton pattern instead of the more usual ring, and three-dot combat sights were fitted.

In addition to the guns being made in Italy, the USA and France, Beretta-type pistols have been made in Brazil (by Forjas Taurus), in Chile (by FAMAE), and in South Africa (by Denel, now abandoned).

The Beretta M8000 Condor pistol was exhibited at the 1984 IWA, Nürnberg, departing from the established '92' practice in the barrel-locking system, which relies on rotation instead of the Walther-type block. However, this design, offered in several chamberings and a choice of three safety systems, has yet to displace the Model 92 and its long-term future is unclear. It is probably too traditional to remain in production for too much longer, and will presumably be replaced by something made largely of synthetic components.

Other Guns

FN Herstal

The currently-available standard Five-seveN is a self-cocking semi-automatic, relying on a delayed-blowback system, and has a trigger mechanism that first 'loads' the firing-pin spring before releasing the firing pin. The 5.7 x 28mm cartridge is considerably longer than the average pistol round, yet the butt, containing a 20-round magazine, does not feel unusually bulky. The recoil impulse is less than that from a 9mm Parabellum cartridge, allowing the gun to be controlled surprisingly easily. Extensive use has been made of synthetic material, and an accessory rail forms part of the frame; a laser spot attachment and a sound suppressor can be obtained to order. A 'Tactical' version is offered with conventional single-action lock work, often preferred by SWAT and CTW teams.

Heckler & Koch

Another major pistol supplier, this company cut its teeth on the G3 rifle before producing the first of its handguns in the early 1960s. This was a comparatively simple blowback general-purpose pistol designated HK4 principally because it could be acquired with four differing barrels chambering 0.22in LR rimfire, 6.35mm Auto, 7.65mm Auto or 9mm Short. However, though the HK4 was well-made and efficient, it had only a minor impact on the export market.

H&K followed with the P9, a large military sporting pistol chambering the 9mm Parabellum cartridge. Renowned for widespread use of synthetic material, polygonal rifling and a roller-delayed breech system, the P9 was quickly upgraded to P9S standards by the addition of a double-action trigger system. The gun was good enough to attract the attention of police and military departments, and saw small-scale use with Special Forces such as the Green Berets, the US Navy SEALs and GSG-9 in the 1970s. But it was too expensive and probably too radical to gain widespread adoption, and the machinery was ultimately sold to Greece where Hellenic Arms Industries made the EP9S for many years.

The PSP or Polizei-Selbstlade-Pistole (subsequently known officially as the P7) was a completely new design relying on a gas-bleed system to delay the opening of the breech until the pressure in the chamber had dropped to a safe level. Another radical departure from conventional practice was the cocking lever down the front of the grip. A pressure of about 7kg (15.5lb) on the lever cocked the gun – previously loaded by operating the slide – after which single-action fire could be continued as long as pressure of more than 500gm (1.25lb) was maintained on the cocking lever. When pressure was released, the firing pin was automatically lowered and the PSP could be carried safely with a live round in the chamber.

The P7, emerging from the German pistol trials with great credit, was an instantaneous success. It was followed by a selection of improved weapons, differing largely in detail or calibre. The P7M13 featured a large-capacity staggered column magazine, whereupon the original single-column gun was renamed P7M8. A short-lived 0.45in ACP P7M45 was developed in the late 1980s, hoping for sales in the USA. Tests showed that the gas-cylinder delay was inappropriate for this ammunition, failing to stop the breech opening too quickly, and an oil-damped recoil suppressor was used. As the slide moved back, the piston head was forced through the oil, and the incompressible fluid passed through the port from one side of the piston to the other. The P7M45 was exceptionally comfortable to fire, but problems arose from the complexity of the valve and only a few prototypes were ever made.

Throughout the 1980s, therefore, the P7/PSP series was used extensively, particularly in Germany. However, its dominance was quickly challenged by the emergence of a new generation of guns, typified by the Glock, and the P7 was never able to match the success of its rival in North America. The replacement for the P7 was the 1993-vintage Universal Self-loading Pistol (USP), which used a Browning-style lock (*see above*).

Soviet/Russian Guns

After the demise of the Tokarev (even though production of modified versions continues in China), the Pistolet Makarova (PM) was the principal handgun of the Soviet bloc. Still being made in Russia – and other lesser states – the Makarov is a simple blowback design chambered for a special 9 x 18mm cartridge generating power midway between that of the 9mm Short (0.380in ACP) and 9mm Parabellum. In spite of Soviet attempts to claim credit for the design, the Makarov is little more than an adaptation of the Walther Polizei-Pistole; it is an efficient personal-defence weapon, but not really powerful enough for special-purpose use. However, this does not stop Makarov pistols, purchased cheaply in eastern Europe, being used in many crimes. Izhevskiy Mekhanicheskiy Zavod currently makes a variety of Makarov-type guns for military and commercial sale, including the PMM, with a 12-round magazine and a revised grip, and the MP448 Skyph with a polymer frame; the Mini-Skyph is a sub-compact version with a short barrel and a short butt.

The improved PSM was designed around a cartridge perfected in 1979. Credited to Lashnev, Simarin and Kulikov (though still retaining Walther-inspired elements), the pistol attracted considerable attention in Western military circles. This was partly because it was unusually flat, had alloy grips, and fired a necked cartridge with the unusually small calibre of 5.45mm.

This choice of calibre was initially assumed to be a production expedient, as it allowed barrels for 5.45mm pistols, assault rifles and light machine-guns to be made on the same basic machinery. However when examples of the PSM eventually reached the West, the standard Soviet cartridge, firing a light bullet at marginally sub-sonic velocity, proved capable of piercing multiple layers of vaunted Kevlar body armour in a way which no Western military handgun cartridge could match at that time.

Thoughts began to turn toward more sinister motives; was the PSM designed for the KGB, perhaps as an assassination weapon? Did its flatness mean that it was designed primarily for covert operations? However, shortly before his death in 1991, Anatoliy Simarin told the Russian historian David Bolotin, author of *Soviet Small-Arms and Ammunition*, that the design specification had always included requirements for light weight, low bulk and good combat characteristics. Clearly, therefore, the PSM was neither developed for second-line forces nor as an officers' sidearm. The gun has had no effect on the design of Western combat handguns, in which the discernible trends are currently towards larger cartridges (for example 10mm Auto, 0.40in S&W) that fill the gap between 9mm Parabellum and 0.45in ACP.

Even the Russians have now followed this trend, with the approval of two new 9mm guns for service. The TsNIITochmash pistol, designed by Pyotr Serdyukov, was developed in response to a Russian Army specification calling for a powerful handgun that had an effective range of 50 metres and could defeat NATO standard body-armour at 100 metres. The result was the Gyurza, chambered for a new 9 x 21mm high-penetration round with a muzzle velocity of about 1,380ft/sec (420m/sec). The gun was about 7.7in (195mm) long and weighed 41.6oz (1,180gm) with a loaded 18-round magazine. The frame was polymer, the locking mechanism was an adaptation of the Walther P. 38/Beretta Model 92 system with a barrel that moved back to depress a locking block in the frame, and the quirky trigger would operate in double-action mode only if the hammer had first been put to a half-cock position. There was no manual safety, though a trigger-locking grip safety and an internal firing-pin lock were fitted. The safety blade protruding from the backstrap is generally reckoned to be much too small, and is customarily taped down in service.

The Russian Army lost interest in the Gyurza in the mid-

1990s, apparently regarding the cartridge as too powerful and the polymer frame as insufficiently durable. However, the Federal Security Service (FSB), impressed by the potential of the 9 x 21mm armour-piercing bullet for use against vehicles, requested that development continue. Finally, in 2003, the Gyurza – also known as the SR-1 Vektor – was adopted as the SPS for the personnel of the FSB and the Russian personnel-protection unit (FSO). Guns have also been used in limited numbers by Russian Army Special Forces (Spetsnaz) teams.

Abandoning the Gyurza allowed the army to accept the MP-443 Grach, a conventional Browning-type tilting barrel design promoted by Izhevskiy Mekhanicheskiy Zavod. Chambered for the 9mm Parabellum cartridge and made largely of steel, the MP-443 has a double-action trigger mechanism that incorporates a de-cocking lever and an ambidextrous safety catch. The grips are polymer, and the back sight is protected by sturdy wings. The Grach is about 7.8in (198mm) long and weighs 33.5oz (950gm) without its 17-round magazine. A commercial derivative, the MP-446 Viking, has a polymer frame-grip unit that reduces weight to about 29.3oz (830gm).

Revolvers

Revolvers are generally much simpler than pistols, and less susceptible to jamming caused by bad ammunition. Mechanical actuation means that a chamber containing a defective round can simply be swung away and the next one fired instead. Revolvers are also less vulnerable to structural failure, though this advantage has been eroded somewhat by the inclusion of transfer bars, mechanical safeties and similar features in the trigger system. However, revolvers are usually bulkier than pistols, particularly across the cylinder (restricting cartridge capacity in some small guns), more difficult to load, and incapable of such a high volume of fire in the hands of anyone other than an expert.

Prior to the appearance of the 0.357in Magnum, most police revolvers were cursed with the poor ballistics of the standard

0.32in and 0.38in Colt and Smith & Wesson cartridges, none of which are anything like as useful as the 9mm Parabellum. Closing the gap between the cylinder and the barrel has also presented insuperable problems, solved only by the now obsolete 'gas-seal' revolvers that cammed the cylinder forward at the instant of firing. However, the best of the revolvers made by Colt, Smith & Wesson and Ruger, joined by the FN Barracuda and other European products, have been widely favoured by police, SWAT teams and individual members of special forces throughout the world.

The most widely distributed Smith & Wesson revolver has been the 0.38in Model 10 Military & Police, nominally the service weapon even of the Metropolitan Police and the RCMP into the 1980s.

The 0.357in Magnum designs are much better man-stoppers, but many police agencies have chosen small-framed 'Magnum' revolvers that cannot handle the continuous battering of full-power ammunition. Instead, practice is supposed to be undertaken with 0.38in Special, the switch to the Magnum cartridges being made only when on duty. As the recoil of the two cartridges differs appreciably, this not only complicates changing from one to the other, but also minimises the value of the training.

For many years, the Smith & Wesson Model 15 revolver was the weapon of USAF aircrew, whilst the FBI specifically requested development of the S&W Model 66 in 0.357in Magnum to improve stopping power. The French 'Presidential Hunting Service', the police CTW team, was still carrying the Manurhin MR-73 and MR-F1 guns in the early 1990s.

Many attempts have been made to smooth the contours of service revolvers to prevent snagging on clothing or in the holster, and a selection of proprietary grips and sights has undoubtedly promoted better snap-shooting over the last two decades. At the time of writing, however, the special forces revolver is fighting a desperate rearguard action against the encroaching automatics.

The modern counter-terrorist operative needs good equipment
and quick reactions. A designator, or an illuminator
of the type shown, helps rapid target acquisition. *Springfield*

Right: The 0.45-calibre Heckler & Koch Mark 23 Model 0 pistol, favoured by SOCOM and US Navy SEALs. The extended muzzle accepts a silencer. *Heckler & Koch*

Below: The Browning GP-35 or 'High Power' has been the principal handgun of many armies for more than sixty years.

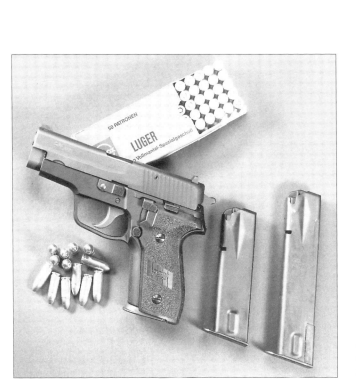

Left: The SIG P228, with standard and over-length magazines. *SIG*

Right: The Kahr MK9 is typical of the modern double-action pistols that are widely favoured by members of police and security teams as 'back-up' guns. *Kahr Arms*

Left: This short-barrelled short-gripped adaptation of the M1911A1 Colt-Browning makes a powerful back-up, though light gun-weight makes the 0.45in ACP round difficult to control. *Springfield*

Right: The Chinese Type 77, although a simple blowback design in an ineffectual chambering, can be charged with one hand. Though this is an old idea, dating back to the First World War, it could have advantages in life-threatening situations where an arm or hand has been disabled.

Right: The 9mm Walther P99, shown here in its militarised form, is an efficient representative of the 'high tech' handgun group. The frame/grip unit is synthetic. *Carl Walther*

Left: A typical modern Smith & Wesson AirLite PD-series revolver. Though chambering the powerful 0.357in Magnum round, this gun weighs only about 12oz. *Smith & Wesson*

Below: The Russian SPP-1M underwater pistol, with a four-round clip of darted ammunition. *Terry Gander*

Above: The Colt CAR-15 is a short-barrelled 'carbine' version of the 5.56mm AR15 (M16) rifle. This example has a grenade launcher beneath the fore-end and an 'after market' MWG high-capacity drum magazine.

Above: Shown here with an image-intensifying sight above the receiver, the Austrian AUG-77 is still renowned as much for its futuristic looks as proven efficiency. The folding handgrip ahead of the trigger guard assists control in burst-firing what is otherwise a muzzle-light bullpup design. *Steyr-Mannlicher*

Below: Among the most important qualities for any serviceable firearm – not only the 'guns of the elite' – is reliability in adverse conditions such as dust, sand and mud. *Springfield*

Above: The G36K, a short-barrelled form of one of the latest 5.56mm assault rifles, renowned for its synthetic grip/frame/receiver unit, with both a 3x optical sight and a red-dot projector built into the carrying handle. *Heckler & Koch*

Above: Made by Zavodi Crvena Zastava (ZCZ) in Kragujevač, this Yugoslavian/Serbian M70B1 is typical of many Kalashnikov derivatives that are to be found throughout the world. Note the folding grenade-launching sight on top of the gas-port block and the short angled compensator.

Below: A US Army marksman takes aim with a 7.62mm M21 rifle in the mountains of Afghanistan. *US Army*

Bottom: The capture of many weapons from the Russians, including the 7.62mm SVD (Dragunov) sniper rifle pictured here, has allowed members of the Taleban and Afghani militia to create problems for the Allied forces.

Below: The short-barrelled version of the Swiss Stgw. 90, the 5.56mm SIG552, has been offered as a lightweight assault weapon. Note the sturdy open sights, and how the transparent-body magazines can be clipped together. *SIG*

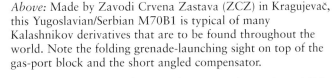

Above: The standard Yugoslavian/Serbian M76 sniper rifle is an adaptation of the Kalashnikov instead of the Dragunov copies used elsewhere. The straight-sided magazine shows that this example chambers the 7.92 x 57mm Mauser cartridge instead of the old 7.62 x 54R. The optical sight, however, is a straightforward copy of the Soviet/Russian PSO-1.

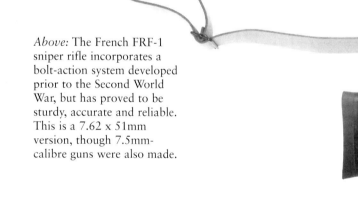

Above: The French FRF-1 sniper rifle incorporates a bolt-action system developed prior to the Second World War, but has proved to be sturdy, accurate and reliable. This is a 7.62 x 51mm version, though 7.5mm-calibre guns were also made.

Right: The 7.62 x 51mm PSG-1, with a special single-action trigger, a heavy free-floating barrel and a multi-adjustable butt, is Heckler & Koch's premier sniping rifle. *Heckler & Koch*

Above: The 7.62mm MSG-90 is a robust, conventional auto-loading sniper rifle based on the G3. Note the bipod beneath the fore-end and the cheekpiece on the butt. The trigger has also been improved.
Heckler & Koch

Left: The British Accuracy International AW (Arctic Warfare) rifle has successfully competed in trials in Sweden and Germany. This 7.62 x 51mm example is fitted with a Schmidt & Bender 10 x 42 optical sight.
Accuracy International

Above: The Barrett L82 Light Fifty long-range sniping rifle, in 0.50in calibre.

Right: The Barrett L82A1 Light Fifty dismantled into its major component groups. Note the design of the butt compared with the M82, and how the barrel is recessed into the top cover of the receiver to facilitate handling. *Barrett Firearms*

Above: The 7.62mm US M14 rifle, though abandoned militarily for everything except sniping, is still being made for the commercial market. This is a Springfield Armory version with a camouflage stock, but is otherwise the same as the US Army guns. *Springfield*

Left: The commercial version of the US Army M21 sniper rifle. *Springfield*

Right: The McMillan Gunworks M87R/M88 'Combo Rifle' was a 0.50in-calibre long-range sniping pattern. The length of the magazine and the impressive muzzle brake show that this chambers the powerful 0.50in machine-gun Browning cartridge.

Below: The Winchester Model 1200 pump-action shotgun, with a luminescent front sight to facilitate target acquisition. *US Repeating Arms Company*

Above: A pump-action 12-bore Beretta M3P shotgun, with a detachable box magazine. *Pietro Beretta*

Below: The Savage Model 69 Riot Gun is typical of the manually-operated pump (or 'slide') action shotguns that have proved popular for SWAT and CTW use.

Below: The Franchi SPAS-12 shotgun was a selectable auto-loading/manual operation design, and one of the first of its type to achieve widespread acceptance for anti-terrorist duties. This was undoubtedly helped by its militaristic appearance!

A US Army soldier carries a short-barrelled 'Para' version of the Belgian Minimi light machine-gun (issued as the M249/M249A1). This particular gun has a CCS (Close Combat Sight) above the receiver, and also has accessory rails on the sides of the fore-end. *US Army*

The US FBI has traditionally been armed with S&W 0.357in Magnum revolvers, though the FBI SWAT teams of the 1980s carried 9mm S&W Model 59 auto-loaders and the FBI Hostage Rescue Teams had specially adapted examples of the FN-Browning GP-35. Then came the infamous 'Miami Massacre' (1986), when eight agents attempted to capture two armed criminals.

The FBI men had revolvers, a basic pump-action shotgun or two, and at least one 9mm S&W auto-loading pistol. Their opponents had handguns and a 0.223in Ruger Mini-14 carbine. Ill-considered tactics left one criminal dead and another dying of wounds, but not before they had killed two of the FBI agents, permanently disabled three, and seriously injured two of the remainder. Only one of ten men involved escaped injury. The bullet that fatally injured the man with the Mini-14, a 9mm jacketed hollow-point, penetrated about a foot into the body tissue. However, as it had passed through several layers of clothing and an arm, the shot was not instantaneously disabling; before he died, the gunman was able to kill two agents.

The outcome was an immediate call within the FBI for a handgun that offered better hitting power. This would clearly have to fire a larger-diameter bullet at a greater velocity. That 9mm JHP bullets would probably have performed acceptably had the Miami gunman been struck from the front, and the possibility that plugs of cloth prevented proper bullet expansion, was apparently overlooked in the hysteria.

A reversion to 0.45in ACP was rejected on the dubious grounds that the ballistics of the cartridge could not be improved, and so the new 10mm Auto was selected instead. The S&W Model 1076NS pistol was subsequently selected to replace the assortment of revolvers and smaller-calibre auto-loaders.

Though revolvers have now lost most of their popularity with police and similar agencies, they are still preferred by many individuals employed by private companies involved in personnel-protection duties. Though sometimes seen only in the role of back-up to an auto-loader with a large capacity magazine, the revolver still has merits. Not least is the absence of any form of manual safety, which allows the guns to be carried in the knowledge that they are perfectly safe in a pocket or a holster, yet can be brought into action instantly. The widespread use of high-strength materials such as titanium alloy has allowed weight and sometimes also the thickness of key components to be reduced, allowing an additional chamber to be squeezed into the cylinder.

Typical of the Smith & Wessons of this type are the Model 340 AirLite Sc[andium], which was introduced in 2001, and the Model 342 AirLite Ti[tanium] of 1999. The hammer of the double-action-only 340 is enclosed within a high-back scandium-alloy frame, and the five-chamber cylinder accepts 0.357in Magnum rounds. The front sight is pinned into the barrel rib, the back sight is fixed, Hogue Bantam grips are used, and the finish is a combination of a grey titanium cylinder and matte 'stainless' barrel/frame. A PD version can be obtained with a blacked frame and barrel, and either a red-insert ramped blade or an orange HiViz sight at the muzzle. The 342 is also a double-action-only design, with an aluminium-alloy frame and a titanium cylinder, but chambers 0.38in Special +P ammunition. Guns of this type have 1.9in (48mm) barrels and weigh only about 12oz (340gm) empty.

Underwater Pistols

The popular belief that guns cannot be fired underwater is true only in certain circumstances; as long as the barrels are completely full of water ahead of the bullet, firing will proceed normally – though muzzle velocity and effective range are greatly reduced.

In 1968, the Soviet Navy formed a special Underwater Anti-sabotage Team (PDSS) to serve the Black Sea Fleet and requested the development of special weapons. These included the APS submachine-gun (*q.v.*) and the SPP-1 pistol, both designed by Vladimir Simonov and made by TsNIITochmash.

The pistol was a simple tip-barrel design that received a

special four-round clip, each barrel being fired sequentially by a striker. The cartridge, however, was much more unusual: a 4.5mm-calibre 205gn (13.2gm) dart in a conventional necked case, but measuring 5.7in (145mm) overall. Ten clips were issued in a special leather pouch, accompanied by three metal single-clip canisters and a waistbelt.

Approved in March 1971, the SPP-1 was 9.6in (244mm) long and weighed about 33.5oz (950gm) empty. It was subsequently upgraded to SPP-1M standards by adding a spring above the sear, improving the trigger pull, and altering the trigger guard to admit a three-finger diver's glove. Performance is said to include a muzzle velocity of 820ft/sec (250m/sec) in air, giving 'lethal ranges' of 20m in air, 17m in water to a depth of 5m, and 11m at a depth of 20m.

The only other underwater pistol to have been made in quantity is the Heckler & Koch P11, introduced about 1980 but formally acknowledged only in 1997. Reputedly used by, among others, the German GSG-9, British SBS and US SEALs, it is little more than a butt, trigger and socket-like frame that accepts a pre-loaded five-barrel module. The special cartridges use an electric primer activated by a battery in the grip, and carry slender dart-like finned projectiles. Pulling the trigger fires the barrels in sequence, launching the darts. When the last of the five barrels has been fired, the empty module is simply replaced.

It has been suggested that the Soviet designers copied the Heckler & Koch pistol, but the opposite is more probable; Simonov had begun work as early as 1969/70.

Chapter 5

Small-Calibre Rifles

Virtually all today's major armies have adopted rifles chambered for either the 5.45mm Soviet/Russian or the 5.56mm US/NATO cartridges. In addition, though the design of the guns varies considerably, almost all of them rely on a rotating bolt to lock the mechanism satisfactorily. Some of the introductions have been comparatively straightforward, including the development of the AK-74 from the AKM, but some of the weapons still attract controversy. The initial problems of the M16 series have been overcome, and the rifle, though not universally favoured, has at least regained much of the praise it was being given in the early 1960s. The Austrian AUG is still seen as a success, and the French 5.56mm FA MAS, which some commentators have claimed to operate only just within the margins of safety, remains in use in a modified form. Only the British L85 still struggles to justify its status.

Despite a protracted development history, the L85A1 was tried and found to be seriously deficient during the Gulf War of 1991. Though large sums of money have since been spent on upgrading the design to A2 status, early feedback from Iraq suggests that the gun is still not performing to the standards set by the M16. The preference of British Special Forces and Marines for the American design is well documented, and there has been a suggestion that the Heckler & Koch G36 could replace the L85 in the not-too-distant future.

The first generations of M16 rivals were often simply scaled-down variants of existing guns, the FN CAL/FNC being derived from the FAL and the HK33/G41 from the G3. However, though sales were soon made in many non-aligned countries, it was some years before major powers adopted weapons of this type. In this period of uncertainty lesser guns such as the Armalite AR-18 simply disappeared. There are many competitive designs on today's scene, ranging from the best of the guns made in Europe to some interesting South American products. Potentially excellent weapons have been made in the Far East, notably by CIS (now STK) in Singapore, whilst a derivative of the M16 has been made in quantity in Taiwan.

The existence of oddities such as a modified version of the Czech vz/58 introduced in Thailand some time in the early 1980s, has led to an extraordinary selection of equipment being carried by some subversive and anti-government units. The rifles recovered in Ethiopia, Sierra Leone, Somalia or the Sudan, for example, provide testimony to this incredible diversity – though, as far as Western special forces are concerned, the AK and AKM are still the rifles most commonly encountered in the hands of terrorists, guerrillas and freedom fighters.

The ready availability of captured Soviet bloc weapons in the West even enabled exercises such as 'Fortress Gale' (USA, 1979) or Operation 'Brave Defender' (Britain, 1985) to be undertaken with genuine equipment to familiarise Allied forces with guns that might be needed in an emergency. In addition, the success of the Kalashnikov within the Soviet bloc, and in the hands of millions of guerrillas throughout the world, has persuaded many Western authorities of its efficiency. Consequently, many attempts have been made to copy it.

Conventional Rifles

The Kalashnikovs

These have been by far the most successful of all the assault rifles, judged quantitatively. Like many Soviet-designed small-arms, the AK and its derivatives were essentially simple and efficient enough to persuade many countries outside the former Soviet bloc – for example Finland, India, Israel and South Africa

– to modify the action in detail before beginning production of their own.

The Kalashnikov rifle has been the traditional weapon of the freedom fighter for many years, particularly those whose leftward-leaning political views were nurtured by the USSR or China. Unfortunately, hopes are waning that fragmentation of the Soviet bloc – and the redrawing of the political map in eastern Europe – would have a beneficial influence not only on the distribution of Kalashnikovs but also on the availability of more powerful weaponry that could ultimately threaten the power-base of the West. Instead, reductions in the military establishments of Eastern Europe have created a vast pool of surplus weapons that can be bought ridiculously cheaply.

Many Western observers have damned the Kalashnikov as clumsy, obsolescent, and firing a poor-performance cartridge. From the purely technical standpoint, the criticism has some validity: the 7.62 x 39mm M43 bullet loses velocity quickly, and its high, looping trajectory magnifies range-gauging errors in a way that contrasts poorly with the comparatively flat-shooting 5.56mm round preferred by NATO.

However, the Kalashnikov is simple, solid, very reliable and, particularly when fitted with the latest muzzle brake, quite effective when firing automatically. Though it undoubtedly benefited from issue throughout the Soviet bloc, to the exclusion of native designs other than the Czech vz/58, the AK has been proven in arctic cold, desert heat, constant drought and tropical rainforest alike. In addition, it is as accurate as the standard M16 in the hands of average shots, though marksmen invariably extract better results from the latter at longer ranges.

The origins of the Kalashnikov are often disputed, and sometimes seem to have been lost in 'official fog'. However, the facts seem to be that the Soviet designers – though experimenting prior to the Second World War with intermediate cartridges – had made very little progress until the first few German *Maschinenkarabiner* and their 7.9mm Kurz cartridges had been captured. The first result was the 7.62 x 39mm M43 cartridge, credited to Elizarov and Semin but little more than the German round adapted to suit Soviet production methods. These had restricted rifles, submachine-guns and handguns alike to a calibre of 7.62mm since Tsarist days, in an attempt to maximise the use of barrel-rifling machinery. However, time was needed not only to perfect the cartridge but also to develop guns chambered for it. This process was not as speedy as the Soviet authorities have claimed; as late as August 1944, the head of the Artillery Operations Department of the Chief Artillery Directorate was still noting, 'a need . . . for increases in the combat efficiency of submachine-guns . . . and an extension of effective range . . . to 500 metres'.

At this time, only the cumbersome blowback Sudaev Avtomat had been submitted to trials. An improved gas-operated Sudaev gun then appeared. Testing showed that it worked well enough for a batch of about fifty to be made for field trials, but the results were not as good as had been hoped. Plans to develop a lightweight version of the gun came to an end when Sudaev died suddenly.

The Soviet authorities then, as an expedient, resurrected the SKS-41, a comparatively conventional 7.62 x 54mm carbine-like diminution of the existing PTRS (Simonov) anti-tank rifle that had been abandoned when the Germans had invaded the USSR. The outcome was the SKS-45, a conventional semi-automatic carbine that was ordered into series production largely to gain experience with the new M43 intermediate ammunition and buy time while a true assault rifle was developed. Though the SKS carbine only equipped the Soviet Army for a short period, it provided the basis for many guns produced in later years in China and Yugoslavia – and is still retained in Russia for ceremonial duties.

The first Kalashnikov was not submitted until 1946, benefiting from the involvement of a designers' collective in Alma-Ata. This prototype performed well enough to allow an improved version to be made in the Kovrov machine-gun factory. Several designers have claimed to have made important changes to the original Kalashnikov rifle, in particular an engineer named Aleksandr Zaytsev; whatever the truth, the modified assault rifle beat off challenges from guns submitted by Demetev and Bulkin, and a large batch of pre-production Kalashnikovs emanated from the Tula small-arms factory in 1948. Field trials showed that the design was extremely efficient and, with purely minor changes, it was officially adopted in 1949.

The layout of the AK was similar to that of the German MP. 43/StG. 44 series, but appreciably less use was made of stampings. Propellant gas was tapped at the mid-point of the bore to strike a piston attached to the bolt carrier, driving the piston/bolt carrier backward and rotating the bolt out of engagement. The assembly then retreated behind the magazine well, riding over and cocking the hammer, and then returned under the influence of the spring to strip a new round into the chamber. The AK was easy to strip for cleaning or inspection – unlike many rival designs.

The original AK, chambering the 7.62 x 39mm M43 intermediate round, measured 34.2in (869mm) overall, had a barrel of 16.3in (414mm), and weighed about 11.3lb (5.12kg) with a loaded 30-round magazine. The four-groove rifling made one turn in 10.2in (260mm). Muzzle velocity was 2,330ft/sec (710m/sec), giving a maximum effective range of 350–400 metres. The cyclic rate of the AK, when firing fully automatically, was about 800rds/min.

The AKM was introduced in 1959, once lessons had been learned from construction of the original gun and Soviet industry had mastered new production techniques. The receiver was a U-shape pressing, permitting a considerable reduction in weight compared with the earlier machined forging, though the lightened gun was more difficult to control when firing automatically. A rate-reducer in the trigger mechanism held back the hammer after the bolt-carrier had depressed the safety sear, relying on the inertia of the hammer to retard the firing cycle. But whether this had any real effect or simply added complexity to an otherwise unusually simple design is still questionable. Some experts have considered the retarder to be no more than an additional mechanical safety, but this is contradicted by the original Soviet manuals.

Though much the same length as its predecessor, judicious use of stampings, pressing and welding reduced the empty weight of the AKM to 8.93lb (4.05kg) compared with 9.48lb (4.30kg) for the AK. Amongst the major constructional changes were the additional rate-reducer, a stamped receiver with riveted-in bolt-lock recesses, and a stamped receiver cover with prominent lateral ribs. In addition, the gas-piston tube of the AKM had semicircular vents behind the gas-port assembly instead of the eight circular holes (four on each side) found on the AK, and the bolt carrier was parkerised instead of bright- or chromed steel.

The butt and fore-end were generally made of laminated wood; pistol grips were usually wooden on the AK, but injection-moulded plastic on the AKM. Soon after the first AKMs had been introduced, a short compensator was added to the muzzle to reduce the tendency of the gun to climb to the right when firing automatically.

The 7.62mm AK and AKM, and their folding-stock 'paratroop' derivatives (AKS and AKMS), were supplemented by the AK-74 in the mid-1970s. This rifle was identical mechanically with the AKM, but fired a 5.45mm cartridge and had a cylindrical muzzle-brake/compensator precluding use of the original bayonet. The origins of the AK-74 appear to lie in the success of the M16/5.56mm M193 cartridge combination, many of which were captured in Vietnam and extensively tested in the USSR. The Russian 5.45mm cartridge was little more than a reduced-calibre derivative of the 7.62mm pattern, but had an odd two-piece bullet with a hollow tip within the jacket. This was intended to improve lethality by allowing the tip to deform when striking the target, but the compromise has been shown to be less effective than the M193.

The AK-74 – chambered for the rimless 5.45 x 39mm M74

cartridge – had a 15.7in (400mm) barrel, but the large muzzle-brake/compensator gave the gun an overall length of 36.5in (928mm). Weight remained much the same as the AKM, though the magazines were slightly lighter and the AK-74 has occasionally been seen with 40-round plastic-body magazines, shared with the RPK-74 light machine-gun. Longitudinal grooves cut into both sides of the butt identified the calibre in the dark.

The AK-74M was approved in the 1980s to overcome some of the weaknesses of the AK series in comparison with Western equipment. First among these was the lack of an optical-sight mounting rail. Though some AKM and AK-74 rifles had been converted for special purposes, the Soviet military authorities demanded that all new guns should be fitted appropriately and a rail was added on the left side of the receiver. The AK-74M also had an improved muzzle brake, a new design of plastic furniture (with a butt that hinged to the left), and a better knife bayonet. Kalashnikovs are still issued in the Russian Army, though a decision was taken in 1994 to replace them with the AN-94 or Nikonov rifle when time (and funding) permitted.

The standard AK/AKM was deemed to be too large and cumbersome for special-purpose use, and so the Soviet designers simply reduced the dimensions to those of a large submachine-gun. Introduced in 1979, the AKS-74U had a folding stock and a 7.9in (200mm) barrel restricting its overall length to 16.5in (420mm) with the stock folded or 26.6in (675mm) with the stock extended.* The standard tangent-leaf back sight was replaced with a two-position rocking sight contained in a special housing on the receiver cover above the ejection port, and improvements were made to the muzzle brake to compensate for increases in flash and blast. The U variant soon proved to be popular with internal security forces and armoured-vehicle crews, and has been used extensively by commandos and the Spetsnaz.

---

* A 'U' version of the 7.62mm AKMS has also been seen, but it is assumed that production was comparatively small – possibly an expedient whilst the AKS-74U was being perfected.

Kalashnikov-type rifles have been fitted with a variety of sights, including the 1PN29 optical, NSP-2 infra-red, NSPU electro-optical and 1PN58-2 electro-optical patterns, and the recent Cobra collimator sight. They may be found with single-shot GP-25 40mm grenade launchers beneath the fore-end, and can also receive silencers (*q.v.*). However, though the Kalashnikov rifle has been widely used by Soviet-bloc special forces, it is insufficiently powerful for snipers' use and the SVD (Dragunov) was developed instead.

By the early 1990s, the Russian Army had become sufficiently disenchanted with the Kalashnikov to invite the submission of potential replacements. The resulting competition, known by the codename Abakan, included the Nikonov or ASN, the A-91 series, and improved Kalashnikov rifles promoted by Izhmashzavod.

The ASN was victorious, but the 'Hundred Series' Kalashnikovs have been marketed commercially in a variety of barrel lengths. Some were chambered for the 5.45 x 39mm round but, with an eye on export markets, others were adapted for 5.56 x 45mm ammunition. The AK-101 (5.56 x 45mm) has been particularly favoured, and most of the series remain in production. They have been joined by the 5.45mm AK-107 and 5.56mm AK-108, which incorporate a 'balanced gas system'.

Developed by Izhmash engineer Yury Aleksandrov on the basis of work undertaken in TsIINTochmash in the mid-1960s, the perfected AL-7 prototype appeared in 1969. However, though it proved to be efficient, the Soviet authorities adopted the small-calibre AK-74. This was seen as a cheaper option at a time when the Soviet economy was weak, and had the additional merit of minimally disrupting Kalashnikov production.

The AK-107 and AK-108, which are regarded as Aleksandrov Kalashnikov ('AK') designs, have duplicated pistons that are blown in opposite directions by gas bled from the bore through duplicated ports. Though this forces the inclusion of a synchronising mechanism, the recoil sensation has decreased appreciably, control when firing automatically is greatly enhanced, and the cyclic rate has risen owing to a reduction in the travel of the bolt. The AK-107 is 47.1in (943mm) long (27.4in/695mm with the butt folded), has a 16.3in (415mm) barrel, and weighs 7.9lb (3.6kg) without its magazine. The selector can be set to give single shots, a three-round burst, or automatic fire.

The rifle developed by Gennady Nikonov, winner of the Abakan competition, was adopted in 1994 to replace the Kalashnikov in the hands of the Army and Ministry of Internal Affairs (MVD) personnel. The AN-94 operates on a patented 'blowback shifted pulse' (BBSP) system, but is really little more than a combination of gas and recoil operation with a separate cartridge rammer. When the gun fires, gas is bled from the barrel to strike a piston, which drives the bolt and bolt carrier backward, rotating the bolt out of engagement. Simultaneously, the entire barrel/receiver group begins to run back within the polymer frame and a rammer transfers a cartridge from the magazine to a small auxiliary feed-way in the underside of the receiver. When the bolt returns, it strips the new round into the chamber, the action is re-locked, and the receiver moves back to its forward position.

The goal is to allow an exceptionally rapid second shot if the selector has been set to auto, when the hammer is tripped the moment the cartridge has been chambered and the gun fires again as the receiver is still moving backward. The result is two rounds fired at a cyclic rate of 1,800rds/min, though the third and successive shots revert to a normal 600rds/min cycle. If the selector is set to fire bursts, however, the two rounds are fired at the normal rate. The goal of all the complexity is to deliver two shots near-simultaneously on the same spot, enhancing penetration of body armour.

The AN-94 chambers the standard 5.45 x 39mm M74 cartridge, measures 37.1in (943mm) overall – 28.7in (728mm) with the butt folded – and weighs 8.5lb (3.85kg) without its 30-round magazine. Separating the awkwardly placed safety catch/selector lever of the Kalashnikov into two components is advantageous, but the selector cannot be reached if the butt is folded.

A five-position aperture sight is fitted above the rear of the frame, a self-cleaning brake is attached to the muzzle, and a bayonet lug on the right side of the muzzle allows a 40mm GP-25 grenade launcher to be mounted without removing the bayonet (one of the weaknesses of the AK series). But whether the complication is justified is arguable, and the AN-94 has not yet reached service in large numbers. This has been blamed on the cost of re-equipment, at a time when the military budget is being reduced, but this excuse may cloak operating problems. The Abakan programme may not be finished, as Izhmashzavod recently announced that trials with an experimental 'AS' prototype were commencing.

Compared with the robust Kalashnikov, the Nikonov does not yet give the impression of a battle-worthy weapon. It will undoubtedly be used to good effect by the Spetsnaz and similarly well-trained units, but it is hard to see it achieving universal issue.

Among the other Russian developments, the compact 9 x 39mm 'assault carbines' deserve mention. The most conventional of these is the SR-3 Vikhr (Whirlwind), based on the VSS silenced sniper rifle and the ASS silenced submachine-gun. These incorporate a reduced-scale version of the SVD (Dragunov) action, and have achieved limited popularity with the Spetsnaz, MVD and FSO units. Though the cartridge is subsonic, it fires a heavy boat-tailed bullet that has a much better combat performance than the 9mm Parabellum or 0.45in ACP rounds chambered in conventional submachine-guns such as the Heckler & Koch MP5, the Ingram or the Uzi.

Initially known as the MA, the SR-3 was developed in the early 1990s by TsNIITochmash engineers Borisov and Levchenko in response to a request for a 'personal defence weapon'. It has an upward-folding butt and a simple pivoting-'L' back sight. The protruding charging handle of the Kalashnikov has been replaced with duplicated buttons above the front of the fore-end, and the selector is a cross-bolt in the front of the trigger guard.

The 9A-91, the only survivor of a series of guns submitted to the Abakan competition, was designed by the KBP design bureau in the Tula factory and entered small-scale production in the mid-1990s. It is more conventional than the SR-3, with the charging handle projecting from the right side of a Kalashnikov-type receiver. The furniture is polymer, the back sight is a two-position 'flip' pattern, and the steel butt folds upward to lie along the receiver-top.

The SR-3 and 9A-91 are each about 24in (610mm) long, or, with their butts folded, 14.2in (360mm) and 15.1in (383mm) respectively. Empty weight is only 4.4–4.5lb (2–2.1kg), without the magazines, which makes the guns virtually modern versions of the US 0.30in M3 Carbine. Though the AKS-74U has been widely used by Soviet and Russian Special Forces and anti-terrorist units, the 5.45 x 39mm round is sometimes judged to be too powerful (and to have too much potential for collateral damage) to be used in urban confrontations. In this context, the use of these 9 x 39mm guns makes perfect sense.

The Kalashnikov design has been extensively copied in former Soviet-bloc countries and the People's Republic of China, where work continues. Many of these guns are difficult to distinguish from their Soviet prototypes, though the selector markings will provide clues – Russian guns are marked 'AB' and 'ОД'. The first letters of *avtomatichisky* ('automatic') and *odinochniy* ('one-shot') respectively; Bulgarian guns are marked 'AB' and 'ОД' or '0' and 'T'; Chinese guns have ideographic selector markings (though export patterns may be marked 'L' and 'D'); Egyptian guns may be marked in Arabic, or display 'A' and 'R'; guns made in the German Democratic Republic were marked 'E' and 'D'; Hungarian products will be marked '1' and '∞'; Korean guns have markings in Hangul characters; Polish guns display 'C' and 'P'; Romanian guns will be marked 'S', 'FA' and 'FF'; and Yugoslavian/Serbian weapons customarily display 'U', 'R' and 'T'.

Many Romanian AKM rifles have an additional handgrip beneath the fore-end, the Chinese guns have folding bayonets attached to a block beneath the muzzle, and some of the Hungarian derivatives have metal fore-ends with a synthetic handgrip projecting downward. The Yugoslavian/Serbian guns are among the most interesting, as they incorporate refinements such as grenade-launching sights and mechanical hold-opens absent from their Soviet prototypes. Additional details will be found in the books listed in the Bibliography.

Finland has produced several versions of the Kalashnikov for military use, and a number of 'semi-commercial' derivations. The unsuccessful Rynnakkokivääri ('assault rifle') m/60 had a plastic fore-end, a tubular steel butt, the back sight on the receiver-cover and an Arctic trigger without a guard. It was replaced by the more conventional m/62, with a different handgrip and a conventional trigger-guard. A commercial variant known as the m/71, reverting to the standard butt, encountered limited success before being superseded by the m/76 – essentially similar to the m/62, but with a more conservative appearance. Used by the Finnish Army in 7.62 x 39mm M43, the m/76 was also offered in 5.56 x 45mm and 7.62mm NATO. There were also minor variants such as the m/76P, m/76T and m/76W – with folding plastic, fixed tubular and wood butts respectively – as well as an m/83S sniper rifle, a semi-experimental m/82 bullpup, and a semi-automatic commercial sporting rifle known as the Petra.

A few thousand improved m/95 guns were then made before Sako-Valmet finally stopped making assault rifles; future weapons will be bought-in when required. The selectors of Finnish service rifles will usually display • (single shots) and • • • (automatic fire).

The Indian armed forces adopted the 5.56 x 45mm INSAS ('Indian Small Arms System') in 1990. Developed in 1988–90 by ARDE[W], Poona, this rifle is basically an adaptation of the Kalashnikov with transparent-body magazines, chromed-bore barrels and a three-shot burst capability built into the trigger system. The plastic furniture has more in common with that of the Israeli Galil (*see below*) than the original Soviet patterns.

The INSAS has been touted as a submachine-gun, an assault rifle or a light support weapon. The assault rifle is about 38in (965mm) overall, with an 18.3in (464mm) barrel, and weighs 9lb (4.1 kg) with a loaded magazine. The back sight is a two-position rocking pattern set for 200 and 400 metres, and the cyclic rate is reckoned to average 650rds/min. The first batches were delivered to the Indian Army in 1995, but about 100,000 assorted 7.62mm AKM-type Kalashnikovs were purchased in 1993 as an expedient.

The Israeli arms industry has also benefited greatly from the success of the Galil, a Kalashnikov derivative. Though the safety system is markedly different, the earliest Galil rifles are said to have been made with unmarked 'Finnish Kalashnikov' receivers supplied by Valmet. The standard service rifle, the 5.56 x 45mm Galil AR, was adopted in 1972: however, guns have also been chambered for the 7.62 x 51mm NATO round. A short-barrelled variant, the SAR, and the bipod-fitted ARM light support weapon could also be obtained, together with a 7.62mm NATO wood-butt sniper rifle with an optical sight.

The semi-automatic 7.62mm NATO Hadar II, intended for police use, has a distinctive one-piece wood stock with a large thumb-hole behind the conventionally positioned Galil-type pistol grip. As the design of the stock precludes the use of the standard Galil safety catch, a radial lever is set into the left side of the pistol grip. All standard Galils have folding metal butts.

Ironically, in view of the fact that the Galil was copied from the Kalashnikov, the South African R4 and R5 rifles were copies of the Galil. The bipod-fitted long-butt Rifle Model 4 (R4) was made in quantity in the Pretoria factory of Lyttleton Engineering Works; the short 'carbine' version was known as the R5.

The Armalites

During the period in which the CETME/G3 was being developed, a new full-power rifle appeared in the USA. In October 1954, the Fairchild Engine and Airplane Company had created an Armalite Division in which to develop modern lightweight small-arms. Development of the AR-10 began in 1954, based on a rifle Eugene Stoner had devised before being appointed as Armalite's chief engineer. The gas-operated rotating-bolt design featured an integral carrying handle and a straight-line layout intended to minimise climb in the automatic mode. By 1956, it had gained a titanium-lined aluminium barrel, a fibreglass stock and a synthetic magazine, all in an attempt to combine lightness with strength.

However, Fairchild had neither the production expertise nor the facilities to contemplate mass production, and the AR-10 was licensed to NWM in the Netherlands in 1957. Changes were made, including the elimination of the original flash suppressor and the removal of the gas tube to a better position above the barrel. However, though belt-fed derivatives appeared, the project was unsuccessful and sales were very poor.

Nicaragua, Sudan and Burma are known to have taken some AR-10 rifles, but a large order for Portugal was cancelled after just 1,200 had been delivered. The Portuguese took the G3 instead, and production of the NWM-Armalite ceased.

In 1957, the Commanding Officer of the US Army's Continental Army Command (CONARC) had issued a specification for an infantry rifle weighing no more than 6lb, with selective-fire capabilities, accuracy comparable with the Rifle M1 (Garand) and lethality bettering the 0.30in M1 Carbine cartridge at distances up to 500 yards. Though no calibre was specified, and the weight requirement seemed completely unattainable, Winchester and Armalite showed interest. Stoner began development of a small-diameter cartridge by loading 55-grain commercial Sierra bullets into 0.222in Remington cases, which developed into the longer-case 0.222in Remington Special (later renamed 0.223in Remington) to compete against Winchester's 0.224in E1 and E2.

The first ten 0.222in Special AR-15 trials rifles were delivered to the US Army Infantry Board at the end of March 1958. At only 6.12lb complete with a loaded 25-round magazine, they all but met the CONARC specifications. Initial reports were enthusiastic, and much interest was shown in the AR-15, despite the standardisation of the T44E4 experimental rifle as the M14 in June 1957.

Both lightweight high-velocity rifles (LWHVR) were extensively tested at Fort Benning, Aberdeen Proving Ground and Fort Greely. Results were generally encouraging, but doubts had already been expressed about the lethality of such small-diameter bullets. During 1958, therefore, a group of generals – the Powell Board – was convened to consider the small-calibre rifles, but rejected 0.223in and 0.224in in favour of an optimal 0.258in. CONARC then requested that a final series of trials should be undertaken by the US Army Combat Development Experimentation Center (ACDEC) at Fort Ord, California, to determine the future of the LWHVR project. The trials began on 1 December 1958 but, before they could be finished, the Army Chief of Staff rejected the LWHVR in favour of the 7.62mm Rifle M14 'on the basis of all available facts'. The high-ranking factions that opposed the 0.223in cartridge on personal grounds, believing that a military weapon should be 'man-size' rather than a 'toy', had covertly disrupted the LWHVR project.

At the end of May 1959, ACDEC reported that the 0.224in Winchester rifle had proved more accurate but appreciably less reliable than the 0.223in AR-15. By this time, however, the US Army had lost interest, cancelled the programme, and turned to the 6mm Special Purpose Infantry Weapon (SPIW) instead. All seemed lost until, in May 1961, the USAF agreed to purchase AR-15 rifles in quantity and classified the 5.56mm Rifle AR-15 (later XMI6, then M16) as standard in January 1962. An Air Force contract for 8,500 guns and 8.5 million cartridges was passed to Colt on 23 May 1962.

While the USAF was finalising its first purchase, the AR-15 had been extensively demonstrated in the Far East and had attracted special attention in Vietnam. In December 1961, the Secretary of Defense authorised the supply of a thousand AR-15 rifles for the Vietnamese Army (ARVN), the first guns being shipped in January 1962. By the summer, trials had been completed; it was clear that the AR-15 was a great success, being hailed as a suitable replacement for most of the guns in ARVN service – including the M1 and M14 rifles, the M1 Carbine, the BAR and the M3 submachine-gun. No parts-breakages were reported in a trial allegedly lasting 80,000 rounds!

General Haskins, Commander of the US Military Advisory Command in Vietnam, was so impressed that he unsuccessfully attempted to order 'substantial' quantities of AR-15 rifles for front-line ARVN troops. Owing to the lack of progress with the 6mm SPIW, US Army interest in the AR-15 grew once more; 338 XM16 rifles were acquired in October 1962 so that tests could be undertaken against the M14 and the AK-47. However, in January 1963, a 'final' report recommended continued acquisition of the M14 during the period in which the SPIW was being perfected.

The AR-15/M16 still had its champions; indeed, the Army Materiel Command had actually recommended it for universal issue. And, when an investigation by the Inspector General of the Armed Forces revealed that trials had been strongly biased in favour of the M14 – the guns that had been used were specially selected, fired match ammunition, and were often shot by experienced marksmen – the Armalite design was given another chance. Finally, in 1963, 85,000 guns were ordered for airborne, assault and special forces units to whom the light weight was advantageous.

As the US Army had been made sole purchasing agency, 104,000 rifles were to be ordered in fiscal year 1964: 19,000 M16 rifles for the USAF and 85,000 XM16 guns for the US Army. By this time, there had been a severe difference of opinion among the services, and the government had toyed with the idea of ordering guns from several contractors simultaneously. The Army then refused to take the XM16 unless some changes were made, the most important being the incorporation of a bolt-assist on the rear right side of the action.

This was intended to close the bolt in the event of problems, though neither the USAF nor the US Marine Corps considered it necessary. Air Force representatives pointed to the phenomenal reliability of the test rifles in ARVN hands, and that normal procedure in the event of a misfire or bolt problem was to retract the cocking handle and try again; they considered the Army's addition to be an unnecessary complication, and even to compromise safety. In addition, a reduction of the twist-pitch from one turn in fourteen inches to one in only twelve – necessary to extend the operating range of the XM16 so that it became -65° to +125°F – seriously compromised the lethality of the M193 bullet.

The new Army rifle was initially designated 5.56mm Rifle XM16E1, eventually reclassified M16A1 in 1967. Until the end of 1965, when purchasing was finally rationalised, the M16 (for the Air Force and the Marines) was made concurrently with the Army XM16E1.

During this period, the US Government's preference for single-source procurement was increasingly questioned, particularly as Colt was not only reluctant to license production to other manufacturers until more than 500,000 assorted M16 and M16A1 rifles had been ordered but was also making more than permissible from the fixed-profit government contracts. Finally, a licence was concluded between Colt and the US Department of Defense on 30 July 1967. The rights had cost the US Treasury no less than $4.5 million, plus a 5.5 per cent royalty on each gun made by companies other than Colt, which at that time also held orders for 632,500 guns extending into 1970. Harrington & Richardson of Worcester, Massachusetts, and the Hydra-Matic Division of General Motors subsequently made M16A1 rifles. Guns have also been made in the Philippines, by Elisco, and by CIS of Singapore.

The service debut of the XM16 was eagerly awaited, but initial enthusiasm soon waned. Jamming soon presented a serious problem and the weapons quickly became unusable. It was due to poor maintenance – the gun had been optimistically touted as 'self-cleaning' – and an unappreciated change in ammunition.

During 1966, so many reports of severe problems with the XM16E1 filtered back from the US forces in Vietnam that representatives of the Army Weapons Command and Colt were immediately dispatched to the Far East. There they found many of the guns in a dreadful state. Their report stated that:

> ... with the exception of ... the 1st Brigade, the 101st Airborne Division, the 173rd Airborne Brigade and the 5th Special Services Group, the weapons were in unbelievable condition ... rust, filth, and lack of repair. The filthy condition ranged from actual dirt, grit and mud on various components of the weapon and ammunition to a heavy deposit on various components. The most significant trouble spots were the chamber, the outside of the gas tube extension in the upper receiver, and the inside of the carrier key. Approximately 5% of the ammunition was found to be unserviceable due to corrosion and an additional 10% would have given trouble due to being dirty. From 30 to 50% of the magazines appeared unserviceable due to bent or spread lips.

The problems were soon isolated. Poor training, appalling maintenance and poor lubrication were easily cured by better instruction and better cleaning procedures, a trap being added in the butt to hold the appropriate implements. Excess copper deposits in the bore had arisen from firing too much tracer; chroming the chamber (also, subsequently, the bore) minimised carbon deposition, corrosion and extraction problems. Alterations were made in the gas system, and a new buffer, designed by Foster Sturtevant, slowed the cyclic rate.

The major problem proved to be the ammunition. Cartridges fired in the early AR-15/XM16 trials had been loaded with the Du Pont IMR (Improved Military Rifle) 4475 propellant customarily used by the US armed forces. However, IMR had generated operating pressures with such low margins of safety that the first 19 million cartridges supplied by Remington to the USAF contained Olin Mathieson WC-846 ball powder instead. This, together with IMR (CR) 8136, was a permissible substitute. During the fiscal year 1964, therefore, 1 million cartridges had been loaded with IMR 4475, 50 million with IMR (CR) 8136, and the remaining 81 million with WC-846.

Though USAF endurance trials in March 1964 had given a mere 55 stoppages whilst firing 162,000 cartridges loaded with IMR 4475, the WC-846 batches not only gave appreciably more fouling but also raised the cyclic rate above the acceptable maximum. Though a minimum fouling requirement had already been added to the ammunition specifications, this applied only to the pre-production deliveries. In theory, a manufacturer could supply a few thousand cartridges to pass the fouling test . . . and then make millions that did not.

Tests undertaken in Frankford Arsenal in December 1965 showed that cartridges loaded with WC-846 were more than five times as liable to stoppages as IMR loads. IMR S20SM powder was adopted in May 1966 – but even as late as August 1967, no USMC unit in Vietnam had received anything other than WC-846 loads. Thus propellant fouling in XM16E1/M16A1 rifles continued unabated until the end of that year, though its effect was minimised by greater attention to maintenance.

In sum, the M16 has been refined into a battleworthy weapon, but only after a decade of hard work and the traumatic experience in Vietnam. The story also illustrates the considerable problems of developing a soldier-proof weapon for general service, even though the M16 and M16A1 are much appreciated by the SAS and other special forces to whom good preventive maintenance is second nature.

Changes made to the gas system, and the addition of a new back sight, produced the M16A2; and the supersession of the fixed carrying handle/back-sight guard in favour of a Picatinny rail (capable of accepting a variety of sights and accessories) led to the current M16A3. In addition, variants of the basic design have been made for military and commercial sale. Apart from the heavy-barrel guns submitted to the SAWS project as a light machine-gun, there was also a shortened version originally known as the Commando, XM16, XM16E1 or XM16E2.

The XM16 carbine was an M16 with a 10-inch barrel and a long flash-hider; the XM16E1 was the army derivative with a bolt assist; and the XM16E2 was an XM16E1 with a grenade launching muzzle attachment. In May 1993, the US Army placed an order for 15,597 XM4 5.56mm carbines, intending to buy 52,000 M4 carbines by 1997. These were to supplement about 5,000 guns acquired for trials and special forces' use in 1985–93.

The M4A1 is the perfected version of the XM16 series, with a three-round burst firing capability in the trigger mechanism and a Picatinny rail instead of the carrying handle. Many guns of this type have been seen in use in Iraq, often fitted with sophisticated collimator, optical or night vision sights. Shorter and handier than the M16A3, the M4A1 has been popular with SOCOM (Special Operations Command) and even touted as a universal replacement for the M16 series. Though the US Navy Surface Warfare Center produced a SOPMOD (Special Operations Modification) kit, which included the Rail Interface System (RIS) instead of the standard handguard, allowing laser-designators and tactical light projectors to be fitted, the M4A1 has not been as reliable as expected. It is well known that the M16 rifle operates at the limit of acceptable pressure in the gas system; the short barrel of the M4A1, which degrades muzzle velocity and range, also raises the pressures to a point where components may fail. The comparatively lightweight barrel also overheats if fire is sustained for even a short period, and complaints have been made by US Special Forces serving in Afghanistan that the M4A1 – which is also comparatively heavy when fitted with all its accessories – places them at a disadvantage in a long-range firefight.

The US authorities seem to have accepted that the forty-year life of the ArmaLite rifle is coming to a close, and have projected the introduction of an experimental batch of XM8 light assault rifles for the 2005 Fiscal Year. The XM8 Lightweight Modular Carbine System ('LMCS') is an outgrowth of the OCIW XM29 – see '*Combination Weapons*' – developed by the Office of the Project Manager for Soldier Weapons at Picatinny Arsenal, in conjunction with the US Army Infantry Center. Thirty guns were delivered for trials in November 2003, followed by a hundred early in 2004.

The XM8 Future Combat Rifle (FCR) is expected to replace the existing M4 carbines and selected 5.56mm rifles, but is part of a family that includes a sniper rifle (XM8 Sharpshooter), a light-support weapon (XM8 Squad Automatic) and an ultra-compact carbine (XM8 PDW). The ability rapidly to alter guns to different configurations, including changes of calibre, is claimed to be a major advantage. This includes the addition of the XM322 40mm grenade launcher and the LSS 12-bore shotgun module without the use of tools.

The XM8 has a charging handle doubling as a bolt-assist, placed centrally; ambidextrous selector, safety-catch and magazine-release controls; and a multiple-position collapsible butt. Magazines may include a 10-round box, the standard 30-round box or a 100-round drum. Most of the parts are made of fibre-reinforced polymer material that can be moulded in a variety of colours to suit individual applications, and to quote the US Army literature, the surfaces 'that interface with the user are fitted with non-slip materials to increase comfort and operator retention'. Sight-rails are integral with the body of the gun, though adaptors will allow Picatinny rails to be used when necessary. The standard sight is a battery-powered 'red dot' close-combat optic (CCO).

The 5.56mm XM8, derived from the Heckler & Koch G36 by HK Defense in Sterling, Virginia, will be manufactured in the USA at a factory close to the US Army Infantry School at Fort Benning, Georgia. The basic carbine is 29.8in (757mm) long with a 12.5in (318mm) barrel, and weighs 6.25lb (2.84kg) without its magazine.

The success of the AR-15, M16 and M16A1 throughout the world (even Britain has acquired large numbers of guns for the Royal Marines and Special Forces) led to a radical revision of tactical doctrines, and the development of similar small-calibre rifles in many other countries. Yet, despite its undoubted efficacy, the AR-15/M16 series requires specialised machine tools and metal-fabricating techniques for effective mass-production, the requisite capital investment being repayable only by lengthy production runs. The US Army contracts for M16A3 rifles are now being placed with Fabrique Nationale Manufacturing of Columbia, South Carolina.

Most small countries simply could not afford to make the M16, though several Far Eastern countries have been interested and small numbers were made by Elisco Tool Corporation in the Philippines. Guns are also being made for the Canadian armed forces by Diemaco of Kitchener, Ontario, as the C7/C7A1 rifles and C8 carbines. Diemaco also successfully tendered to provide the Royal Netherlands Army with these guns, paying Colt a suitable royalty, and the British Army has acquired C8 carbines for Special Forces use.

The military success of the AR15/M16 series has been mirrored in commercial demands, which have been satisfied not only by Colt but also by small customising businesses that have transformed the basic weapons into high-grade ones suitable for use as target rifles by adding heavy free-floating barrels, chroming the bore, fitting bipods, and replacing the military-style fore-end with special tubular guards that do not contact the barrel. Guns marketed by ArmaLite (owned since 1995 by Eagle Arms), DPMS, Olympic Arms and Professional Ordnance have proved popular with SWAT teams. Though outclassed by 7.62mm ammunition at long range, the exceptional accuracy of match-grade 5.56mm cartridges allows the smaller bullets to be placed with unerring accuracy at ranges up to 500 metres.*

FN Designs

The gas-operated CAL was a lightened version of the FAL introduced in 1966, but was complicated, expensive and

---

* Ironically, ArmaLite now offers a range of 7.62 x 51mm AR-10 rifles created by reverse-engineering the 5.56mm guns. The original (and largely unsuccessful) AR-10 was the prototype of the AR-15, but differed in many important respects.

insufficiently durable. Its replacement, the FNC-80, has advanced through several developmental models since 1975 and a Para model may be obtained with a folding butt.

Several European countries have considered the FNC for adoption. However, apart from Belgium, only Sweden has translated this interest into large-scale purchase. Known as the Ak-5, the Swedish rifle was adopted in 1984 to replace the Ak-4 (7.62mm Heckler & Koch G3). Tooling began in the Eskilstuna factory of FFV in 1986, the first guns being delivered a year later.

Heckler & Koch Designs

H&K strenuously championed the 5.56mm HK33 and then the 5.56mm G41, both being diminutions of the standard roller-locked G3, but too much effort was put into the caseless-cartridge G11 – a remarkable project whose story has yet to be wholly told – for even the perfected roller-locked 5.56mm-calibre gun to be entirely successful.

The West German government cancelled the G11 to save money after reunification, but the G41 remained in limbo until being replaced in the 1990s by the 5.56mm G36, a much more conventional gas-operated design locked by a rotating bolt. Though initially seen as little more than an expedient, trials showed that the G36 was extremely efficient; consequently, it was adopted by the Bundeswehr to replace the ageing 7.62mm G3 series and also by the NATO Rapid Reaction Force.

The G36 has a skeletal butt/frame/receiver unit, made of fibreglass-reinforced polymer, and a combination optical sight/red-dot sight built into the carrying handle above the breech.* The magazine well is detachable – the gun will accept a 100-round drum as well as the standard translucent 'snap-together' box magazines – and the trigger can incorporate burst-firing capabilities in addition to the standard semi- and automatic fire settings. A bipod, a single-shot break-open AG36 grenade

---

* The G36E, the 'Export' version, has a simple 1.5x optical sight instead of this particular combination.

launcher, or the H&K Universal Tactical Light (UTL) can be fitted beneath the fore-end.

Modular construction allows the basic G36 to be configured in several different ways, including the G36C. This special short-barrelled carbine has a short flash-hider and a low Picatinny rail above the receiver fitted with auxiliary open sights. It is only 28.3in (720mm) long with the butt extended, compared with 39.3in (998mm) for the full-length rifle. Cyclic rate remains about 750rds/min.

Beretta Designs

The Italians announced their original competition to replace the venerable BM-59 (Garand) rifle as long ago as 1980. However, though substantial numbers of Beretta AR-70 and SC-70 rifles were acquired for the Special Forces (GIS, NOCS) and the Italian Air Force, flaws were found in the basic design. The result of the remedial work was the 70/90 rifle, introduced in 1985. Finally, in June 1990, the perfected version was selected to replace the BM-59; the first large-scale deliveries were made in 1992, and the Italian armed forces have now re-equipped with the 5.56mm rifles.

The bolt of the AR-70 had reciprocated on rails pressed into the receiver, but hardened steel rails inserted in the AR-70/90 frame extended service life considerably. Raising the heel of the butt created a 'straight-line' configuration, but forced the addition of a carrying handle/sight rail to the receiver. The SC-70/90 has a folding butt, and the otherwise comparable short-barrelled SCP-70/90 – intended for the paratroops – has a grenade launcher on the muzzle, and an auxiliary folding sight on the gas-port block.

CETME Designs

The Model L is a 5.56mm diminutive of the 7.62mm Spanish CETME, developed in the late 1970s and made by Empresa Nacional 'Santa Barbara'. Like most of its rivals, the small-calibre CETME has undergone searching trials during development. During this period, the original drum sight was replaced by a simple two-position pattern and the burst firing mechanism – in the opinion of many commentators, a needless complication – was finally abandoned. The original 20-round magazine was replaced by a standard NATO 30-round pattern shortly before the Model L was adopted by the Spanish Army in 1984 to supplement and ultimately replace the 7.62mm rifles, the first large-scale deliveries being made in 1987. The guns had already seen extensive use with the Spanish Special Forces.

The L1 pattern, intended for export, also accepted the NATO standard US M16-type 30-round magazine. It had a three-position selector and a simplified two-position back sight. The LC version was a 'compact assault rifle' with a sliding butt, and a 12.6in (320mm) barrel with a short expansion chamber behind the flash suppressor. It was only 26.2in (665mm) long, with the butt retracted, and weighed about 7lb (3.2kg) empty.

SIG Designs

The first Swiss SIG rifles were originally based on the StGw. 57, which itself owed something to the wartime German FG. 42 and MG. 42. The StGw. 57 was replaced in the mid-1960s by the SIG510 series. These rifles proved to be too expensive for most of the armies of the time, though a large quantity went to Chile; once 5.56mm became popular, therefore, SIG produced the unsuccessful SG530-1 – a diminutive form of the roller-lock SG510 series – before proceeding to SG540 and SG541 (5.56mm) and SG542 (7.62mm), all of which included gas operation and rotating-bolt locks. The 540-series was designed with an eye to simplifying production. During the mid-1970s, the SG540 series was licensed to Manurhin, which made substantial numbers of 5.56mm rifles for the French Army whilst the FA MAS was being perfected.

The SG541 was upgraded to SG550 standards in the early 1980s, and adopted by the Swiss Army in 1984 as the Sturmgewehr Modell 90; the first series-made rifles were delivered in 1986, issue being completed by 1996. The three-round burst-firing mechanism is standard, the plastic butt is a skeleton design, the magazine body is transparent plastic, and a rail above the receiver accepts optical or electro-optical sights.

The SG551 'headquarters weapon', with the barrel cut to 14in (357mm), has been promoted as the Sturmgewehr 90 Assault Carbine. A short-barrelled SWAT Model, with a Picatinny rail above the receiver, has been offered to police and counter-terrorist forces, and there is also a sniper-rifle derivative (SSG550, *q.v.*).

Bullpup Patterns
FA MAS
Virtually all of the rifles mentioned previously have followed the conventional design, with the barrel, receiver and butt virtually in a line. However, there are also battle-worthy representatives of the so-called 'bullpup' class, which, by placing the pistol grip ahead of the magazine, allows the butt to be eliminated in favour of a shoulder pad on the rear of the receiver. This allows overall length to be shortened, though placing the chamber alongside the firer's face does not meet with universal approval.

The French Fusil Automatique F3 MAS (better known as the FA MAS) was developed in the government factory in Saint-Étienne and introduced to the French Army in 1973, though development problems prevented adoption for six years and substantial quantities of the Manurhin-made (but SIG-designed) 5.56mm SG540 rifles were acquired in the interim.

Nicknamed *le clairon* (the bugle), owing to the curious combined carrying handle/sight base, the FA MAS displays some very unusual features; for example, it is readily convertible for left- or right-hand ejection. The trigger system, packaged in a replaceable synthetic box, incorporates a ratchet escapement to fire three-shot bursts. In the finalised design – substantial numbers made at the beginning of production lacked the burst-firing capability – the selector in the trigger guard could be moved from 'S' to '1' for single shots. With the main selector set to 'R' and the burst-fire selector under the trigger on '0', the FA MAS would fire fully automatically; if the settings were 'R' and '3', a three-round burst ensued.

Light and comfortable to fire on the credit side, the adequacy of the delayed-blowback action for the high-pressure cartridge has often been questioned. In 1995, however, the French Navy (soon followed by the Army) adopted the improved FA MAS G2. The new gun has an enlarged trigger guard, a more robust breech-block buffer, a NATO-standard magazine interface, and a lipped fore-end preventing the firer's hand slipping in front of the muzzle. The rifling, a compromise design making a turn in 9 inches (228mm) allows M193 and SS109 ball ammunition to be fired interchangeably.

British Designs

Experiments with the original 4.85mm guns dated back to the 1970s, the first public exhibition occurring on 14 July 1976. The XL64E5 rifle was entered in NATO trials in 1977, which eventually standardised the 30-round US M16A1 magazine, the French grenade launcher, and the Belgian FN SS109 5.56mm bullet. However, this left the British isolated, and the XL64E5 was redesigned to accept the 5.56 x 45mm round. This created the XL70E3 of 1981, which could be identified by the straight under-edge of the receiver.

The first series-production guns were made in the Enfield factory in 1983 for field trials and issued in the summer of 1984 with the 4x magnification Sight, Unit, Small Arms, Trilux, L9A1 (SUSAT), the combination performing well enough to permit the SA-80 to be adopted in 1985 as the 5.56mm Rifle L85A1. It bore an external affinity to the old EM-2, but looked more conventional than the FA MAS.

The rifle was originally seen as part of a system that included a light machine-gun (L86A1), and perpetuated the post-war British belief that infantry weapons should have optical sights. It was fitted with a compact 4x magnification SUSAT optical unit, though emergency open sights were contained in the pistol grip.

Yet, despite its protracted development, the L85A1 was not particularly successful. So many problems arose during the Gulf War (1991) that British newspapers were full of scare stories. The *Observer*, claiming to quote from a Ministry of Defence report, suggested that:

> The Individual Weapon [IW or L85A1] and the Light Support Weapon [LSW, L86A1] did not cope with the sand. Infantrymen faced the enemy in combat unsure whether their weapons would fire or stop. Tactical drills were affected, in that provision had to be made to cover a man with a stoppage. Some section and platoon commanders considered that casualties would have been suffered because of weapons shortages . . . had the enemy put up more resistance in close combat.

It was suggested that the problems arose from very poor standards of manufacture; that the gun and its accessories had effectively been 'designed down to a price' by financial constraints applied by the Treasury; or that the project – having been many years in creation (the prototype of the L85A1 had been announced as 'The British Army's New Rifle' as early as 1976) – was rushed through to sweeten the sale by the government of Royal Ordnance. One senior British military commander complained that the L85A1 was basically 'a poor rifle with good sights', and this is a reputation that, to date, it has failed to shake off.

Extensive alterations created the L85A2, which is undoubtedly an improvement. Problems have been reported during the recent fighting in Iraq, but these have been blamed on troops disembarking into clouds of dust and sand thrown up by their helicopters – an environment in which, British officials claim, few rival designs would work.

Steyr Designs
Once regarded as the most curious-looking of guns, the AUG-77 is now so well established that its looks no longer seem excessively futuristic. The Armee-Universal-Gewehr was

developed and manufactured by Steyr-Daimler-Puch, its flowing lines, facilitated by extensive use of synthetic material, hiding a gas-operated turning-bolt action efficient enough to have convinced the Australians, Irish, Malaysians, New Zealanders and others to adopt it at the expense of the British SA-80/ L85A1. The AUG has also been seen in the hands of the SAS, in addition to Austrian counter-terrorist units operating at Vienna airport.

Though the standard rifle chambers the 5.56mm SS109 cartridge, it can be converted instantly into light-support configuration merely by changing the barrel. Alternatively, a 9mm Parabellum conversion unit transforms the AUG into an efficient submachine-gun.

FN Designs

Introduced in 2001, the F2000 is a 5.56mm-calibre assault rifle embodying a modular concept. The gun looks extraordinary, made largely of polymers, with a slab-sided butt, a 1.6x optical sight module attached to the bolt/barrel unit, and a streamlined shroud protecting the attachment rail beneath the fore-end. The selective-fire F2000 ejects spent cases forward, requiring no alteration for left-handed firers, and can accept accessories such as FN 40mm grenade launchers, the compressed-air XM303 non-lethal projector (which fires 12-bore pellets loaded with dye or tear gas), or a computerised fire-control system for the rifle and the grenade launcher.

The gun is 694mm long, with a 400mm barrel, and weighs 4.6kg with the grenade launcher in place. Standard 30-round NATO/STANAG magazines can be used, inserted into the feed-way immediately behind the pistol-grip aperture.

Singaporean Designs

The success of the CIS Multimax light machine-gun and the associated SAR-88 assault rifle has led to the creation of the SAR-21, developed by the Kinetics Division of Singapore Technologies (STK, formerly CIS). Introduced in 1999, the gas-operated SAR-21 is replacing the M16A1, SAR-80 and SAR-88 rifles in the hands of the Singapore forces. Similar in layout to the AUG, the SAR-21 is locked by a seven-lug rotating bolt and is made largely of impact-resistant polymer. A 1.5x magnification optical sight is built into the carrying handle and a large 'gloved hand' trigger guard extends to the base of the pistol grip. The feed-way for the 30-round magazine lies directly behind the pistol grip, but, unlike many rivals, the SAR-21 can only eject to the right. Consequently, it is not suitable for left-handed firers.

The standard gun has a well-shaped fore-end with an integral laser-aiming module or LAM, but the SAR-21 P and SAR-21 RIS have Picatinny rails on the top (P) and sides (P and RIS) of the fore-end, the charging handle on the left side instead of beneath the carrying handle, and an additional forward pistol-grip. Handling characteristics are reportedly very good. The gun is 31.7in (805mm) long, with a 20in (508mm) barrel, and weighs 9.8lb (4.4kg) with a loaded magazine. The selector is restricted to single shots or fully-automatic fire at a rate averaging 550rds/min. M203 or CIS/STK 40GL grenade launchers can be attached when necessary.

Russian Designs

The Abakan assault-rifle competition held in the 1990s, leading to the standardisation of the AN-94, gave designers an ideal opportunity to present much more radical designs than the well-established Kalashnikov. They included the A-91 and A-91M, developed by the KBP design bureau in Tula arms factory, which originally had the 40mm grenade launcher mounted integrally above the barrel. The carrying handle lay above the receiver, and the pistol grips accompanying the main and grenade-launcher triggers were connected by a strut. These features were unacceptable militarily, and changes were made. By 2002/3, the launcher had been moved beneath the barrel and its trigger moved back into the main trigger guard. Only about 25.6in (650mm) long, with a carrying handle doubling as a sight rail, the current version of the A-91M also ejects spent cases forward. It has been offered in 5.45 x 39mm and 5.56 x 45mm.

The OC-14 Groza ('Thunder', sometimes listed as OS-14 or OTs-14) was developed by the Central Bureau of Sporting and Hunting Guns in response to a specification for a convertible assault rifle/grenade launcher for the Ministry of Internal Affairs (MVD), and has been made in small quantities in the Tula arms factory. The design of the OC-14 receiver and pistol grip shares an affinity with the Kalashnikov, though the grip lies directly beneath the elevated carrying handle/sight rail, ahead of the protruding box magazine, and a butt-plate is attached directly to the rear of the receiver. The standard version chambers the 7.62 x 39mm M43 round, which is still used by the MVD. However, a short-barrelled variant for the subsonic 9 x 39mm SP-6 round is available; this weapon can mount an efficient silencer. Alternatively, the standard assault-rifle trigger guard can be replaced with a module containing the 40mm grenade launcher, the grenade-launching sights, and a single selectable trigger mechanism. The standard 7.62mm Groza-1, with a 16.3in (415mm) barrel, is 27.6in (700mm) long and weighs about 7.1lb (3.2kg) without its 30-round AK-type magazine. The fire-rate is usually listed as 750rds/min.

Others

The South African Defence Force is experimenting with the CR-21 assault rifle, which is essentially a conventional R4 action (a licence-built Israeli Galil) clothed in a curvilinear polymer stock with a pistol grip, an 'all hand' trigger guard, and a non-magnifying optical sight with a recticle illuminated not by battery power but instead by its inherent light-gathering capability. The CR-21 retains the selector of the R4 on the rear of the butt, the charging handle protrudes from the left side of the stock, and the safety catch is a cross-bolt in the trigger guard.

The People's Republic of China also accepted a bullpup design for service in the late 1990s, the first guns being seen when the Chinese took possession of Hong Kong in 1997.

Designated QBZ-95, chambered for a 5.8 x 42mm cartridge (and 5.56 x 45mm for export purposes), the gun is believed to be an updated Kalashnikov action in a polymer stock. The charging handle lies on top of the action, beneath the carrying handle, and the front of the trigger guard is expanded into a rudimentary forward pistol grip. A polymer butt is attached to the rear of the receiver, ejection is to the right, and the 30-round plastic magazines have prominent strengthening ribs. The QBZ-95 has also been made in carbine form, with a short barrel and an even shorter sight radius, and can be fitted with a single-shot bolt-action grenade launcher.

Chapter 6

Full-Power Rifles

The FAL Series

If the Kalashnikov assault rifle can be said to represent the first, highly successful efforts of the Soviet bloc design-school, the Fusil Automatique Léger (FAL) developed by Dieudonné Saive of Fabrique Nationale is its Western equivalent. Though the inspiration of the FAL was the Garand and the SVT rather than the MP. 43, its worldwide success from 1953 into the 1970s is a tribute to its efficiency.

FN's pre-war experiments with a tilting-block locked rifle were interrupted by the German invasion of Belgium in 1940. However, Saive and many other FN technicians escaped the clutches of the Wehrmacht by fleeing to Britain, where work continued at the Royal Small Arms Factory at Enfield. The experimental SLEM automatic rifle became the post-war SAFN, ABL or Modèle 1949, adopted by the Belgian Army and sold to Egypt and some South American countries. The success of the ABL bought the time necessary to perfect the prototype FAL.

Immediately after the end of the Second World War, the newly-formed NATO alliance sought to standardise equipment in its constituent armies. The three principal entries in the rifle trials were the US T44 (a modified Garand), the British EM-2 and the Belgian FAL. By 1947, the US representatives had rejected the British 0.280in cartridge – though ironically, not only did this embody many of the ideal characteristics of the later 7.62mm NATO and 5.56mm rounds, but also bore an appreciable resemblance to the 0.276in pattern 'adopted' by the US Army in the 1930s. The Americans were not impressed by the revolutionary EM-2 rifle either, and the project foundered in 1953. Piqued, the British then backed the FAL against the US T44. A strange agreement was finally struck: the American-backed 0.30in T65E3 became the 7.62 x 51mm NATO round, but *both* rifles were accepted. In June 1957, the US Army accepted the perfected T44E4 as the Rifle M14, while most major European armies other than the French adopted the FAL.

The FAL was a conventional, sturdy semi- or fully-automatic rifle, made in a variety of guises for export to the armed forces and paramilitary organisations in more than fifty countries. Locking was achieved by a tilting block, displaced downward into the receiver immediately behind the magazine well. When the gun fired, gas bled from the barrel impinged on the head of the piston rod. The rod struck the bolt carrier, which, as it moved backwards, lifted the locking block out of its recess; the bolt and bolt carrier recoiled together, clearing the magazine well and cocking the hammer, and then returned to strip a new round into the breech.

The FAL, therefore, was a lightened and improved ABL with a much-modified trigger mechanism and appreciably lighter construction. It was, however, large, heavy and cumbersome by the standards of the M16 and even the AKM. This eventually militated against it, even though the gun was sufficiently accurate at short range to be used for sniping by many regular armies. During the Falklands war between Britain and Argentina (1982), the FAL was successfully employed by both sides, alongside the FN-designed GP Mle 35 pistol and the MAG.

The tremendous export success of the FAL hindered the development of semi-automatic rifles for several years, particularly as the US Army was satisfied with the M14. For much of the period prior to the American embroilment in Vietnam, which effectively began in 1961, the NATO powers were firmly wedded to the concept of full-power/long-range performance, intermediate weapon needs being satisfied by submachine-guns – or, in the case of the British, Australian and New Zealand SAS units, shotguns or the US M1 Carbine.

The CETME Series

The dispersal of German small-arms technology at the end of the Second World War allowed Fabrique Nationale to create a monopoly that lasted for a decade. The FAL was even adopted by the armies of Federal Germany (as the Gewehr 1) and Austria (StG. 58). During this period, however, wartime expertise was kept alive by German technicians working in the Iberian Peninsula, where an ex-Mauser engineer named Ludwig Vorgrimmler continued development of the Gerät 06, the most promising entrant in the StG. 45 competition that had remained unresolved when the Second World War ended. Mauser's roller-lock system had been developed from the MG. 42 by Ernst Altenburger and Herbert Illenberger, and was potentially very efficient. It was subsequently appropriated for the abortive British Thorpe Rifle (EM-1).

During the 1950s, however, the system was refined at the Centro de Estudios Técnicos de Materiales Especiales (CETME) in Madrid, under the direction of Dipl.-Ing. Heynen and General José Canteró. The first CETME rifles fired a distinctive intermediate cartridge with an extra-long and unusually light bullet, the 7.9 x 40mm, to combine good long-range performance with a recoil effect that was low enough to facilitate accurate burst fire. The rifle was perfected by about 1955, and a licensing arrangement was concluded with NWM – though NWM-marked rifles were actually supplied from Spain. Ultimately, a successful demonstration for the Bundesgrenz-schutz attracted the attention of a Bundeswehr far from enamoured with the G1 (FAL). After a false start with a 7.62 x 40mm cartridge, the West Germans requested redevelopment for 7.62 x 51mm NATO, though the resulting wholesale changes lost many of the advantages of the original lightweight CETME. Once agreement from the remainder of NATO had been forthcoming, the Bundeswehr retrieved the licence from NWM to enable production to begin in Germany.

After successfully negotiating stringent trials, the new rifle was adopted as the Gewehr 3 (G3). Initially made by both Heckler & Koch and Rheinmetall, the weapon was a great success, and the subsequent exploits of H&K – who have produced everything from minimal submachine-guns to belt-fed sustained-fire machine-guns on the basic action – have now largely overshadowed CETME's contribution.

All the original CETME and H&K guns incorporated a delayed blowback system in which two rollers, between the bolt-head and the bolt carrier, locked into the barrel extension. When the gun fired, part of the backward pressure on the cartridge case attempted to force the rollers into the breechblock. The bolt carrier and firing-pin assembly moved backward to make sufficient room. However, this was opposed by the remainder of the recoil force acting outwards into the receiver body. A brief period of delay ensued, allowing the chamber pressure to drop to a safe level before the rollers re-entered the bolt and the whole unit began to move backwards against the recoil spring. Once the bolt and its carrier had cleared the magazine well, and cocked the hammer, the recoil spring reasserted itself, returned the bolt and stripped a new round into the chamber. When the bolt-head stopped against the chamber, the cam-shoulders on the separate locking piece in the bolt carrier (which was still moving) pushed the rollers out into their recesses. This halted the mechanism and firing could take place again.

The roller system lacked something of the solidity of the genuine locked-breech designs, but the G3 and its derivatives gained a reputation for reliability under adverse conditions or with a wide variety of cartridge-loadings. They were adopted in Norway, Portugal and elsewhere, and have been used by US Army Rangers, US Navy SEALS, the SAS and other special forces from Aden to the Arctic.

The M14 Series

The modernisation of the M1 Garand rifle, begun experimentally during the Second World War, stopped in 1951 when the Korean War began. Eventually, however, the action of the T20E2, the gas cylinder of the T25 and the magazine of the abortive T31 were combined to create the T44. This was tested at length in the mid-1950s, vying with the T25 and the FN FAL (T48 to the US Army) to become the standard weapon of the NATO powers. The US Army did not want the FN rifle, and, on 1 May 1957, adopted the perfected T44E4 as the 7.62mm Rifle M14.

The M14 was essentially similar to the Garand internally, but a detachable box magazine replaced the 'en bloc' clip, the gas tube was shortened, and a pistol-grip half-stock was fitted. The earliest M14 rifles had wooden stocks and hand guards, but the guard soon became ventilated fibreglass-reinforced plastic; finally, a durable synthetic stock was adopted and a ribbed non-ventilated hand guard was used.

Introduced in 1960, the M14A1 was a selective-fire M14 with a wood pistol grip behind the trigger, a bipod attached to the gas cylinder, a strap on the butt plate, and (on guns intended for use in support roles) an auxiliary folding hand-grip. The standard M14 action was used, but a stabiliser fitted over the compensator prevented use of the bayonet.

Not surprisingly, the M14A1 performed no better than the abortive M15, which at least had had the advantages of a heavyweight barrel. The selector on many guns (unofficially known as 'M14 M[odified]') was subsequently plugged to restrict them to semi-automatic fire, though a standard three-position selector could be substituted when required.

The comparatively unsuccessful heavy-barrel M15, known during development as the T44E5, was declared obsolete in December 1959; the M21 sniping-rifle derivative is described in greater detail below. Production ceased in the USA in 1963, and the machinery was sold to the government of Taiwan in 1967. However, the perpetual popularity of the M14/M21 series for sporting purposes has allowed Springfield, Inc. (formerly Springfield Armory) to market new guns. These range from facsimiles of the military patterns to match-quality target rifles that have been used by SWAT units and other security teams in the USA.

Chapter 7

Sniper Rifles

The sniper continues to be an integral part of most armies, police organisations and virtually all special forces. His brief remains the elimination of key opposing personnel (particularly officers or terrorist leaders) and counter-sniper activity. He is both well trained and specifically equipped, taking great pride in his marksmanship and – equally importantly – an ability to hide.

The widespread service introduction of intermediate cartridges, with their comparatively limited effective range, has failed to displace the traditional full-power cartridge and sniper rifle combination necessary to engage targets successfully at 800 metres or more. At ranges below 500 metres, this chance must become a virtual certainty and few of the current 5.56mm cartridges, particularly those fired from 1-in-12 pitch rifling, perform well enough to merit consideration. Thus, the 'old faithful' designs were retained. Britain, the USA and most of the NATO-aligned powers kept the 7.62 x 51mm NATO round for many years; the French persisted with 7.5 x 54mm; and the Russians (and many former Soviet-bloc countries) still cling to the venerable 7.62 x 54mm rimmed cartridge dating back to 1891.

The rifles, however, are subject to appreciably greater variation. This is partly due to the marked divergence of military and target-shooters' views of acceptable construction, and also to the varied theatres in which the sniper is expected to ply his trade. The target marksman, firing in relatively benign circumstances, simply seeks the perfect strike on his target with total reliability; but an army or a counter-terrorist unit must also consider the logistical implications, durability, and performance of man and equipment under the stress of shooting to kill. The delicate sights, triggers and accessories of many of the best target rifles are quite out of place on a battlefield, while, conversely, the performance of standard military rifles rarely allows a certain 'kill' at 500 metres.

Sniper rifles and their sights, therefore, almost always represent a compromise. In addition, the counter-terrorist sniper often holds a watching brief and the provision of bipods on most of the new designs reflects the necessity to spend hours motionless, without losing concentration, yet remain sufficiently alert to make the first shot count.

Countries that still maintain something of a global presence – the USA, Britain, Russia and France – have relied on well-tried military-style rifles, accepting proven reliability and robustness at the expense of performance.

When the US Army became embroiled in Vietnam, the North Vietnamese snipers wreaked considerable havoc. The Communists initially had little appreciation of the subtleties of sniping, and one-shot kills at ranges greater than fifty yards were rare. American counter-sniping was extremely effective at such short ranges and many of their opponents were soon killed. Ironically, this provided a form of natural selection; only the best North Vietnamese survived, becoming well-respected adversaries effective at ten times the early fifty-yard maximum. Most of the sniper rifles recovered from the Communist Vietnamese were Hungarian-made 48M Mosin-Nagant rifles, interspersed with a few Russian 1891/30 and Czech vz/54 examples.

Rifle-Calibre Guns

Though SWAT teams are often satisfied with heavy-barrel versions of the AR15/M16 series or modifications of commercially-available hunting rifles, special forces customarily seek pinpoint accuracy at long range. This has meant retaining the 7.62 x 51mm NATO round, even though most infantry rifles are now chambered for 5.56mm ammunition. The armies of the former Soviet bloc, facing the same problem, have accepted the same solution by retaining the $7.62 \times 54R$ rifle cartridge to compensate for the comparatively poor long-range performance of first the $7.62 \times 39mm$ M43 round and then the $5.45 \times 39mm$ M74 derivative.

Though arguments still rage over the relative merits of bolt-action and auto-loading rifles, most authorities are agreed that power is the key to long-range performance. This can be seen in the move away from even 7.62mm NATO towards 0.338in Lapua (also known as 0.338/416 or $8.58 \times 71mm$), derived from the British 0.416in Rigby sporting cartridge, and to the rise in enthusiasm for cartridges as large as 0.50in Browning and the 14.5mm Soviet/Russian machine-gun round.

US Designs

Realising the obsolescence of the M1C and M1D (Garand) sniper rifles, with M81, M82 and M84 telescope sights, the US Army began to experiment with better weapons shortly after becoming embroiled in Vietnam. Known during development as the XM21, a derivative of the M14 National Match Rifle was thoroughly tested against the Marine Corps Remington 700, the MAS FR-F1 and the Steyr SSG-69. Proving to be as accurate as any of its rivals at long range, particularly when fired with M118 match ammunition, the modified Garand was preferred. Conversion of National Match (NM) pattern M14 rifles to XM21 standards began in Rock Island Arsenal in 1970, and standardisation as the M21 followed in December 1975. Fitted with the 3–9x Leatherwood Adjustable Ranging Telescope, the gun remained the standard US Army sniper rifle until the bolt-action 7.62mm Remington Model 24 was approved in 1987.

The USMC, disapproving of semi-automatic sniper rifles but in dire need of efficient alternatives, standardised the M40 as early as April 1966. This 'militarised' Remington Model 700 commercial bolt-action rifle was originally issued with a 3–9x Redfield optical sight, and then with a fixed-magnification 10x

Unertl pattern. The M40 had a standard barrel and a wooden stock; the improved M40A1, which shared the same action, had a stainless steel barrel and a fibreglass stock.

Severe problems were soon encountered in the hot and humid Vietnamese climate and unannounced inspections sometimes showed that as much as sixty per cent of the equipment was unserviceable. Though the sniper rifles were reasonably durable, excepting for the wood stocks that warped and mouldered, the optical sights proved to be the Achilles' heel. Detail complaints included the unnecessary zoom mechanism of the variable-power sights, poor focus at maximum magnification, ingress of moisture, poorly-marked control drums, and failure of the mechanical range-finding systems. All these faults were to be expected when commercial telescopes attempted to withstand the rigours of military service, but were a nuisance in the field.

One of the conclusions, despite the often strident opinions of the M14NM/M21 champions, was that the bolt-action rifles offered two considerable advantages: their shooting was generally better, owing to the lack of moving parts and more precise lock-up; they also benefited from the absence of the mechanical noise generated by an auto-loader. With this in mind, Research Armament Company of Rogers, Arkansas, delivered a few Model 300 CLRRs (Convertible Long Range Rifles) to US special forces. The bolt-action M300, which fed from a box magazine, could be chambered for either the 7.62mm NATO round or 0.338in Lapua. Only the barrel, bolt-head and magazine needed to be substituted to change calibres.

RAP reasoned that excellent long-range performance was indispensable to a sniper, and that this was easier to achieve by *increasing* cartridge power than by attempting to extract the maximum performance possible from the existing 7.62mm NATO cartridge. The ultimate expression of this view was the RAP Model 500 in 0.50in Browning, which offered frighteningly potent performance in a gun weighing only a little over 30lb.

The bolt-action M24 rifle was adopted in 1987 to replace the

Garand-type M21. The most important component of the XM24 Sniping System, it was an improved version of the M40A1 with a kevlar/graphite composite half-stock with an aluminium bedding-block in the fore-end. The butt plate could be adjusted, and a Picatinny rail for optical or electro-optical sights appeared on the receiver. The M40X adjustable trigger mechanism was an adaptation of the M40 Match Rifle design, and the barrel was rifled specifically for the 173-grain 7.62mm M118 bullet. A 0.300in Winchester Magnum conversion was produced in small numbers, in an attempt to enhance long-range accuracy, but the 7.62 x 51mm NATO pattern remains standard.

Many US SWAT and police teams still use commercial derivatives of the M21 or, increasingly, heavy-barrelled commercial versions of the M16 series. The FBI Hostage Rescue Team retained the M40A1 for many years, while, in Canada, the Royal Canadian Mounted Police issued an optically-sighted commercial Winchester Model 70 bolt-action rifle.

Several bolt-action rifle makers also offer guns, usually derived from well-proven hunting patterns, that can serve security personnel surprisingly well. They include the Dakota Longbow Tactical Emergency Response Rifle, offered in 0.300in and 0.330in Dakota Magnum and 0.338in Lapua Magnum; the Magnum Research Magnum Lite Tactical Rifle, in calibres ranging from 0.223in Remington to 0.300in Winchester Magnum; the Savage Model 110FPXP-LE Tactical, with skeleton butt, in 0.223in Remington or 0.308in Winchester (5.56 x 45mm and 7.62 x 51mm respectively); and the Winchester Model 70 Stealth from the US Repeating Arms Company, in 0.22-250, 0.223in and 0.308in.

The Barrett M98, introduced in 1998, chambers the 0.338in Lapua Magnum round. Unlike many of the current US-made guns in this calibre, however, it is a gas-operated semi-automatic. In an innovative attempt to improve the accuracy of auto-loading designs, a rotating bolt inspired by the ArmaLite series – which in turn drew inspiration from the Johnson rifle –

has been combined with a free-floating barrel on an aluminium base and a gas-piston mechanism contained in the butt (though the gas is still drawn from a port in the bore). A detachable 10-round box magazine protrudes beneath the black polyamide half-stock, which has a thumb-hole pistol grip, and a bipod attaches to the fore-end. A large two-port muzzle brake helps to reduce the recoil sensation. A Picatinny rail directly above the ejection port allows virtually any US/NATO standard sight to be attached. The M98 is about 46.25in (1,175mm) long and weighs 15.5lb (7.03kg)

The best of these 'rifle-calibre' guns claim accuracy bettering half a minute of angle, which theoretically allows them to deliver 2-inch groups at 400 yards. Performance of this class gives credence to the view that rifles adapted from sporting guns will regularly outshoot those that have been purpose-built for military service. But it is equally probable that the 'civilian' guns would not withstand the rigours of combat in theatres such as Iraq, where conditions are harsh and maintenance facilities are limited.

British Designs

Though optical sights were tried on the L1A1, including the modern SUIT and SUSAT patterns, the auto-loader never proved entirely suitable for long-range work. Consequently, British snipers were issued with a 7.62mm NATO conversion of the Rifle No. 4 Mk 1 (T) or Mk 1* (T), known as the L42A1 or – for the police Blue Berets – a civilian variant marketed as the Enfield Enforcer. The L42A1 was used with great success by the SAS, Marines and Paratroopers in Aden, Northern Ireland and the Falklands, with a 4x fixed-power L1A1 telescope sight adapted from the Sight, Optical, No. 32 Mk 3 of the Second World War era. The Enforcer, an adaptation of the Envoy target rifle, was usually encountered with a 4–10x Pecar telescope sight. It was more delicate than the L42A1, its variable-power sight and rather better trigger befitting less demanding police services.

Experiments undertaken in the 1980s to find a replacement for the L42A1 resulted in the introduction of a new rifle developed by the late Malcolm Cooper and marketed by Cooper's company, Accuracy International. The resulting PM, accepted for military service as the L96A1, soon replaced the L42A1 in the hands of the regular army and the Finnish-made Tikka guns that had been favoured by the SAS.

The basic L96A1 was soon upgraded to the Arctic Warfare version (AW), developed in 1986–7 for trials in Sweden, where it was eventually adopted as the PSG-90. The bolt action was improved, an anti-icing system allowed the rifle to operate reliably in ultra-low temperatures, and a three-position safety lever lay on the right side of the receiver behind the bolt handle. The bolt could be locked ('full lock') or left free to open ('half lock'). A muzzle brake could be attached to the stainless-steel barrel to reduce the recoil sensation, and a modified Parker-Hale QD bipod could be fitted. Open sights could be provided to support the standard Schmidt & Bender Mk 2 6x, 10x or 3–12x telescopes, and the rear section of the thumb-hole butt could be adjusted vertically.

Among the variants of the AW rifle are the AWP (Police), introduced in 1997 in 0.243in Winchester or 7.62 x 51mm (0.308in Winchester), with a medium-weight stainless-steel barrel and a 3–12 x 50 Schmidt & Bender sight. The AWS ('Suppressed' or 'Silenced') had a full-length sound suppressor, and the SM (or 'SM-94', 'Super Magnum') chambered the 0.338in Lapua Magnum cartridge. The SM-type bolt was strengthened and had six lugs instead of the standard three. The standard AW is about 48.2in (1,225mm) long, has a 27in (686mm) barrel, and weighs 15.5lb (7kg) with sights and bipod.

The AW has now been adopted by a number of European armies – including that of Germany, which could have been expected to have taken Heckler & Koch auto-loaders. However, a few dissenting voices have been raised, highlighting the perennial difference of views between target-shooters and hunters. Common complaints about the L96A1 concern the angularity of the stock, and a safety catch placed where the firer cannot reach it unless the firing hand is taken from the trigger.

The original Parker-Hale sniper rifle, the Model 82, was built on Santa Barbara Mauser actions imported in unfinished state from Spain. The M82 was a strong, plainly-finished gun offering the excellent performance expected from a company with generations of experience of target shooting. It was adopted by Australia, Canada and New Zealand, and used in small numbers by British special forces. Some guns were fitted with Pecar 4–10x optical sights, but the Australian and Canadian guns, at least, had fixed-power 6 x 42 Kahles Helios ZF69 sights. The improved Parker-Hale M85 ran the Cooper/AI design a close second in the British trials, being recommended as 'fit for service', but many of the most expensive European submissions fared badly. The M85 was soon supplemented by the shorter and lighter M87 (which once interested the Metropolitan Police), but the manufacturer then decided to leave the rifle-making business. The stock and goodwill were acquired by the Navy Arms Company of the USA, and production was switched to the Gibbs Rifle Co. Consequently, the Parker-Hale sniper rifles were soon replaced by other designs.

Soviet/Russian Designs

The standard Kalashnikov rifles, in 7.62 x 39mm M43, had much too looping a trajectory – and insufficient long-range accuracy – to be suitable snipers' equipment. For much of the post-war period, therefore, the Soviet Army and its satellites retained the bolt-action Mosin-Nagant M91/30 sniper rifle, fitted with the 3.5x fixed-power PU telescope sight. Though rather clumsy, and offering poor optical performance by Western standards, this combination proved in Vietnam that it was to be feared out to 500 metres or more.

However, by the mid-1950s, the Soviet Army was seeking something different. Trials were subsequently undertaken with a variety of rifles, including heavy-barrelled AK adaptations made by Mikhail Kalashnikov, but the principal contenders were the guns submitted by Evgeniy Dragunov – an experienced designer of sporting guns – and Aleksandr Konstantinov. The contest was keenly fought, but the accuracy and reliability of the SSV-58 (Dragunov prototype) eventually overcame its rival, even though the Konstantinov design was easier and cheaper to make.

The semi-automatic Snayperskaya Vintokva Dragunova (SVD) was approved in 1963, firing the full-power 7.62 x 54mm rimmed round. Generally similar to the Kalashnikov, the gas-operated turning-bolt action relied on a long-stroke piston and two locking lugs. In Soviet service, the rifle has been accompanied by the PSO-1 and PSO-1M, 4x fixed-power optical sights that can double as passive infra-red detectors. A variety of infra-red and image-intensifier night sights has also been used.

By the best Western standards, the SVD is somewhat crudely made, and its sight falls short of comparable German systems; however, like virtually all Russian-made sniping equipment, the SVD and PSO-1 are robust, effective and issued on a surprisingly large scale. Whether it is particularly accurate is questionable. Published Russian figures indicate 100 per cent dispersion at 600 metres of 395mm (12.6in) compared with 440mm (17.3in) for the 91/30-type Mosin-Nagant, noting that the NATO acceptance figure is 15in at 600 *yards*. The implication is that the SVD would meet NATO criteria. However, the NATO standard is a minimum; most armies would be happier with guns that could deliver minute-of-angle accuracy at 600 yards, which would be a group measuring merely 6in/15cm. On this yardstick, the SVD does not perform nearly as well as (for example) the Finnish Tikka, and could not be guaranteed to strike a head target at more than 300–400 metres.

The SVD is about 49.8in (1,220mm) long, with a 24.4in (620mm) barrel, and weighs about 9.6lb (4.35kg) with the PSO-1 sight in place. The earliest guns had four-groove rifling making a turn in 12.6in/320mm, but this was subsequently changed to 9.4in/240mm to improve performance with tracer and API bullets. Accuracy with the standard 7H2M steel-core ball rounds deteriorated perceptibly, however, and muzzle velocity dropped by 20m/sec. The latest guns, which are made in Izhevsk by Izhmashzavod, have furniture of fibreglass-reinforced polyamide. Guns will also be seen with the new PKS 3–9 x 42 Minuta or Giperon optical sights.

An improved version known as the SVDS, designed by Azariy Nesterov, was finalised in 1994. The changes were made principally to allow sniper rifles to be carried in aircraft, helicopters and armoured personnel carriers, and used – if necessary – through firing ports. The original SVD was too long, so the barrel and flash-hider were shortened and a folding butt was developed. It was accepted that this would reduce rigidity, and possibly accuracy, but was deemed to be an acceptable price to pay. The tubular butt folds laterally to the right, and has an adjustable three-position cheekpiece; a separate pistol grip is fitted. Changes to the design of the muzzle brake allowed the unit to be shortened without losing efficiency.

A typical SVDS is about 44.7in (1,135mm) long, with a 22.2in (565mm) barrel, and weighs about 10.25lb (4.65kg) with the PSO-1. Series production has only recently begun in the Izhevsk factory.

The unsuitability of the 7.62mm rifle cartridge for ultra-accurate shooting has been recognised in Russia for some time. Though the SVD has proved to be sufficiently robust in conditions ranging from the cold of Siberia to the deserts of Afghanistan, a search for something better has culminated in the introduction of a new cartridge – the 9.0mm SN – and the advent of a bolt-action rifle derived from target-shooting practice.

The new round has allowed the SVD to be adapted, resulting in the SVDK ('K', *kruptokaliberniy*, 'large-calibre'). This is little more than a strengthened SVDS, with a bipod, a detachable 10-round box magazine, a folding butt, and a sight-rail that can accommodate equipment ranging from optical sights to image-intensifiers. Derived from a 9.3 x 64mm sporting round, the SN (*snayperskie*, 'sniper') cartridge fires a 262 grain (17gm) bullet at 2,495ft/sec (760m/sec).

The SA-98 sniper rifle, offered in 7.64 x 54R or 7.62 x 51mm NATO chamberings, is a modification of the Rekord-CISM target rifle. It has a synthetic thumbhole-type half stock, a bipod, and a detachable 10-round plastic box magazine. Unusually, the magazine catch is part of the magazine. The SV-98 has a conventional tangent-leaf back sight, but will usually be encountered with the PKS-7 fixed-magnification (7x) optical sight on a rail above the bolt. The three-lug front-locking bolt, free-floating barrel and 'sports' trigger ensure that the SV-98 will produce five-shot groups within 2in (5cm) at 300 yards – considerably better than minute-of-angle, and an improvement on the SVD. Rifles of this type (which are about 50in/1,270mm long and weigh 13.7lb/6.2kg without sights) have already been used by the Russian Special Forces, and are likely to find increasing application as their good shooting qualities are realised.

If the introduction of the 9.0mm SN cartridge and the SV-98 rifle conform with the universal trend towards more power and better accuracy in conventional sniper rifles, the SV-99 presents a complete departure from modern practice. Developed expressly to satisfy Spetsnaz needs, it is a 0.22in LR rimfire adaptation of the Izhmash biathlon rifle! There are many precedents for the use of small-calibre sniping equipment,* which have the merits of being quiet (and thus easily silenced) and easy to handle. Accuracy at short range is good enough to ensure the precision strike that the lack of power demands, and the short effective range minimises the risk of collateral damage.

The SV-99, designed by Vladimir Susloparov, is very small – merely 39.4in (1,000mm) long – and weighs 8.3lb (3.75kg) with its optical sight, detachable telescoping-leg bipod and silencer. It can be dismantled into sub-assemblies that are small enough to fit an attaché case, including the receiver/bolt unit and the

---

* These are said to include the use of Soviet-made sporting rifles by the Vietcong, and, more recently, by the opponents of the Russians in Chechnya. The Chechens have even used plastic bottles clamped over the muzzle of rimfire rifles to act as rudimentary silencers.

laminated plywood skeleton butt. The standard detachable box magazine holds 5 rounds, though 8- and 10-round sporting patterns will fit; two additional 5-round magazines can be carried in the butt. Accuracy is claimed to be half-inch (12mm) groups at a distance of 100 yards, but one of the great assets of the SV-99 is the rapidity with which the toggle-locking action can be cycled.

French Types

Owing to the adoption of the 5.56mm FA MAS rifle for general issue, the French Army also retained bolt-action rifles for snipers and special forces. The efficient Fusil à Répétition Modèle F1, Tireur d'Élite (FR-F1), with a fixed-power 4x Modèle 53bis optical sight, was used to good effect by GIGN personnel at Djibouti in 1976 and in the hands of French paratroops at Kolwezi, Zaire, in March 1978, when European hostages were successfully released from the clutches of Communist guerrillas. The FR-F1 bolt system was a simple adaptation of the pre-war MAS-36, but the basic rifle was then upgraded to FR-F2 standards by adding a thermal jacket around the barrel, substituting synthetic furniture for wood, and relocating the bipod. Guns of this type remain in service with the French forces and counter-terrorist units.

The guns made by PGM Précision (now being distributed by FN Herstal)* offer an alternative to the FR series that has proved popular with security and anti-terrorist agencies, including the GIGN. Another bolt-action design, with three lugs and a 60-degree throw, the rifles are chambered for either the 7.62 x 51mm NATO round or 0.338in Lapua Magnum, can be issued with special Athena armour-piercing ammunition, and have detachable 10-round box magazines. A sturdy modular construction allows them to be configured in several ways. The original UR (Ultima Ratio) design, for example, was supplied in Intervention or Commando style, the latter with a short barrel,

---

* The PGM name, deemed to be too unfamiliar, has now been abandoned in the USA.

and could also be fitted with a full-length suppressor that reduced the noise signature of subsonic ammunition from 113dB to 83dB.* Accuracy was less than minute-of-angle at ranges up to 250 metres.

The Intervention UR was about 40.6in (1,030mm) long, with the 18.5in (470mm) barrel option, and weighed about 12.1lb (5.5kg). It could be dismantled and concealed in a special case. The guns are easily identifiable by the position of the bipod, at the tip of the fore-end beneath the free-floating barrel – which is finned, later plain (UR), or deeply fluted (Commando).

The Mini-Hecate, essentially a modernised form of the UR, is a derivative of the Hecate II 0.50in-calibre rifle offered with barrels of 470mm, 550mm, 600mm or 650mm. Weight averages 6.3kg without the optical sight. Butts may include a recoil absorber and a monopod, a variety of different bipods is available, and there are two different silencers. Conventional ring-type optical-sight mounts can be provided, though a Picatinny rail is an optional extra.

Austrian Types

Few remaining NATO-aligned powers are required to protect interests as diverse as the Falklands and the Far East, or Alaska and Vietnam. They can be far more discerning where sniper equipment is concerned, but unanimity is still curiously absent. One of the most impressive of the bolt-action designs was the Austrian Scharfschützengewehr 69 (SSG 69), made by Steyr-Daimler-Puch on the popular Mannlicher-Schönauer bolt system and now made under licence by Hellenic Arms Industries in Greece. This beautifully-made rifle was usually extremely accurate; indeed, its manufacturer claimed that, with RWS Match ammunition, ten-shot groups of less than 40cm diameter could be achieved at 800 metres. At 400 metres, dispersion was a mere 13cm (5.1in) and a hit could be all but guaranteed.

The SSG 69 generally had a wood or rot-proof synthetic

* Measured, according to PGM literature, '5 meters from the muzzle and 5 meters parallel to barrel axis'.

stock and a fixed-power 6 x 42 Kahles Helios ZF69 telescope sight. It was adopted by the Austrian Army, and has since been used by military and paramilitary units worldwide, notably the German counter-terrorist unit, GSG-9. In recent years, however, it has lost ground to purpose-built rifles such as the Accuracy International PM/AW series.

The Steyr Scout Tactical is a short-barrelled rifle that has often been carried as a back-up by SWAT and police CTW teams. Originally developed in consultation with the American marksman and CTW authority Jeff Cooper, the Scout is essentially a bolt-action sporting rifle with a 19.3in fluted barrel, a polymer stock (generally black, green or 'camo'), a fore-end that doubles as a bipod and a spare magazine inserted into the underside of the butt. Chamberings are restricted to 0.223in or 0.308in, the commercial equivalents of 5.56 x 45mm and 7.62 x 51mm respectively. Sights are customarily an emergency 'Ghost Ring' aperture and an optical sight, often with unusually long eye relief so that it can be set forward above the barrel to clear the breech. There is also an SBS Tactical Elite series, usually with longer heavy barrels, which can have adjustable cheek pieces, Picatinny rails, large bolt-handle balls, and a variety of other special features.

German Types

Not convinced by the claims of the proponents of bolt-action sniper rifles, Heckler & Koch developed several special variants or the G1/HK33/G41 series. The original G3A3 Zf was simply a selected standard rifle, specially finished and fitted with an optical sight, but was too much of an expedient to be successful and was replaced by the G3 SG-1. These were based on unusually efficient and accurate G3 actions, identified at proof stage and fitted with a special set-trigger. Zeiss Diavari 1.5–6 x 42 optical sights were standard. Many G3 SG-1s were purchased by West German state police forces and the similar MSG-90 was issued in the Bundeswehr, but they have never been entirely successful; the handling characteristics are not particularly pleasant, the trigger is not good enough to capitalise on real accuracy, and the fluted chamber – which suggests an action that opens rapidly – is not ideal in a sniper rifle. Some police units have preferred the HK8, which is actually an adaptation of a heavy-barrelled light machine-gun.

Heckler & Koch subsequently progressed to the Präzisions-Scharfschützen-Gewehr 1 (PSG-1). This much-modified G3 had a heavy barrel, a greatly-improved single trigger mechanism, a competition-style adjustable palm-rest pistol grip, and an adjustable butt. A 6 x 42 Kahles Helios ZF69 optical sight was initially regarded as standard, and performance proved to be very good indeed.

Mauser offered an SG66 variant of its standard System 66 bolt-action rifle with one of the shortest of all actions and the highly sophisticated 2.5–10 x 56 Schmidt & Bender telescope sight, though the greatly restricted magazine capacity – merely two rounds – was an unnecessary weakness. Guns of this type were to be seen in the hands of many German state police Special-Einsatz-Kommando, the Spanish Grupo Especiale de Operaciónes (GEO) and Israeli border guards, but have since been withdrawn.

The SG66 was superseded by the Model 86SR, chambered only for the 0.308in Winchester round (7.62 x 51mm NATO). It retained the basic shape of the Model 83 sporting rifle, but the bolt-lugs locked into the receiver ring instead of the bridge to improve accuracy. The sight-rail above the breech was lowered, and a laminated stock was used exclusively until a synthetic thumbhole stock was introduced in 1989. The barrel was fluted to save weight, and had an efficient flash suppressor/muzzle brake.

Made only in small numbers for trials with the Bundeswehr, the SR-93 was a simplified Model 86 in 0.300in Winchester Magnum or 0.338in Lapua Magnum. The bolt handle could be moved from the right side of the breech to left when required, the synthetic stock bolted to an alloy chassis was clearly inspired by British designs, and the barrel was allowed to float.

Unfortunately for Mauser, the Accuracy International AW performed best in the German trials!

Swiss Types

Sauer and SIG collaborated on the highly sophisticated SSG2000, distinguished by an unusually effectual trigger system and built around the Sauer Model 90 bolt system with triple rear-locking lugs. The rifle was offered in four chamberings – 7.62 x 51mm NATO, 5.56mm, 7.5mm Swiss M11 and 0.300in Winchester Magnum – but never sold in large numbers, owing to its high price.

The SSG3000, introduced in 1992, was based on the Sauer 200 action, which reverted to a front-locking system. This was believed to offer better accuracy than the rear-locking 'wedge' lugs of the earlier gun. Modular construction allowed the guns to be configured with differing barrels or trigger systems. The sliding safety catch locked the trigger, bolt and firing pin, and an indicator pin protruded from the breech when a round had been chambered. The stock was a single piece of wood, synthetic material or a warp-resisting laminate, and the butt plate and cheek piece were both adjustable. The receiver rail was designed to accept a 1.5–6 x 24 Hensoldt optical sight, but an alternative NATO-standard pattern or Picatinny rail was available to order.

The SSG3000 was touted as a replacement for the SSG2000 in Swiss service, but the Army decided to issue a special heavy-barrelled version of the standard 5.56mm Stg. 90 (SIG) assault rifle as the SSG. 90. Known commercially as the SG 550 Sniper, this was submitted for evaluation in 1991. It had a heavyweight barrel and a special adjustable trigger mechanism restricted to semi-automatic fire. The butt, cheek-piece and pistol grip could be adjusted to suit the preferences of individual marksmen, and a variety of sights could be attached to the receiver rail.

Finnish Types

For such a sparsely populated country, Finland retained a sizeable firearms industry for many years. Commercial Tikka and Sako rifles were purchased by many agencies, including the SAS and the Pakistani special security services, and Valmet (later Sako-Valmet) made a semi-sporting variant of the standard Kalashnikov-type assault rifle under the brandname Petra.

The purpose-built bolt-action Valmet M86 sniper rifle was purchased in small numbers by the Finnish armed forces. This impressive gun, though long and heavy (47.6in/1,210mm, 12.6lb/5.7kg without sights), derived more from traditional army-type sniper rifles than the target shooter's dream and, despite the bipod and adjustable cheek piece, presented an unusually conventional appearance. It was designed expressly to guarantee hitting a 150mm (5.9in) diameter target at 500m, with specially selected ammunition, and was claimed to group its shots inside 65mm (2.6in) at 300m. The Sako TRG-21 has also sold in small numbers, though the Finnish Army, probably for reasons of economy, elected to produce an adaptation of the tried and tested Mosin-Nagant bolt action. This is an extraordinary story; many of the actions, though refurbished many times, were originally provided by the former Tsarist arsenal in Helsinki when the Finns gained independence in 1919!

Super-Calibre Guns

When *Guns of the Elite* was first published in 1987, attempts to interest the military in large-calibre sniping rifles had made very little headway. Though small quantities of AMAC LRRS (0.338/416 or 0.50in) and Barrett Light Fifty guns had been sold, often for special forces, their public profile remained low. Much of the initial lack of enthusiasm stemmed from the fact that 0.50in machine-gun ammunition was not designed for extreme accuracy, but instead to give sufficient 'scatter' when fired continuously.

Once improvements in the cartridges began to be made, the value of hitting helicopters, vehicles and similar valuable equipment at long range could be seen much more clearly. Literature published as early as the 1980s by Barrett, makers of the M82A1 Light Fifty, drew attention to the fact that:

Armored personnel carriers, radar dishes, communications vehicles, aircraft and area denial submunitions are all vulnerable to the quick strike capability of the Barrett M82A1 . . . With decisive force, and without the need for manpower and expense of mortar or rocket crews, your forces can engage the opposition at distances far beyond the range of small-arms fire.

The lesson was not really new; throughout the Second World War, the Red Army had retained its powerful 14.5mm anti-tank rifles for use against vehicles long after their value against tanks had declined.

The original M82 Light Fifty was a recoil-operated semi-automatic measuring about 61in (1,550mm) overall, and weighing about 32.5lb (14.7kg). It fed from a detachable box magazine containing 11 rounds, was usually encountered with 10x optical sights, and fired 0.50in M33 Ball ammunition with a muzzle velocity of 2,800ft/sec. Recoil was claimed to be not unlike that of a 12-bore shotgun, and the gun could be fired from the hip if the firer was able to lift it.

The success of McMillan (no longer trading), Barrett and other guns of this general type in their intended role, and the usefulness of large-calibre machine-guns to down small helicopters, including one destroyed in Northern Ireland by the IRA, has inspired work to begin elsewhere. It is now unusual to find a manufacturer of sniping equipment that does not offer a large-calibre gun alongside the rifle-calibre patterns.

US Designs

The Barrett Light Fifty is still in production, as the M82A1. A recoil-operated auto-loader, with a detachable 10-round box magazine, it is about 57in (1,447mm) long and weighs 28.45lb (12.9kg) empty. The short-lived M82A2 was a bullpup design, with an auxiliary fore-grip, but retained the auto-loading action; the Models 90, 99 and 99-1 are simple single-shot bolt-action bullpup rifles; and the Model 95 is a variant of the Model 90 with a detachable 5-round magazine.

In August 2003, the US Army adopted the Barrett M82A1M as the M107 Long Range Sniper Rifle, with a few minor modifications that included provision of a monopod beneath the butt; a contact to supply 3,100 guns by the end of 2007 was also signed. The 25mm XM109 is a modification of the M107 chambered for 25mm ammunition, which allows a wide range of projectile types including a HEAB (high-explosive air burst) pattern. The gun is a recoil-operated auto-loader, feeds from a detachable 5-round box magazine, and is 46in (1,170mm) long. It weighs 33.3lb (15.1kg) empty.

The Harris Gunworks/McMillan guns, typified by the M93, were bolt-action designs fed from detachable box magazines. Distinguished by its size, multi-port muzzle brake, and synthetic thumb-hole stock (with a butt that can be folded laterally), the M93 is 53in (1,346mm) long and weighs about 21.5lb (9.75kg) without its magazine. This is very light by 0.50in-calibre standards, and the absorbent butt-plate is more of an essential than an option.

European Designs

Accuracy International has recently introduced a 0.50in-calibre rifle in Britain, by enlarging the highly successful PM/AW sniper-rifle series. PGM Précision in France offers the Hecate II derived from the Ultima Ratio rifle-calibre guns. The Hecate II has a turning bolt with three locking lugs, a bipod attached to the fore-end, and a floating barrel that delivers excellent accuracy. A substantial muzzle brake is required to reduce the recoil sensation of the powerful 0.50in Browning cartridge to reasonable levels, and the adjustable butt can be fitted with a monopod. The guns weigh about 29.75lb (13.5kg) with an empty magazine, and are about 54.3in (1,380mm) long. Muzzle velocity is claimed to be 2,790ft/sec (850m/sec) with standard ball ammunition.

The Hungarian M1 Gepard is an interesting single-shot rifle, chambered for the 12.7 x 108mm Soviet machine-gun cartridge. The bolt and the pistol grip are combined in one unit, which is withdrawn from the gun to allow a single round to be inserted, whilst a combination of an effective muzzle brake and a buffer is used to keep the recoil sensation within reasonable bounds. The Gepard, about 60.6in (1,540mm) long and weighing 34.2lb (15.5kg), is designed for use at ranges up to 1,200 metres. However, the demise of the Soviet bloc has left it temporarily without a role; attempts are apparently being made to re-chamber it for the 0.50in Browning cartridge but have yet to be satisfactorily concluded.

Designer Istvan Fellegi has also produced rifles chambering the 14.5 x 114mm cartridge developed for the original Soviet anti-tank rifles. This is a particularly potent round, much more powerful than the 0.50in Browning, and could ultimately find an important niche for special purposes. The manually-operated M3 has a detachable box magazine holding 5 or 10 rounds, and weighs about 20kg (44lb) empty; the semi-automatic Elefant is longer and heavier.

The Russians – mindful of the pedigree of the PTRD and PTRS anti-tank rifles of the Second World War – have also shown interest in super-calibre sniping rifles in recent years, though the service status of the prototypes revealed in the 1990s is unclear. The V-94 or OVS-96, designed in Tula by the KBP bureau, has been used by Ministry of Internal Affairs (MVD) units serving in Chechnya. The rifle is a gas-operated semi-automatic with a rotating bolt, and can be folded in half for transportation. The barrel is allowed to float, as the bipod is attached to a frame extension. The V-94 has a sturdy synthetic butt with a rubber recoil pad, and is usually found with optical or electro-optical sights. It is about 69in (1,750mm) long and weighs 28.5lb/12.9kg without sights (now usually the POS 13 x 60) or the detachable 5-round box magazine. The 865 grain (56gm) bullet develops a muzzle velocity of about 2,395ft/sec (730m/sec).

The KSVK is a manually operated bolt-action rifle, developed in Kovrov from the unsuccessful SVN of the late 1990s. Though sharing the same barrel length as the OVS, 39.4in (1,000mm), the bullpup design keeps overall length to only 55in (1,400mm). Weight is about 26.5lb (12kg) without sights or the 5-round magazine. A massive muzzle-brake/sound suppressor is a standard feature, distinguished by circumferential bands of short slots.

The guns chambered for the 12.7 x 108mm machine-gun cartridge, developed in the Soviet Union for the old DK machine-gun of 1934, face much the same problem as the users of 0.50in-calibre Browning ammunition did before the development of match-grade cartridges became a priority. The Russian patterns, though made in a useful variety of armour-piercing, explosive and incendiary combinations, still lack the ability to hit head-size targets at much greater than 300 metres. The problems encountered with the 14.5 x 114mm round are similar, though it has to be admitted that projectiles of this size are exceptionally destructive when used against vehicles, helicopters and aircraft.

Rifles chambering the 12.7 x 108mm were also made in Yugoslavia (and now Serbia) and are occasionally encountered elsewhere. The 12.7mm Crna Strela ('Black Star') is a conventional bolt-action design, with a 5-round box magazine and a large muzzle brake. It has an adjustable butt sliding on two parallel steel rods projecting from the rear of the pistol grip. The single-shot Macs M3 uses a similar action, but the pistol grip has been brought forward beneath the fore-end, and the shoulder plate of the butt lies immediately below the chamber. The designers sought to create a compact rifle that was no longer than the barrelled action, but achieved their goal only at the expense of magazine capacity.

Chapter 8

Shotguns

The use of the shotgun in war has a long pedigree, dating back to the swivel guns that were used to clear the decks of warships from the sixteenth century onward, and the flintlock blunderbusses beloved by eighteenth-century coachmen. The goal was always to provide a large number of projectiles that, by spreading as they flew, increased the chance of a hit. Though essentially short-range weapons, they had an awesome destructive power.

Though double-barrelled guns became popular for sporting purposes, particularly in Europe, they had no military application. The emergence of mechanically-operated repeating shotguns in the USA – particularly the Winchesters of 1893 and 1897 – brought greater potential. A few guns were used by US Army personnel during the Philippine Insurrection, when the regulation 0.38in-calibre revolvers and 0.30in-caliber rifles often proved unable to drop Moro fanatics effectively, and the experience was recalled when the American Expeditionary Force reached Europe in 1917. More than 30,000 shotguns were purchased, often to be fitted with ventilated sheet-steel barrel guards that carried a bayonet boss and lug. Though many of these guns were used for guard duties, freeing magazine rifles for front-line service, trench warfare favoured short-range weapons; many shotguns, therefore, found their way into the combat zones.

After the war had finished, the shotgun became a preferred weapon of the American gangsters, used in far greater numbers (and sometimes to much better effect) than the legendary Thompson submachine-gun. The recoil-operated Remington

Model 11 was favoured by Bonnie Parker (of Bonnie & Clyde), who used several cut-down 20-bore guns in her short but murderous career. Similar 12-bore guns were widely used in the Pacific Theatre during the Second World War against the Japanese alongside the Stevens 520 and 620, sturdy slide-action guns, dating from the 1920s, that served on into the Vietnam era. Prior to the advent of the M1 Carbine US troops found that the shotgun was exceptionally useful in jungle fighting, a view confirmed by British experience in the 1960s and by the US forces in Vietnam.*

During the Second World War, 'lethal ball' rounds were loaded for the British Local Defence Volunteers (later known as the Home Guard), whose shotguns often represented the sole deterrent to German invasion, and were often to be seen in the hands of soldiers guarding key military installations.

Though shotguns remained popular with US police units after the Second World War had ended, and were regularly carried aboard patrol cars, the renaissance of the fighting shotgun occurred during the Malayan Emergency. FN-Browning auto-loaders were issued to the British-backed police forces in Malaya and, subsequently, to the SAS. They were then used in Borneo, during the period of Indonesian insurgency. In 1960s Vietnam, the Delta reconnaissance teams of the Special Operations Group (SOG) favoured the Ithaca M37, while the USAF Combat Security Police used a selection of slide-action guns: the Remington M870, the Ithaca M37 or the venerable Winchester Model 12.

The rapid rise of urban terrorism, and counter-terrorist warfare (CTW) operations, renewed interest in the combat shotgun. Its advantages include awesome close-range firepower and the ability to handle not only a wide variety of loads, but also, with suitable adaptors, a selection of grenades. For military use, the disadvantages are comparatively minor. However, the

* Leroy Thompson, in *Combat Shotguns* (2002), claims that studies undertaken by the British forces have shown the shotgun to have a 'hit probability' 75 per cent greater than any other gun.

issue of conventional shotguns to a small CTW squad can, by taking away an assault rifle, reduce firepower and make the shotgunner – even though he may be carrying a pistol as a back-up – particularly vulnerable in a firefight with determined, well-armed opponents.

The shotgun has also proved to be indispensable in urban confrontations, even if its tactical use can be a political minefield. Though the shotgun can have a psychological effect, the perceived indiscriminate nature of its buckshot often pacifying individuals (and even small crowds), it is important that collateral damage is limited; too much penetration can present a problem at close range, and too much shot-spread past the target can endanger bystanders. Problems such as these can be limited by judicious choice of ammunition, but should never be underestimated: a 450-grain 12-bore slug can blow a small rock into powder at close range.

Virtually all modern combat shotguns are chambered for 12-bore ammunition, either standard (3-inch case) or Magnum (3.5 inches), though limited use has been made of 20-bore guns for short-range tasks. Ithaca once made a 10-bore 'Roadblocker' gun, specifically for use against vehicles, but this role has now been assumed by special high-penetration 12-bore projectiles. However, the Russians have recently introduced a 6-bore gun intended to handle a range of specialist anti-personnel ammunition and large-diameter baton rounds. This gun will undoubtedly be brutal to fire, owing to its comparatively light weight, and is unlikely to set too much of a trend in Western anti-terrorist circles.

Among the most discernible recent trends have been towards shorter barrels, folding stocks, better sights and more efficient magazines. In addition, attempts have been made to provide MILSPEC guns – ensuring that designs that were originally conceived for less arduous sporting purposes become durable enough to withstand active service.

The most popular operating system is still the manually-operated slide, allied with a rotating bolt or (nor more rarely) a tilting block to lock the breech at the moment of firing. The guns generally have barrels measuring 18–20in, weigh about 6.5–7lb, and have under-barrel tube magazines holding 7–8 rounds. They have emanated from a wide variety of gunmaking businesses, particularly in the USA.

The Ithaca Gun Company has offered a selection of guns, including the M37, Deerslayer, Handgrip and Stakeout (the last, a particularly compact design). These guns have gained a reputation for reliability and exemplary accuracy when firing slugs. They also eject downward, simplifying use by left-handers, and the design of the trigger mechanism – which lacks a disconnector – allows the gun to be fired continuously simply by holding back the trigger and cycling the slide. Mossberg has promoted the Model 500 Milgun (now advanced to Model 590), the P6 and P8, all pump-action. Remington still makes the Model 870; and Winchester has a selection of pump-action guns, including the Model 1300 Defender that derives from the legendary Model 12.

The Mossberg has been widely used by the US armed forces, and a new double-action-only version has proved popular with police. Though guns such as the Stevens 620 (introduced in 1927) and Winchester Model 12 (introduced in 1912) were still serving in Vietnam in the 1970s, the most popular of the post-Second World War combat shotguns has undoubtedly been the Remington 870. Used by the US Army, the USAF (having beaten off a challenge from High Standard in the final trials), the USMC and the USN, the Remington has also been the choice of countless police forces. It is still the most popular choice for customisation, which is undertaken by a variety of specialist gunsmithing businesses. Among the most popular changes are to the furniture, which is usually replaced by non-slip synthetics, and the sights; quick-loaders are also often attached to the receiver.

Though European makers have brought the double-barrelled shotgun to the pinnacle of development, only in recent years has the slide-action repeater been pursued with enthusiasm. Even the auto-loader has struggled hard to gain widespread acceptance, despite the manufacture of thousands of Browning-type guns by Fabrique Nationale d'Armes de Guerre (subsequently FN Herstal) in Belgium.

Both FN and Beretta make pump-action patterns though, owing to the purchase by FN of the US Repeating Arms Company, the FN-Police shotgun is little more than a variation of the Winchester Model 1300. Beretta designs have included the RS202 and RS202P, subsequently known as the M1 and M2.

Benelli of Urbino recently introduced the Nova SP, with steel bolt-slide inserts in a fibreglass-reinforced polymer receiver, but it is too soon to judge the claims being made for this particular gun. Luigi Franchi of Fornaci/Brescia has offered the PA-8 and the SAS-12 (Slide-Action Shotgun), relatively conventional pump-action designs. The SAS-12 has a pistol-grip butt that gives 'straightline' construction, and is regarded as unusually comfortable to shoot even though the standard sights are not only too low but also ineffective in combat; a ghost-ring sight on a riser block would be an improvement. Elsewhere in Italy, Fabarm makes the FP-6, a good-quality gun that is sold for police use in the USA under the Heckler & Koch banner; and Valtro offers a small range of box-magazine guns, including some with short barrels.

The China North Industries Corporation (Norinco) makes slide-action shotguns based on North American prototypes, customarily the Winchester Model 12 or Remington 870. These are sturdy, inexpensive and offer surprisingly good value. The Russian arms industry has also belatedly realised the value of slide-action shotguns for sporting and anti-terrorist use. Current products include the Baikal IZh-81, made in Izhevsk, which has a box magazine; the conventional slide-action turning bolt TOZ 194 and the TOZ RM-90 series (emanating from Tula), which amalgamate a swinging block locking/feed mechanism with a tube magazine above the barrel and a slide that must be pushed *away* from the firer to load and cock. The most extraordinary of these guns are the TsNIITochmash KS-23 and KS-23M, with fixed butts and pistol grips respectively, which are chambered for 6-bore ammunition. Designed to fire baton rounds and discarding-sabot anti-vehicle projectiles, the guns are large, heavy, and have a fearful recoil.

The only other shotgun to feature a slide that moves forward is the revolutionary South African Neostead, designed by Tony *Neo*phytou and Wilmore *Stead* and patented in 1991–3. Its unique features include two 6-round magazines placed on top of the receiver, which can be set to feed separately – or alternately, if required. This gives an unusual tactical flexibility, as the magazines, if necessary, can be loaded with entirely different types of ammunition. When the operating handle is pulled forward, the entire barrel is pulled away from the standing breech to allow the ejection/reloading cycle to take place. The system allows the Neostead to be a bullpup design, with a barrel that is virtually as long as the gun, but necessitates a carrying handle on top of the receiver to support the rudimentary iron sights. Marketed by Truvelo, the guns have excited considerable interest. A few have been acquired for CTW or SWAT use, but have yet to convince a major purchaser of their undoubted merits. The Neostead is about 27.1in (690mm) long, has a 22.4in (570mm) barrel and weighs 8.6lb (3.9kg) empty. It ejects downward, beneath the butt, suiting it to right- and left-handed firers alike.

Though the slide-action shotgun is still seen in great numbers, it has always been challenged in the USA by autoloading designs since the introduction of the first Remington and Winchester designs prior to the First World War. There is no doubt that the auto-loader has certain tactical advantages: it is easier to handle; can be used with one hand – useful if the firer is injured or attempting a task such as opening a door; and fires second and subsequent shots much more rapidly than any of the mechanically-operated designs. To their debit, gas-operated guns are potentially susceptible to propellant fouling, undoubtedly less durable, and dependent on the quality of the ammunition.

No recoil-operated guns remain in production in the USA at the time of writing, the principal manufacturers preferring tried-

and-tested gas operation and the advantages of a fixed barrel. Among the auto-loaders, the Mossberg 9200A1 has been purchased in quantity by the US armed forces and the Drug Enforcement Agency. A sturdy gas-operated MILSPEC 3443E design, with a heavyweight barrel, synthetic furniture and parkerised finish, the 9200A1 is compromised only by the half-length magazine, which, while protecting the magazine tube within the fore-end, restricts magazine capacity to merely five rounds. The Remington 11-87P (Police) is also gas operated, with polypropylene furniture and a parkerised finish. The guns have a full-length magazine tube beneath the barrel, and can be loaded simply by cycling the charging handle. The Mossberg and Remington shotguns can both be obtained as 'entry guns', with 14-inch barrels instead of the standard 18-inch type.

In Europe, most of the auto-loaders are gas-operated semi-automatics, offering good quality but, perhaps, too many legacies of their sporting-gun past – ineffectual combat sights and cartridge-drop levers and similar loading buttons that must be activated before a cartridge can be chambered. These can slow and inevitably complicate a response when speed is paramount.

Benelli makes 'inertia-operated' guns, and has also supplied actions to Beretta. The Benelli M1 Tactical Shotgun embodies this system, which relies on a floating block in the action moving forward as the gun fires before being forced back by recoil to rotate the locking lugs out of engagement with the breech. This mechanism is claimed to be less sensitive to variations in ammunition pressure than gas operation. However, the guns have a rapid recoil cycle that takes time to master. Benelli was the victor of the US Joint Services Combat Shotgun program (JSCS), the M4 being approved for limited issue in 1999. The first of 20,000 guns was delivered in 2001. It is gas-operated, with automatic power regulation, duplicated gas tubes, an extended bolt handle to facilitate clearing the chamber of misfired rounds, a Picatinny rail above the receiver, and a collapsible stock. Interestingly, the testers decided to retain the integral tube magazine instead of a detachable box pattern. It has been suggested that combat experience will soon show this decision to be mistaken.

The Beretta M1200 and M1200P retain the Benelli 'inertia' recoil action and cartridge-drop lever, but are light for guns in their class and have become quite popular. The Fabarm FAST-20 is another gas-operated design, with a Picatinny rail above the receiver, extended safety catch and charging handle, and a variety of short-barrel or folding-butt options. Franchi's LAW-12 is basically a gas-operated version of the SAS-12, sharing the pleasant shooting characteristics of the manually operated version. Distinguished by a one-piece synthetic butt/pistol grip and a 'quick action safety catch' in the front of the trigger guard, it also has a notably 'straightline' configuration.

Other auto-loaders include the Chinese Norinco SPS-12, a surprisingly heavy gun which amalgamates a detachable box magazine with a short-stroke gas system inspired by the US 0.30in M1 Carbine. One strange feature of this particular shotgun is the excessive distance from the rear of the receiver to the trigger, which does not suit the SPS to small-handed firers.

Undoubtedly the most interesting combat shotgun is the Russian Sayga (also listed as 'Saiga'), which is little more than an adapted Kalashnikov assault rifle. The basic components of the AK-74M, without the rate reducer and the full-automatic trigger setting, are amalgamated with a simplified fore-end and a smoothbore barrel chambered for 0.410in, 20-bore or 12-bore shotgun cartridges. The short-barrelled 12-bore gun, with detachable box magazine and either a folding butt or a simple pistol grip, makes an exceptional weapon that capitalises on the legendary strength and efficiency of the Kalashnikov action. Guns of this type have been seen in the hands of Spetsnaz and FPB troops, and there is no good reason why the principle of adapting assault rifles should not be applied elsewhere. However, this should not include the Korean Daewoo USAS-12. Based very loosely on the M16 rifle, fitted with a 10-round box or 20-round drum magazine, the USAS is 38.1in (968mm) long and far too heavy (12lb/5.5kg with loaded box magazine) to succeed; the Sayga-12K is merely 26.4in (670mm) long with its butt folded, and weighs 7.7lb (3.5kg) with its 6-round magazine. The Daewoo gun has the additional ability to fire automatically, but the power of 12-bore shotgun rounds is really too great for even the heavyweight USAS to be controlled satisfactorily.

There has also been a move towards guns that can be set to operate semi-automatically or manually at will, even though, in the view of some highly qualified observers, they bring an unnecessary complication to guns that work best at their most simple. The addition of selectors can hinder response if the firer is unsure of the state of loading, or the mode that has been selected.

The Franchi SPAS-12 and its prototype, the SPAS-11 (Special Purpose Automatic Shotgun), were gas-operated semi-automatics. Manipulating a function selector under the black high-impact polymer fore-end allowed the SPAS-12 to revert to pump action if desired. The shotgun had a pistol grip and a folding stock; the under-barrel magazine tube was loaded, with the breechblock closed, by depressing a catch on the left side of the receiver. The magazine could hold eight 2.5in or 2.75in cartridges, or nine 2in. These could even be intermixed without affecting the auto-loading action. The muzzle of the 20.3in barrel was threaded for chokes, grenade-launchers or Franchi's shot diverter, which changed the shot-pattern from circular to a flattened oval – useful in close-quarter firing when the chance of hitting bystanders is absent.

The SPAS-12 encountered considerable commercial, police and paramilitary interest, and was joined by the SPAS-15 and SPAS-16 developed for the US Army CAWS trials (*see below*). Though the basic convertible manual/automatic action has been retained, the newer Franchi designs have featured detachable box magazines. Though these were bulky, protruding some way beneath the receiver, they greatly facilitated loading and, by no means unintentionally, the selection of specific cartridges for particular tasks. This is always hindered by a conventional tube magazine, in which the state of loading can be difficult to determine.

The Beretta M3P was another convertible manual/automatic shotgun, with a detachable box magazine, developed for the CAWS competition and not unlike the Franchi SPAS-15.

An alternative approach to combat-shotgun design can be seen in the South African-made Striker-12, which amalgamates a spring-driven drum magazine and a double-action trigger system. This allows the mechanism to be compact; with the butt folded back over the top of the receiver, the Striker-12 is only about 28in (710mm) long. However, it weighs 9.25lb (4.2kg) with its 12-round drum and is quite a handful. Neither has it proved to be particularly reliable, despite early publicity successes.

Another alternative is provided by bolt-action shotguns, once widespread in North America but out of favour for several decades. Savage, however, has offered a version of the Model 110 rifle – known as the Model 210 – chambered for 12-bore shotgun ammunition. The gun has the 24in (61cm) barrel characteristic of bolt-action designs, finely-adjustable sights and special slow-twist rifling designed to stabilise slugs. Though the capacity of the magazine is restricted to two rounds for the commercial market, there is no reason why a 5- or 8-round detachable magazine could not be provided for CTW purposes. The hybrid could appeal to police SWAT teams armed with Savage sniping rifles, owing to the similarity of the controls.

Ammunition Flexibility

Among the greatest attractions of combat shotguns is the ease with which they can fire a variety of ammunition, and the ease with which this can be changed to suit particular operations.

Even the traditional charge of shot can be varied from small-diameter 'dust shot', which minimises tissue injury even at close range, to heavy buckshot designed to stop an attacker with maximum force. In recent years, however, shotgun ammunition has undergone an amazing transformation with the advent of a large number of specialist designs. Some police and CTW units have purchased shotguns that are not only rifled, but also have 'ghost ring' sights, light projectors, laser-designators or electro-optical sights. Rifling enhances accuracy when slugs are fired, and the provision of proper sights is generally accepted to improve performance (even when firing shot) by defining a point of aim. One proprietary load, MK Industries' Quadrangle Shot (QS), departs from normal practice by providing eight segmental hardened-steel wedges arranged as two discs of four ahead of the wad. These are designed to shred wiring and control gear, which they have proved to do most effectively on targets such as helicopters and radar installations. Some projectiles are designed specifically for penetration, including the French Balle Flêche Sauvestre (BFS), which relies on a sub-calibre projectile and a discarding sabot, and a ball bearing inserted in a plastic carrier. One projectile has rotating vanes on the nose to act as a tiny – and very destructive – circular saw. The Dust Buster is a frangible lead bullet that dissolves into dust if it strikes a hard object, preventing unwanted collateral damage from ricochets in close-quarter fighting. Special loads have been developed to allow locks and hinges to be blown off doors at close range and in great safety, owing to the elimination of splash-back effects; non-lethal alternatives include baton rounds ('plastic bullets') and ballistic bags, which are virtually a bean bag fired at enough velocity to have a knock-down effect.

Distraction Munitions can contain projectiles filled with magnesium powder, giving a brief million-candlepower flash, and enough explosive to produce a sharp crack that can exceed 170 decibels.* Among the shotgun loads with the greatest

---

* For comparison, a Boeing 747 attains about 130dB on take-off; and the report of a 0.22in LR round being fired in a Marlin 780 rifle – at 140dB – is reckoned to be on the danger level for impulse sound, hearing protection being mandatory. An ex-Soviet 122mm howitzer recorded 183dB in tests undertaken in Finland, and, at 220dB, according to NATO literature, an observer can actually be killed by mechanical damage arising from the pressure wave. See Alan C. Paulson, *Silencer History and Performance*, vol. 1 (1996).

pedigree is the 'bolo', which derives from the whirling chain-and bar-shot used at sea to bring down masts and rigging, or as anti-personnel weapons on land. Bolo rounds can be obtained either to kill or disable, or to bring down escapers. The former usually contains two large buckshot joined with stout metal wire; the latter has three balls attached to sturdy cord in the form of a 'Y' – the CTW equivalent of the *bolas* of the Argentine *gaucho*.

Chapter 9

Combination
Weapons

The fighting in Vietnam, together with the extensive urban experience of SWAT teams, persuaded the US authorities to investigate a variety of short-range weapons. The Special Purpose Infantry Weapon (SPIW) programme was adjudged a failure, as attempts to fire flechettes – small-calibre dart-like projectiles, enthusiastically promoted by Irwin Barr of Aircraft Armaments – as well as 40mm grenades from a single 'infantry weapon' failed to challenge the established M16 rifle/M203 grenade-launcher combination. The AAI-designed XM19 was finally rejected in 1973, but the Close Assault Weapons System project (CAWS), promoted under JSSAP later in the same decade, continued to investigate the perfection of a combat shotgun. The goal was a versatile weapon that could be used on raids, in close combat, in ambushes, on search-and-destroy missions and in poor visibility, as well as for guard duties, policing and survival. Among the more arcane developments, such as Heckler & Koch's extraordinary combat shotgun, were a variety of more conventional submissions, typified by the Franchi SPAS-12, SPA-15 and SPAS-16 described above.

However, the CAWS project was not conclusive enough to satisfy the armed forces, and another series of tests ensued. Though a conventional gas-operated Benelli M4 shotgun was approved in 1999, rather surprisingly retaining a tube magazine, more innovative solutions are still being touted.

One obvious solution to the problem of equipping anti-terrorist units with rifles and shotguns is to provide a weapon that has the characteristics of both. This is hardly new; multi-barrelled guns combining rifled and smooth-bore barrels have been made in Europe for more than a hundred years – the first three-barrel *Drilling* was patented in Germany in 1891 – and many break-action guns combining a small-calibre rifle barrel (often 0.22in rimfire) with a shotgun (often but not exclusively 0.410in) have been made by Harrington & Richardson and their successors since the 1930s. The Finnish Tikka M07, which could be supplied for a variety of high-power rifle rounds, was one of the best guns of this type.

The major drawback of these designs is simply that each of the barrels is restricted to a single shot, which limits fighting potential. The challenge that faces developers of combat-worthy combination guns, therefore, lies in combining two barrels, two magazines (for cartridges of greatly differing diameters) and an appropriate selection mechanism in a package that is short and light enough to be acceptable. To put this into context, most of the slide-action guns are about 38 inches long, weigh about 7 pounds, and have magazines containing 7 or 8 rounds; modern military rifles, excepting the bullpups, are about the same length, but weigh as much as 10 pounds with a loaded 30-round magazine. Yet the combination weapon has to include everything within an envelope no larger than that of the assault rifle!

The Crossfire, promoted by LLC of La Grange, Georgia, USA, is currently among the most promising designs. It combines a 5.56mm rifle barrel, fed conventionally from a detachable box magazine (including the standard 30-round M16 type), with a 12-bore shotgun barrel fed from a 4-round tube magazine that forms the comb of the butt. The gun is only 38in (965mm) long and weighs 8.5lb (3.9kg) with the standard 5-round 5.56mm magazine. Though it is still quite large, and the superimposition of the barrels makes the receiver unusually deep, similar to the Heckler & Koch G3, the Crossfire is undoubtedly approaching the optimum for a weapon of its class.

From a combat viewpoint, combination guns suffer one of

the drawbacks of the selectable manual/autoloading shotguns – the potential confusion of barrel/mode selection in a stressful situation – but their advantages may soon be too great to ignore.

Another approach to the problem is provided by the OCIW or Objective Combat Individual Weapon under development in the USA as the 'lethality element of the Land Warrior program'. Known as the XM29 and expected to reach service in 2008, this represents another attempt to integrate primary infantry weapons – in this case, the rifle and the grenade launcher.

The XM29 is essentially a two-barrel weapon, one chambering the 5.56 x 45mm round and the other firing newly developed 20mm HEAB fragmentation projectiles. The 20mm ammunition is seen as a replacement for the short-range 40mm M203 grenade launcher commonly encountered on M16 and M4 rifles. It is hoped not only to increase effective range to 1,000 yards but also to reduce weight by integrating the launcher with the structure of the gun. A 6-round magazine in the butt holds the 20mm rounds, which are designed to burst 1–1.5m above the target. This is particularly useful against men who may be prone, concealed in a trench or behind a breastwork. The projectiles can also be used in 'window mode', allowing the initiator to delay explosion long enough for the projectile to enter a room or a thin-walled fuel tank. An eight-second self-destruct is designed to ensure that no unexploded rounds remain.

The main sight of the XM29 target acquisition/fire-control system (TA/FCS) is a 'Direct View Optic', essentially a small television-like screen onto which the image can be projected and magnified if required to 3x. An electronic compass and an inclinometer are built into the sight, and a laser-ranger, assisted by environmental sensors, feeds information to a ballistic computer that sets the electronic HEAB projectile fuze for each individual target.

Being developed by HK Defense (gun) of Sterling, Virginia, and Brashear LP of Pittsburgh (sight), the XM29 is fairly conventional – though, at 14lb (6.35kg), questionably heavy.

In addition, the ability of such sophisticated electronics to function effectively in a battlefield environment is unknown. Firing a few hundred 20mm HEAB rounds has apparently convinced the US Army Fuze Safety Board that work can proceed, but the experience of many other 'smart' munitions has not always been encouraging; some of the claims being made for the OCIW, therefore, may ultimately prove to have been overstated.

One argument in favour of the XM29 is that it is lighter than an M16 or M4 fitted with a separate grenade launcher and an intensifier sight, but there are those who see the weight as the result of unnecessary complexity. It is probable that the XM29 will only be a long-term success if there is a wholesale change of attitude in the US Army – particularly as the intention seems to be only to issue four OCIWs to each nine-man squad. The progress being made with the XM8 5.56mm rifle, which is reckoned to cost less than $1,000 per gun once series production gets underway, may ultimately jeopardise the OCIW ('at least' $10,000 apiece) simply because the cost of large-scale issues will be too great.

Chapter 10

Light Automatic Weapons

The future of classical submachine-guns remains uncertain. Though phenomenal numbers of Heckler & Koch MP5s have been sold around the world, to military and police forces alike, there has been a perceptible move towards compact versions of assault rifles such as the AK and AKM. This has been most evident in Soviet-bloc and similarly aligned countries. These guns, however, unlike the MP5 or the 9mm AUG, still offer virtually the same power as an assault rifle.

The increased popularity of the assault rifle, particularly after the introduction of the US 5.56mm cartridge, has brought an appreciable decline in the fortunes of the submachine-gun. The US Army has effectively ceased to use it, even though stocks of the 0.45in ACP M3A1 are held in reserve, and many others have questioned its utility. Consequently, the esteem in which guns such as the Thompson, the MP. 40 and the Sten Mark 5 were held by special forces of the Second World War – or the Shpagin-designed PPSh by Russian *tankoviy desant* (tank-borne infantry) forces – is no longer relevant.

An alternative approach to the problem of providing a suitable intermediate weapon, the so-called Personal Defence Weapon or PDW, has been actively touted by several leading gunmakers, including FN Herstal and Heckler & Koch. The specification for these guns, ironically, is similar to the one that created the US M1 Carbine – regarded by some as a catastrophic combat weapon, and by others as one of the greatest compromise weapons developed during the Second World War. The goal has been to create a weapon that can arm second-line personnel effectively, offering more power than the pistol or the submachine-gun but less powerful, lighter and less cumbersome than a full-size infantry rifle. The principal stumbling block has been the cartridge; the 0.30in US M1 Carbine pattern was too weak, and too close to a glorified pistol round to be successful. The current 5.56 x 45mm is regarded as too powerful, and so the proponents of the PDW concept have been forced to develop new rounds that are in essence reduced-scale rifle cartridges such as the FN 5.7 x 28mm and the Heckler & Koch 4.6 x 30mm designs, developing power that lies about mid-way between 9mm Parabellum and 5.56 x 45mm. Some people have hailed these rounds as a means of fulfilling additional special-purpose tasks, and even as replacements for the 5.56mm pattern – particularly if the gun is a combination weapon firing 20mm or 25mm ammunition as well. The case is not proven, and some trial reports have suggested that the PDW cartridges cannot provide enough hitting power on the limits of normal combat ranges to be acceptable.

Consequently, though FN Herstal has developed the F2000 bullpup 5.56mm assault rifle, work is continuing with the FN P90 PDW. This is an interesting selective-fire 5.7mm-calibre blowback that is remarkable for its futuristic appearance. Heckler & Koch has also embarked on a similar approach, developing a 4.6 x 30mm cartridge for the H&K M7 PDW for NATO trials.

Traditional Submachine-Guns

Sterling

Almost alone among the major powers, Britain clung to a traditional submachine-gun into the 1990s. The Sterling, developed from the 1944-vintage Patchett prototype to replace the crude, cheap but surprisingly efficient Sten Gun, was adopted by the British Army in 1956. Its design was un-remarkable by later standards, with a conventional in-line barrel/bolt layout, but it was simple, reliable, easy to make and shot well. Among the differing models were the standard Mk 4

(British Army designation L2A3), the silenced Mk 5 (L34A1), a long barrelled semi-automatic Mk 6, several variants of the Mk 7 Para Pistol, and a special semi-automatic Mk 8.

The silenced Sterling was a much underrated gun, capable of firing fully automatically without unduly damaging the silencer system, while the Mk 7 Police Carbine was specifically developed at the request of Metropolitan Police D11 marksmen to provide a handy carbine with an adjustable butt and optical sights. It was replaced in the 1980s by the Heckler & Koch MP5. The Mk 8, developed specially for the British security forces to provide greater accuracy, fires from a closed bolt.

Owing to its adoption in the British Army, Canada and elsewhere, the Sterling may have been made in greater quantities than any post-war submachine-gun excepting the Uzi. It even attained a measure of notoriety as the weapon used to kill WPC Yvonne Fletcher outside the Libyan People's Bureau in London, in 1984.

The Sterling Mk 7 Para Pistol was a much shortened version of the standard Mk 4 (L2A3) with barrels of 3in or 8in and a shortened receiver. Though the Mk 7 was abandoned with the demise of Sterling, which was sold to Royal Ordnance in 1988, a similar gun has been made by FAMAE in Chile.

Uzi

During the early 1950s, the Israeli Uziel ('Uzi') Gal perfected a submachine-gun by taking many features from Czech prototypes and adding ideas of his own. The Uzi submachine-gun used an overhung bolt, running forward above the barrel to restrict overall length, while the magazine ran up through the grip. With the stock folded, the gun measured only 470mm – appreciably shorter than the majority of its contemporaries – and performed efficiently under virtually any conditions. It was adopted by the Israeli forces, being made by Israeli Military Industries (IMI) in Tel Aviv, and was subsequently licensed to Fabrique Nationale. Guns have also been made in South Africa, and are being copied in the People's Republic of China; the Croatian Ero (and the Mini-Ero) is a minor adaptation of the basic design.

These AN/PVS-7B night-vision goggles are typical of the head-sets used
in conjunction with image intensifiers working in the infra-red spectra.
The picture also shows the restrictions placed on peripheral vision
by the earliest designs.

Below: The Striker, developed in South Africa, is a unique double-action shotgun fed from a drum magazine.

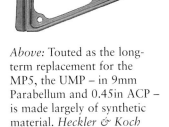

Above: Touted as the long-term replacement for the MP5, the UMP – in 9mm Parabellum and 0.45in ACP – is made largely of synthetic material. *Heckler & Koch*

Above: Chambered for a unique 4.7 x 30mm high-performance cartridge, the Personal Defense Weapon seeks to replace a variety of weapons. *Heckler & Koch*

Above: A typical 9 x 19mm MP5A4, with a fixed butt and an additional three-round burst-firing capability. *Heckler & Koch*

Below: The Czechoslovakian vz/61 Skorpion machine pistol.

Above left: Distributed throughout Western armies, the 7.62mm FN MAG is one of the leading support weapons. It can be fired from a bipod, a tripod or a variety of vehicle and aircraft mounts. *FN Herstal*

Above: The current version of the 0.50in-calibre M2HB-QCB machine-gun. *FN Herstal*

Above left: The Israeli Negev is a clever combination of assault rifle and light machine-gun, shown here with a belt-pouch hanging beneath the feed-way.

Left: The blowback GMG fires 40mm grenades from a linked belt. *Heckler & Koch*

A 5.56mm Steyr AUG-77 set to fire a rifle grenade. Note the special sight, which is used in conjunction with the tip of the grenade-head to estimate range. *Steyr-Mannlicher*

Above: A silenced sniper rifle dismantled into its unobtrusive carrying case. Note the folded butt. *Accuracy International*

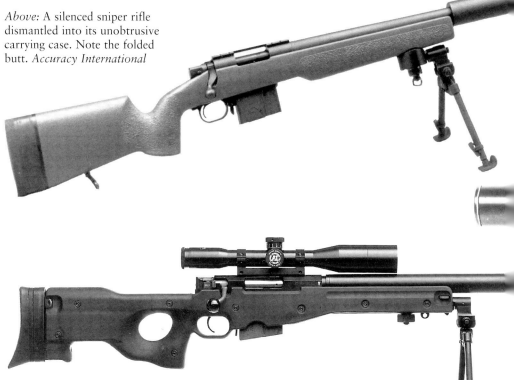

Right: The Soviet/
Russian PSS silent
pistol, chambered for
piston cartridges.
Terry Gander

Left: A McMillan bolt-action
rifle with a half-length
suppressor. Fittings of this
type generally work best with
subsonic ammunition.

Below: A typical silenced submachine-gun, this MP5SD1 has
the suppression chamber built integrally with the receiver.
Heckler & Koch

Left: The British Accuracy
International AWS ('Arctic
Warfare Silenced') rifle, with
a full-length annular
suppressor. *Accuracy
International*

A combat-type adaptation of the M1911 Colt-Browning, with many customised features and additional slide-retracting grips at the front. This gun also has a laser-designator beneath the muzzle. Fittings of this type are now small, light and comparatively unobtrusive. *Springfield, Inc.*

An M1911-type pistol with a light projector beneath the frame. *Springfield, Inc.*

The participation of such a well-known manufacturer as FN in the Uzi programme brought greatly increased success and the Uzi prospered, being widely adopted for police, paramilitary and special-purpose use. The 1980s variant, available in 9 x 19mm or 0.45in ACP, was a particularly 'safe' submachine-gun: in addition to the manual safety on the left side of the receiver above the grip, there was a grip safety and an additional ratchet to prevent the bolt flying shut if the firer's hand slipped during cocking. Compact and sub-compact versions have also been made (*see below*).

Heckler & Koch

The most popular submachine-gun of the late twentieth century was the Heckler & Koch HK54, a 9mm gun adopted by the Bundeswehr as the Maschinenpistole 5 (MP5, the name by which it is best known) to replace the Walther MPK and MPL that had been used by West German police during the counter-attack after the 1972 Munich Olympic Games tragedy. The MP5 has been used by a wide variety of Special Forces, including SAS personnel who used them in active service for the first time during the Iranian Embassy siege in 1980. The guns have also been popular in Germany (with GSG-9), Italy (NOCS) and in the USA.

Unlike most submachine-guns, which fire from an open breech, the Heckler & Koch featured a scaled-down roller-lock delay system adapted from the G3 rifle. This supported the cartridge case until the bullet had all but left the barrel, and accuracy was greatly enhanced as a result of firing from a closed bolt. The MP5 was reasonably heavy, too, and had a reputation for excellent single-shot performance. In addition, the MP5 had far better open sights than most submachine-guns. This facilitated accurate shooting in a way that is usually impossible with a pistol, minimising the chance of collateral damage occurring in urban terrorism. Experiments with various kinds of 9mm projectile also improved performance, as Teflon-coated man-stoppers and special SFM-made Très Haute Velocité

(THV: extra-high velocity) penetrator bullets could be used when required.

The MP5 could also be fitted with optical sights, image intensifiers, infra-red sights and aiming projectors in pursuit of operational flexibility. The success of the design permitted a constant updating programme, leading to constructional refinements, the addition of burst-firing capabilities (often at the expense of the fully-automatic feature), and better handling characteristics.

The current range includes four basic patterns: MP5A2 and MP5A4 with fixed butts, MP5A3 and MP5A5 with retractable butts. The first in each pair has a conventional trigger system, but the second pair has additional three-round burst-firing capabilities. SF in the designation indicates guns that are restricted to semi-automatic fire. The MP5-N, with fixed or retractable butts, was developed for US Navy SEAL teams, and incorporates a 'Navy' trigger group (though this is little more than the standard three-position pattern with the 'safe' position at the bottom).

Highly effective silenced variants have been marketed, the SD1, SD2 and SD3 being fitted with receiver end caps, fixed butts and retractable butts respectively; three otherwise comparable guns – SD4, SD5 and SD6 – have additional burst-firing capabilities. The MP5K series are short-barrelled, with additional fore-grips ahead of the magazine, and often lack butts. MP5KA4 has a burst-firing mechanism, and the MP5K-PDW (Personal Defense Weapon) has a folding butt.

However, in pursuit of economy – the MP5 is expensive and difficult to make – Heckler & Koch has now developed a cheaper blowback gun known as the Universal Machine Pistol (UMP). Originally intended for the 0.45in ACP round, though now also offered in 9 x 19mm, the UMP has the G36-type frame/receiver unit of fibreglass-reinforced polymer and a folding butt. The roller-locking mechanism of the MP5 has been abandoned in favour of blowback, reducing complexity and cost, and an internal firing-pin safety is fitted. Picatinny rails will be found on the top of the receiver, and on the sides and base of the fore-end. The 0.45-calibre guns are 23.6in/600mm long with the butt extended (17.7in/450mm folded) and weigh only about 4.9lb/2.2kg without the detachable 30-round box magazine. Cyclic rate is about 700rds/min.

Bizon

Also known as the PP-19, this Russian design originated in an Izhmashzavod design bureau in the early 1990s but was not made in quantity until 1995 or later. It has an obvious affinity with the Kalashnikov assault rifle, sharing many of its components with the AKS-74, but the receiver is shortened to chamber pistol ammunition. The first guns were chambered for the 9 x 18mm Makarov round and had a cylindrical spiral-feed magazine beneath the barrel where it could double as a handgrip. Experience showed that the cartridge was not powerful enough to impress the personnel of the Spetsnaz, MVD and FSO, and a modified version appeared. This may be chambered for the 9 x 19mm Parabellum or 7.62 x 25mm Mauser round, the latter being shared with the obsolescent Tokarev pistol and most of the Soviet-era submachine-guns. Indeed, it is said that the 7.62mm guns – which will normally be found with a cylinder magazine – can be accompanied by old 35-round box magazines originally intended for the PPS of the Second World War. The Bizon is about 425mm long with the butt folded, and weighs about 2.1kg without its magazine; capacity is either 64 9mm or 45 7.62mm rounds.

Others

Many efficient submachine-guns have been made throughout the world since the end of the Second World War, but only a few have had much effect on the export market. The Steyr MPi-69, which bore some affinities to the Czechoslovakian vz/23 and the Uzi, was designed to be made as easily as possible. The receiver was a steel pressing inside a nylon sheath, and the minor parts were usually brazed or welded together. The bolt was an overhung type, and the trigger doubled as the selector – pulling it part-way fired single shots, but pulling all the way allowed the gun to work automatically until pressure was released. The safety catch was also quirky as it could be pressed to an intermediate position where the gun would fire single shots only. The magazine ran up through the pistol grip, the butt was a retractable twin-rod pattern, and, curiously, a pull on the sling (attached to a handle protruding from the front left side of the receiver) charged the gun. The Steyr design was used in small numbers by the Austrian security forces and also attracted a few export orders. It was replaced by the MPi-81, with a conventional charging lever and a few insignificant manufacturing improvements.

The Beretta M12 was another conventional design, made largely of steel stampings, with an overhung bolt. Chambered for the 9mm Parabellum cartridge, it had a magazine that ran up into the action ahead of the trigger, an automatic safety let into the front face of the pistol grip, and a fore-grip under the muzzle. Most of the selective-fire guns also had a rod-like butt that folded to the right to lie alongside the receiver. The sights were sturdy, protected by folded sheet-steel 'wings', and performance was good. The M12S was an improved version with a new safety catch/selector system, a stronger end-cap catch, a better shoulder piece on the butt, and an epoxy-resin finish.

Guns of this type were sold in quantity by FN Herstal (imported from Italy) and made by Taurus in Brazil; consequently, they were supplied to a wide range of security agencies in Italy and abroad. Individual guns were sometimes accompanied by image-intensifying sights, laser-designators or illuminating equipment, particularly when intended for anti-terrorist units or special forces. The M12S was about 26in (660mm) long, with the butt extended, and weighed 7lb (3.2kg) without its detachable box magazine, which could hold 20, 32 or 40 rounds depending on length. Cyclic rate was 500–550rds/min.

The Spectre M-4, developed in Italy by Sites of Turin, was introduced publicly in 1984 and attracted the attention of many security agencies before being abandoned in the late 1990s. A unique 50-round quadruple-column magazine also attracted favourable notice, but the most unusual feature was a double-action trigger system, which allowed the gun to be carried with the chamber loaded. The hammer could be dropped against its stop by a de-cocking system, but the Spectre could then be fired simply by pulling through on the trigger.

Compact Submachine-Guns

Credit for shortening submachine-guns until they were scarcely longer than large pistols has often been given to Gordon Ingram, but is really due to Giovanni Oliani, working for FNA in Italy in 1942, and Václav Holek, designer of the Czechoslovakian vz/23 of the late 1940s – the first gun to introduce the telescoping-bolt construction that allowed the chamber to be set back above the trigger and a magazine introduced through the pistol grip.

The Uzi and the Ingram are just two of many designs that have followed this particular lead, which has allowed the creation of compact and 'sub-compact' patterns. The former is usually short-barrelled, often with a retractable or folding butt; the latter is reduced to an absolute minimum, with barrels that may be no longer than those of a handgun and an end-cap instead of a butt. Sub-compact designs can often be used with one hand, and are difficult to distinguish from true machine pistols.

Uzi

A shortened variant known as the Mini-Uzi, just 14.2in (360mm) long, will be encountered, together with semi-automatic 'civilian' carbine derivatives. The success of the vz/61 Scorpion and the Ingram Model 10, particularly, encouraged other manufacturers to reduce their submachine-guns to the dimensions of a large pistol. The Micro-Uzi is a 'one-hand' version of the popular Israeli submachine-gun. Without its folding stock, the Micro-Uzi measures just 9.8in (250mm) overall and weighs 4.3lb (1.95kg) with an empty magazine.

Ingram

The success of the MP5 has rather eclipsed the Ingram Model 10, which, for much of the early 1970s, looked as though it would achieve universal approval. Developed by Gordon B. Ingram, the short-barrel 9mm Parabellum gun measured merely 10.6in (270mm) overall with the stock retracted and weighed only 7.7lb (3.5kg) with its loaded 32-round magazine. Unfortunately, the Military Armament Corporation (MAC), the original promoter, was liquidated in 1976 and interest in the Ingram lapsed until SWD of Atlanta, Georgia, became involved. Reintroduced as the Cobray, the Model 10 proved popular in South America, and also among American police SWAT teams.

Ingrams were carried by the Israeli 259 Commando on Operation 'Thunderball', the raid on Entebbe airport in 1976, where their compact design – smaller even than the Uzi – was beneficial in the cramped confines of the raiders' aircraft. Small quantities were even bought by the British forces in the 1970s, principally for the SAS, but were found to be too inaccurate to protect bystanders – vitally important in raids such as that undertaken by GSG-9, with SAS advisers, on the Lufthansa jet hijacked to Mogadishu in 1977.

By 1980, the SAS (and many other agencies) had replaced the Ingram with the Heckler & Koch MP5, and the once-popular Ingram has lost much of its reputation. Ingrams were usually chambered for 0.380in ACP/9mm Short (as the 'Model 11') or 9mm Parabellum (Model 11/9).

Steyr Types

Particularly interesting in this class is the Steyr Tactical Machine Pistol of 1988, which owed something to the abortive Pi-18 and the AUG. The TMP, made largely of synthetic material, had the appearance of a large pistol – excepting that the magazine protruded beneath the butt and a folding hand-grip could be found under the fore-end. Though basically a blowback design, an element of delay was introduced by rotating the barrel, which released the bolt after the parts had moved back about 0.5in

(12.7mm). The synthetic receiver/frame unit accepted a detachable box magazine, running up through the pistol grip, and had a lipped fore-grip beneath the muzzle. Overall length of the weapon was about 11in (279mm), with a 5.1in (130mm) barrel; the TMP weighed about 2.9lb (1.3kg) without its box magazine, which held 15 or 30 rounds. Cyclic rate was 850–900rds/min.

Polish Types

The Polish wz/63 shares a similar concept to the Czechoslovakian vz/61 Skorpion machine-pistol, though it is much more like a submachine-gun in shape. The most distinctive features of the wz/63 were the long compensator at the muzzle and the folding forward handgrip. Though comparatively uncommon in the West (but apparently still being copied in the People's Republic of China), the efficient little wz/63 offered a good combination of firepower with the size of a large pistol and was particularly favoured in the 1980s by aircraft hijackers. One was used to assassinate Shlomo Argov, the Israeli Ambassador in London, in 1982.

Russian Designs

The success of the AKMSU in the hands of anti-terrorist units of the MVD initially restricted the popularity of the submachine-gun in the USSR. Evgeniy Dragunov, designer of the SVD rifle, had developed a prototype PP-71 compact gun in the early 1970s, but the Army soon lost interest. The rise of organised crime in the early 1990s persuaded the MVD to resurrect the project as the Kedr. Small quantities of the Izhevsk-made guns were purchased, but operational experience soon revealed that the 9 x 18mm Makarov cartridge was not particularly effective – especially when the criminals had more powerful weaponry – and the 9 x 18mm PMM round was substituted in 1994. The gun was then renamed Klin. The Dragunov submachine-guns are blowback designs, distinguished by a short barrel protruding from a squared stamped-steel receiver. The magazine projects downward ahead of the trigger guard, and a simple butt can be folded up and over the top of the receiver. Silencers and designator units can be attached to the muzzle when required. The Klin is 12in (305mm) long with the butt folded, and weighs about 3.4lb (1.5kg) without its 20- or 30-round magazine.

Other Russian designs have included the AEK-919 Kashtan, derived from the Steyr MPi-81, which was developed in Kovrov in the early 1990s and is believed to have been used in small numbers by the MVD and security agencies. Developed by the KBP team in the Tula small-arms factory, the PP-93 resembles a large semi-automatic pistol, with a short projecting muzzle and a butt that folds up and over the top of the elongated receiver. The design is unusually flat, and the charging handle takes the form of a roller beneath the receiver ahead of the trigger guard. It was derived from the earlier PP-90, which could be folded into a large rectangular 'box' for covert operations – but was unacceptable in service, as the designers had forgotten that it had still to handle comfortably as a gun! The PP guns chamber the standard 9 x 18mm PM (Makarov) cartridge.

Underwater Submachine-Gun

One of the most unusual guns in this class is the Soviet/Russian APS, designed by Vladimir Simonov and made largely of pressings. Though vaguely resembling the AK, it has an unmistakably-shaped magazine accepting the 5.66mm MPS cartridge. The sliding butt can be locked into the pistol grip, reducing overall length from 32.4in (823mm) to 24.2in (615mm); the gun weighs about 7.6lb (3.45kg) without the 26-round magazine, which adds another 1.25lb (570gm).

The MPS cartridge, about 4.7in (120mm) long, is loaded with a dart-like projectile weighing 318 grains (20.6gm). Credited with a muzzle velocity of 1,200 ft/sec (365 m/sec), it is said to have a lethal range of 30 metres in water up to 40m deep, and can also be used in air. The simple pressed-steel back sight, however, is set for 30m.

Machine Pistols

A plausible alternative to the minimal submachine-gun is the truly automatic pistol, very few of which have ever been successful despite a pedigree stretching back by way of the Mauser Schnellfeuerpistole and its Spanish copies to a Borchardt of 1893. The problem has simply been that cyclic rates as high as a thousand rounds per minute are valueless in light pistols, which climb too quickly. Though designers have added shoulder stocks, supplementary hand grips, and burst-limiters (generally restricted to three rounds), few have been able to solve the inherent instability.

However, though almost universally derided, there are a few champions of machine pistols. T.J. Mullin noted in his book *Special Operations Weapons and Tactics* (2003) that weapons of this type:

> . . . can be truly devastating when used by the first man on the door in raids . . . But the person who is . . . armed in that fashion must keep in constant practice to maintain the all too perishable skills necessary to dominate the machine pistol. My experience tells me that anything less than 1,000 rounds of proper practice *each month* [italics added] will simply not suffice . . .

The problem is still one of balancing the power of the cartridge with the need to keep recoil within controllable limits. Though Glock and Heckler & Koch have made guns of this class, the Beretta 93R was among the best. Purchased in small quantities by the Italian NOCS and Carabinieri, it was only marginally larger than the standard Model 92SB pistol, about 9.5in (240mm) overall and weighing merely 41.3oz (1170gm) with an empty 20-round magazine. The 93R had a multi-port muzzle-brake and a selector above the left grip, marked • for single shots and • • • for three-shot bursts. An auxiliary hand-grip pivoted downward ahead of the enlarged trigger guard, whilst an extending shoulder stock could be supplied to order.

The pistol was just about light enough for effective one-handed use, but its special features were only beneficial during burst fire; ideally, the fore-grip was then folded down and grasped with the fingers of the non-firing hand, the thumb of which could then be hooked around the front of the elongated trigger guard. This allowed the muzzle to be held down during firing, counteracting the tendency to climb.

The Czechoslovakian vz/61 Skorpion was also basically little more than an enlarged pistol firing the 7.65mm Browning cartridge from a detachable box magazine in the frame ahead of the trigger guard. Even though it could be fitted with a retractable skeletal shoulder stock and an elongated box magazine, the vz/61 was very small indeed – just 10.7in (270mm) overall, with its stock retracted, and weighing 4.4lb (2kg) with a full 20-round magazine. The rate of fire was restricted to about 700rds/min by a reciprocating-weight retarder mechanism built into the pistol grip. Though adopted by the Czechoslovak Army and internal security forces, and evident during the Prague riots in August 1969, the feeble 7.65mm cartridge restricted its utility. Consequently, variants were made for the 9mm Short, the 9mm Makarov and the 9mm Parabellum (vz/63, vz/64 and vz/68 respectively). It was also made under licence in Yugoslavia.

Chapter 11

Light Support Weapons

As the majority of the operating principles for weapons of this type had been established by 1945, most current guns are merely adaptations of older designs. The Brownings, particularly, had been perfected prior to 1939. But if this is a reasonable assumption, contemporary assessments of the machine-gun's tactical role do not reflect former opinions. This is partly due to the adoption of comparatively low-powered intermediate ammunition with poor long-range performance, and also to the blurring of the distinction between infantry rifles and light machine-guns by the assault rifle.

Machine-Guns

The light support weapon (LSW) category contains a proliferation of belt- and box-fed guns, and a few, such as the Czech vz/52, which are convertible. Though belt-fed guns offer a higher rate of fire, they are useless if replacement belts are unavailable. Box-fed guns, conversely, may be reloaded with loose cartridges taken from accompanying riflemen – as long as the guns share common cartridges.

The poor long-range capabilities of the US M193 5.56mm ball have led to some armies retaining 7.62mm NATO support weapons such as the US M60 series or the FN MAG. However, the recent relaxation of the US Army requirement to pierce a standard US steel helmet at '800 metres or more' to '*up to* 800 metres', has permitted adoption of the 5.56mm belt-fed FN Minimi as the M249.

Many European arms-makers – including Beretta and Steyr-Daimler-Puch – have offered 'machine rifle' derivatives of their basic 5.56mm assault rifles. However, despite the provision of heavy quick-change barrels, it is difficult to see these fulfilling the traditional light machine-gun role. This class shows the deficiencies of the all-purpose 5.56mm round most clearly, and it is hard to avoid the conclusion that the British 0.280in EM-2 or 6.25mm cartridges would have provided better overall performance in assault and sniper rifles, as well as light and even medium machine-guns.

US Designs

The M60 light machine-gun was adopted in November 1956, though series production did not begin until 1960 and large-scale issues were delayed until 1962. The action is locked by rotating lugs on the bolt head into the walls of the receiver, the gas piston and its extension being placed beneath the barrel. However, the bipod was fitted to the barrel and the carrying handle was attached to the barrel-casing, making barrel-change exceptionally awkward. In addition, the reliance on the back sight for zeroing meant that a barrel change could be accompanied by an appreciable change in impact-point unless the sights were adjusted. The M60 was also found to lack sufficient power to lift lengthy ammunition belts, though this did not stop the Saco Defense Systems Division of the Maremont Corporation making more than 250,000 guns by 1985.

The standard mount is the M122 tripod, though the Saco MSGH 60 may be used on vehicles, boats and helicopters. Laser-designators and optical, electro-optical or thermal-imaging sights can be fitted to mounting brackets attached to the right side of the receiver.

The M60C, commonly fitted to helicopters, had a solenoid-operated trigger and a hydraulic charger; the M60D, developed by Saco as a helicopter doorway gun, was a modified 'C' with spade grips and a thumb trigger on the back plate. The M60E1 was the 'product improved' version of the M60, with the bipod attached to the gas tube, and the lightweight M60E3 was adopted by the USMC in 1983; by 1986, all existing Marine Corps' M60 guns had been converted to E3 standard, with straight-comb butts, lightweight barrels, and auxiliary pistol grips beneath the barrel. The standard full-length M60E3 was merely 42.4in (1,077mm) long and weighed 19.4lb (8.8kg).

The 1994-vintage M60E4 is an improved E3, with an integral sight-mounting rail, a short barrel and an improved gas-regulation system. It has been introduced to service in small quantities, but combat experience has shown that it is still comparatively unreliable. The US Navy has sponsored development of a 7.62mm version of the M249A1 (Minimi), which is seen as a potential replacement for the M60 series. M60-type guns, however, are still being marketed by American Ordnance, though they are gradually being superseded in US military service by adaptations of the M240 – the ubiquitous FN MAG.

The Belgian Minimi light machine-gun was adopted as Standard A in 1982, orders being placed with FN Manufacturing for 60,000 guns. Teething troubles ensued, however, and the contract was suspended in 1985 until a 'product improved' version was finalised in 1987. Known as the M249E1 during development, the M249A1 had an improved recoil buffer, a heat shield above the barrel, a fixed gas regulator and a folding carrying handle. The shape of the butt was revised, and a Picatinny rail could be attached to the receiver.

The M249A1 has proved to be extremely successful, and has been used by the US Army in Iraq in huge numbers. The US Navy, which issues the standard 5.56mm as the Mark 26 Model 0, subsequently sponsored the development of a 7.62 x 51mm enlargement of the basic design. Made by FN Manufacturing in Columbia, South Carolina, the first Mark 48 Model 0 guns were issued to SOCOM units in 2003. Trials have shown them to be more reliable than the M60E4, the dual box/belt feed system is advantageous, and the guns weigh merely 18.2lb (8.25kg). They have the Rail Interface System (RIS) with no fewer than five

Picatinny rails – one on the receiver and four on the fore-end – to allow accessories to be attached.

During the Vietnam War, abortive trials were undertaken with many machine rifles and light machine-guns, including the Colt-backed CMG-2 and the Stoner M63 series promoted by the Cadillac Gage Company. Colt, in fact, still offers the detachable heavy-barrel variant of the M16A1 that was once greatly favoured by US Special Forces, SWAT Teams and other paramilitary groups.

During the 1960s, the US Navy equipped many of its SEAL teams with the Stoner Mk 23 Model 0 light machine-gun for covert operations in Vietnam, arguing that the superior firepower of the comparatively light Mk 23 (which weighed only 11.7lb) and its capacity for sustained fire outweighed its suspect reliability and the occasional tendency to 'go auto' while in the single-shot mode. As the SEALs paid great attention to maintenance and could be relied upon to clean the guns almost daily, few operational troubles were encountered. It is interesting to speculate that the Mk 23 and its companion rifle, the XM22, could have been developed to a fully satisfactory service status, had the project been given the indulgence granted to the M16.

British Types

Trials undertaken in Britain in the mid-1950s showed than the gas-operated Belgian FN MAG was the best all-round weapon. It was adopted for the British forces in 1958 and the first large-scale issues of Enfield-made guns were made in 1963 as the Gun, Machine, General Purpose, 7.62mm L7A1. Though customarily fitted with a bipod, the guns may be issued with the Mounting, Tripod, Machine Gun, L4A1 and Sight, Unit, Infantry, Trilux C2 (SUIT) to provide a medium support weapon. The L7A2 was an improved version with an additional feed pawl and mounts for a special 50-round belt bag on the left side of the receiver. There are also a variety of specialist tank and vehicle guns, a helicopter version, and a heavy-barrelled L19A1, rarely encountered, which can sustain fire better than the standard L7.

The British-made variants of the FN MAG performed well enough in the Falklands campaign of 1982, without entirely displacing the supposedly obsolete L4A4, a Bren Mk 3 converted to 7.62mm NATO. With its top-feed box magazine, the L4, which weighed 21lb, was undoubtedly more accurate and handier than the belt-fed L7 series. Its principal drawbacks were limited magazine capacity and a comparatively light barrel that overheated too rapidly.

The Bren Gun was destined to be replaced in the late 1980s by the 5.56mm L86 Light Support Weapon, but even the SS109 bullet performed poorly at long range compared with the 7.62mm pattern, and the guns themselves suffered serious teething troubles. The standards of manufacture were poor, leading to excessive failures in service, and accuracy was judged to be unacceptable. Eventually, the authorities decided to withdraw the surviving L86A1s into store – only for survivors to be reissued in 2003 to serve in Iraq. This was largely due to there being insufficient supplies of Belgian-made Minimi machine-guns and ammunition to answer the needs of all the British troops in the combat zone.

French Types

Most NATO armies are satisfied with the MAG. However, the French have clung to the curious semi-delayed-blowback Arme Automatique Transformable (AAT) Mle 52 after the adoption of the 5.56mm FA MAS rifle, but suffer accordingly. The AAT 52 operates on the very margins of safety and trials have shown that it is particularly prone to jamming in adverse conditions. As barrel changing is also problematical, it is hard to see the AAT in the vanguard of technology.

German Types

The Rheinmetall-made MG3 (and its various predecessors) derived directly from the wartime MG. 42. The roller-locking system was simple, effective and reasonably reliable, though, in some tests, the MG3 has not performed as well as the MAG or the Russian PK (*see below*). Barrel change is simplicity itself, and the feed is particularly smooth and effective.

The Austrians, the Italians, the Portuguese and the Spanish have all used variants of the MG. 42, MG. 42/59 or MG3 at one time or another, though the Austrians are now issuing the heavy-barrelled LSW variant of the Steyr AUG and the Italians are experimenting with a number of LSWs submitted by Beretta, Franchi and others. The Swiss MG51 was essentially similar to the G3, but had a flap-lock rather than rollers.

Heckler & Koch has also made a variety of 7.62mm-calibre machine-guns, though they have never displaced the MG3 in the Bundeswehr. However, the H&K guns have been popular with special forces owing to their variety, flexibility and light weight. All share the standard roller-locking system, associated with the G3 rifle. Users of the H&K guns include GSG-9, whose G6 features an integral 4x optical sight and a special linkless feed system that can be loaded with clips or loose rounds, and replenished at any time. The ill-fated US Delta Force mission to rescue the hostages in Iran in 1980 apparently selected the 7.62mm HK21A1 (an unsuccessful contender in the US JSSAP Squad Automatic Weapon competition) in the absence of a suitable full-calibre indigenous light machine-gun.

The HK21 was little more than a variant of the HK11 light machine-gun, adapted to feed from a belt instead of a box magazine – though it could be converted to use box magazines simply by replacing the feed unit and changing the bolt, which blurred the distinction between the two patterns. The HK21A1 was a minor upgrade of the HK21, with a modified butt allowing a support-hand grip, and 'multiple bullet' markings replacing the 'S', 'E' and 'F' accompanying the original selector. The standard 7.62 x 51mm HK21A1 could be easily altered to chamber the 5.56 x 45mm cartridge by changing the barrel, the magazine and the bolt. Cyclic rate was about 800rds/min for both types of ammunition.

The HK21E was an improved HK21A1 with a burst-firing capability built into the trigger mechanism, an extended barrel casing, and a longer sight radius. HK21-type guns have also been made in Greece by EBO, under the designation EHK21A1 and in Portugal by Fábrica Militar de Braca de Prata, a division of Industrias Naciónais de Defesa de Portugal (Indep).

The 5.56mm HK MG43 is a new design, clearly owing much to the Belgian Minimi in layout, but has been provisionally adopted by the Bundeswehr as the MG4 to fill a gap between the LSW version of the G36 and the belt-feed MG3. The M43 is gas operated, locked by a rotating bolt, and can feed from boxes or belts selectively. It has a readily detachable barrel, ejects downwards, has a bipod, and can be fitted with Picatinny rails to receive a wide variety of optical and electro-optical sights.

Belgian Types

The leading contender for widespread adoption appears to be the FN-made Minimi, which caught the attention of the US Army – though a minority of its experts apparently favoured the CIS Ultimax – and was standardised in 1982 as the 5.56mm Squad Automatic Weapon M249 (*see US Designs, above*). It is an interesting design, feeding from box or belts. The basic 5.56mm US Navy Mk. 46 Minimi has served as the basis of a 7.62 x 51mm adaptation known as the Mk 48.

Soviet/Russian Types

The Soviet bloc approached machine-gun requirements in a different way from the West, largely due to the early adoption of the 7.62 x 39mm M43 intermediate cartridge. Soon after the appearance of the Kalashnikov assault rifle, development of a suitable 'squad automatic' or light support weapon commenced. The RPD appeared in 1952–3 and remained in production for thirty years with only minor modifications. Obsolescence in the Warsaw Pact countries then permitted countless thousands to be dispatched to terrorists, guerrillas and 'freedom fighters' throughout the Developing World.

The RPD was gas-operated, weighing only about 15.7lb empty, with a 100-round disintegrating-link belt carried in a detachable drum. Though reasonably reliable, its belt-lifting capabilities proved to be marginal in unfavourable conditions, and newer versions with non-reciprocating cocking handles could jam solid if attempts were made to cock them with the safety catch applied. In addition, the RPD lacked a detachable barrel and was incapable of sustained fire; this, and the comparatively poor long-range performance of its cartridge, compromised its effectiveness appreciably.

The RPD was replaced in Soviet service in the 1960s by the RPK, a 'machine rifle' derivative of the standard Kalashnikov. Like the RPD, the RPK lacked a detachable barrel and was similarly incapable of sustained fire. Its principal advantages were light weight – 12.9lb with a loaded 30-round box magazine, 15.7lb with the 75-round drum – and a bipod that enhanced accurate shooting. However, the excessive protrusion of the 40-round box magazine below the receiver must often have made covert shooting very difficult. Though top-mounted magazines such as the Bren type undeniably cause a blind spot to the front right of the firer, they also undoubtedly facilitate firing from cover.

The poor long-range performance of the 7.62mm intermediate cartridge has forced the ex-Warsaw Pact forces to retain the rimmed 7.62 x 54mm cartridge for sustained-fire weapons. The needs were satisfied by two comparatively old designs – the SGM and the RP-46 – until a competition between the Kalashnikov (PK) and Nikitin-Sokolov (NS) designs was resolved in favour of the former, which entered service in 1961 as a replacement for the SGM.

The PK took features from many of its predecessors: the rotating-bolt lock came from the Kalashnikov rifle, part of the feed system was taken from the SGM and the Czech vz/52 light machine-gun, and inspiration for the trigger mechanism was provided by the RPD. Made largely of stampings and pressings to simplify production, the first version weighed about 19.8lb (9kg). The feed belt was originally a single 250-round strip, but is now made in 25-round sections and an 'assault magazine' –

little more than a box holding 100 rounds – can be attached beneath the receiver when required.

Dating from the mid-1960s, the PKM was an improved version of the PK, with a light plain-surface barrel, a stamped feed cover and a hinged shoulder plate on the heel of the butt. The PKT and PKMT were tank guns, fired by solenoids; the PKMB was a vehicle gun, with distinctive spade grips and a 'butterfly trigger' on the backplate; and the PKMS was a medium-support version of the PK mounted on Samozhenkov or Stepanov tripods. In addition, M80 copies of the PKM were made in Yugoslavia (now Serbia) by Zavodi Crvena Zastava of Kragujevač. The M80 has a solid butt, instead of the cutaway pattern preferred by the Soviets and the Russians, and may mount 3x ONS-1 optical or 5x PN80 passive night sights.

The PK series fires rimmed ammunition from closed-pocket belts, inevitably complicating the feed system, though the guns have built a reputation for reliability matched only by the MAG.

Czech Types

The success of the PK series has rather overshadowed other achievements in the Soviet bloc. The Czech firearms industry, for example, was allowed a measure of autonomy, resulting in several distinctive machine-gun designs. The interesting vz/52 light machine-gun offered convertible belt/box feed, with the trigger doubling as fire-selector, but was too complicated for its own good. Performance in dust and mud, particularly, was very poor: rather surprising, considering the achievements of the Holek brothers and their collaborators prior to 1939, when they had designed the precursors of the Bren Gun. The vz/59 machine-gun was a simplification of the vz/52, offering better performance but is rarely encountered except in the hands of some guerrilla forces. There was also a vz/68, alternatively known as Nachot, but this again is rarely seen in the West.

The Far East

In spite of ever-increasing technological prowess, developments in the Far East have been few and far between, though the Japanese introduced an efficient (if somewhat complicated) belt-fed general-purpose machine-gun known as the Type 62. The most impressive design has been the CIS Ultimax, made in Singapore, which attracted the interest of many special forces. The Ultimax 100 Mk 2 and Mk 3 (the latter with quick-detachable barrel) were remarkable developments, among the lightest in their class, weighing, with a loaded 100-round drum magazine, a mere 14.3lb. Empty, the guns weighed just 10.5lb with the bipod. The gentle recoil characteristics even permitted single-hand firing in the manner of a large pistol . . . if the firer's arm was strong enough.

Many independent trials showed that the Ultimax jammed very rarely, though early semi-disposable nylon-reinforced plastic 100-round spring-feed magazines were troublesome. However, CIS (now STK) does not have the influence of large gunmaking businesses such as FN Herstal or Heckler & Koch, and the Ultimax has never been purchased in quantity by a major army – even though some US Army observers of the trials that led to the standardisation of the M49 Squad Automatic Weapon (a modified Belgian Minimi) are said to have favoured the Singaporean design.

Grenade Launchers

The simplest way of firing grenades from military rifles has always been to add a discharger cup to the muzzle. Though this type of grenade has been used for many years, its special blank ammunition complicates logistics and courts the potentially disastrous use of ball cartridges by mistake. In the 1960s, however, the Belgian Mecar company developed and patented a 'universal bullet trap' allowing conventional ball ammunition to be used in safety.

The Mecar-BTU device trapped the bullet in the grenade-tail, using the energy of the ball-cartridge propellant to project the grenades. The system would handle virtually any modern military round (including 7.62 x 39mm M43 Russian,

7.62 x 51mm NATO and 5.56 x 45mm M193 or SS109) assuming that the rifle had an external flash-suppressor diameter of 22mm. This has been standardised on NATO guns, initially largely by agreement among the manufacturers themselves, and so the utility of the Mecar-BTU ammunition is immediately apparent.* Most of the grenades of this type seen in 2004 prove to have been made by IMI in Israel, though they may bear a variety of promoters' marks.

Though the versatility of the shotgun and the introduction of lightweight machine-guns to provide additional fire support has often weakened the case for specialised grenade-launchers, this has not prevented the development of a variety of differing designs. These can usually be classed in two groups: rifle-mounted launchers, which are usually single-shot designs firing low-velocity ammunition, and the automatic launchers – firing high-velocity rounds – that are intended for close-range fire-support roles. The recent enthusiasm for high-explosive airburst fragmentation grenades, for use with the XM29 OCIW and similar weapons, must be tempered by the developmental difficulties involved in accurately ranging then predicting the burst of individual munitions. Though the developers are confident that the performance of the ballistic computers in the guns and 'smart' fuzes will answer their critics, the margins of error are very fine. It remains to be seen how useful *individual* weapons of this type will be in combat conditions . . .

The independent hand-held launchers, typified by the obsolescent single-shot US M79 or the Heckler & Koch HK69A1, popular though they were with the soldiers, gave way to lightweight launchers fitted to the guns – usually under (or replacing) the standard fore-end. The M79 weighed about 6lb (2.72kg), which was often considered to be too much to carry in addition to an M16 and two types of ammunition.

---

* The muzzle diameter of the M16 series, however, has tended to be nearer 21mm and the grenades did not fit sufficiently tightly for optimal performance. This problem was cured by fitting a special clip between the suppressor and the rifle barrel.

US Special Forces came to rely on the M203 40mm launcher, developed by AAI and adopted in August 1969. By 1 January 2000, more than 300,000 of these had been made, including a few 'product improved' or PI examples produced in the mid-1990s before budgetary restrictions intervened.* The single-shot M203 was comparatively light, adding about 3lb (1.36kg) to the basic weight of the M16 rifle, though the latter's fore-end was discarded.

The M203 unit comprised a breech-loaded barrel assembly (revealed by sliding the barrel forward), together with its trigger system, a quadrant sight and a new M16 hand-guard, squarer than normal and pierced with holes. To load the M203, the catch on the left side of the barrel was depressed, the barrel unit was slid forward, and a fixed 40mm round could be inserted in the breech. The barrel was then replaced, the safety catch in the front of the trigger guard was pushed to its forward position, and the launcher trigger could be squeezed.

The M203 relied on a quadrant sight attached to the left side of the M16A1 carrying handle, and a ladder-type sight on the hand-guard that could be used for rapid firing in conjunction with the standard rifle front sight when precise shooting was not required. The maximum effective range of the combination was about 350 metres; minimum safe firing range was about 80 metres for the high-explosive grenades.

Colt is still offering the Colt Launcher System, which is little more than an M203 fitted into the M16 or M4 stock. This produces a single-shot 'standalone' gun weighing 6.5lb/2.95kg (M16 stock) or 6.1lb/2.77kg (M4)

British police and Special Forces have made limited use of the electrically-fired Grenade Discharger L1A1 – recognizable by its FAL-like pistol grip – which can project grenades to 100 metres, though the Special Forces have always preferred the M16A1/M203 combination. As a safety feature, the safety button protruding beneath the action immediately behind the

* There were two M203 PI patterns: one with a 12in (305mm) barrel and the other with a 9in (229mm) barrel.

L1A1 discharger cup must be depressed with one hand while the other squeezes the trigger. The 1.5in Webley-Schermuly and the 37mm ARWEN have also been used to project smoke, CS gas and baton rounds for anti-riot purposes.

Heckler & Koch, with typical inventiveness, have made a number of grenade-launching systems, including the 40mm Granatpistole (Gr.P.) and a special barrel insert/discharger cup conversion for the P2A1 signal pistol. The Granatpistole and the similar MZP-1 (with a smaller 100m sight) were special single-shot launchers firing standard US 40mm ammunition. The Gr.P. was operated by pressing down on the locking latch on the left side of the standing breech, and tilting the barrel downward to allow insertion of a cartridge. The breech was then pushed shut until the locking latch engaged its grooves; the hammer was thumb-cocked, the radial-lever safety catch was rotated downward to 'F', and the Granatpistole could be fired. A large-leaf ladder sight on top of the breech was graduated from 150 to 350 metres in 50-metre increments, being used in conjunction with the muzzle sight. There was also an auxiliary back sight, shared with the MZP-1, with a standing block for 50m and a small pivoting leaf for 100m. The Granatpistole measured 28.9in overall, with the sliding tubular stock extended, and weighed 5.8lb with its sling.

The West German equivalent of the M16A1/M203 combination was the TGS system (a G3 or G41 fitted with the HK79 launcher), used in small numbers by the Bundeswehr and GSG-9. The grenade-launcher consisted of a pivoting barrel unit, combined with a new fore-end. To load, the latch under the breech was released and the rear end of the barrel dropped down under gravity. A 40mm grenade round was inserted and the barrel was closed until it could be caught by the latch. The bolt-type firing pin protruding from the HK79 ahead of the rifle magazine was pulled back, and, assuming the cross-bolt safety catch displayed red, the trigger on the mid-point on the left side of the fore-end (immediately below the cocking handle) could fire the gun. An additional ladder sight, graduated 50–200 metres in 50-metre increments, lay on the receiver immediately ahead of the standard rifle back sight.

The HK79 added about 1.5kg to the standard rifle, the G3-TGS weighing about 5.5kg and the G41-TGS 5.35kg. The current G36 can be fitted with the 40mm AG-36 grenade launcher, which attaches beneath the fore-end and has its own pistol grip and trigger. Its breech opens sideways, which experience in Kosovo and elsewhere showed was better than the vertically-dropping breech of the HK79. The AG36 will fit many NATO-standard rifles without alteration, including the G36, G41, L85, M16, M4, C7 and C8.

Other fore-end type launchers include the Soviet/Russian GP-25, also listed as the BG-15, which was introduced about 1980 and fires 40mm low-velocity ammunition. It will fit most Kalashnikov rifles, and many of the copies made outside the USSR or Russia. The GP-95 is a short-barrelled version developed for the A-91 submachine-gun, accepting a reduction in effective range (about 75m instead of 100m) in return for ultra-compact dimensions. The BS-1 is a silent launcher, firing special 30mm low-velocity grenades with the assistance of a 7.62mm blank, fed from a box magazine in the pistol grip attached to the fore-end of the silenced AK-74UB.

The Polish Army uses the Pallad, chambered for a different 40mm low-velocity cartridge, the 40-GL is a Singapore-made pattern with a side-swinging breech; both can also be obtained in 'standalone' form, with additional butts and sights. There have also been several successful attempts to develop disposable grenade launchers (DGLs) which promise to be simpler, cheaper, and equally suitable for rifle-mounting.

Several multi-shot launchers have been made, including the comparatively new Russian 43mm GM-94, a large-bore derivative of the slide-action RM-93 shotgun. Distinguished by an operating slide that is pushed forward before pulling it back – the opposite of normal practice – the gun fires special low-velocity grenades from a bulky 4-round tube magazine. The GM-94 weighs about 10.6lb (4.8kg) and has an effective range of about 100 metres.

The US armed forces have used an automatic 40mm grenade-launcher, developed by the US Naval Ordnance Station in Louisville, Kentucky and introduced for riverine patrols in Vietnam in January 1968 as the Mark 19 Model 0. The Model 1 was approved in 1971, earlier launchers being upgraded, but the Model 2 was a failure and the Model 3 did not appear until the 1980s. By the beginning of 2000, about 21,000 launchers had been supplied to the US armed forces by Saco Defense of Saco, Maine. They could be mounted on the M3 Tripod, the M31C or M14 pedestals, the Mk 16 Stand or ring mounts. Belts of 32 or 48 high-velocity 40mm rounds were fired automatically, using advanced-primer-actuation to restrict recoil. The Mk 19 Model 3 weighs 77.8lb (35.3kg) without its mount and can fire a selection of high-explosive, dual-purpose anti-tank/anti-personnel grenades with an effective range of 200–250 yards. The most recent approval for service with the US Navy SEALs is the Mark 27, the 40mm Striker/CG-40 high-velocity launcher made by a combine of Saab and General Dynamics.

The Russians have also used a comparable automatic launcher, the 30mm medium-velocity AGS-17 Plamya ('Flame'), which belt-fed 29 rounds using blowback principles. The gun had a 2.7x optical sight, and an effective range of 140 metres. Known as the AG-17A on helicopter mounts, it has also been offered in a four-gun laser-ranging combination designated 6S5 Mius. The original launcher was superseded after 1994 by the AGS-30, which is much simpler and weighs merely 35.2lb (16kg) compared with 68.3lb (31kg) for the AGS-17.

Copies of the AGS-17 have been made in China, but the indigenous W-87 pattern (35mm medium velocity ammunition) was preferred. This could be fitted to either a purpose-designed tripod or, with a suitable adaptor, the tripod of the PK machine-gun. The gun had a wooden butt and pistol grip, weighed about 14kg and could feed from a 6- or 12-round drum. The QLZ-87 is a modernised version, with a longer barrel and an additional 15-round drum magazine that will not fit the feed-way of the W-87. Effective range is about 210m.

Elsewhere, Heckler & Koch makes the GMG or Granate-Maschinengewehr, an advanced-primer-ignition blowback weapon with reversible feed, mounted on a lightweight tripod. The receiver is a sturdy aluminium-alloy extrusion and there are several independent safety features, including a bolt lock and an automatic firing-pin block. The gun is 46.5in (1,180mm) long and weighs 64lb (29kg) without its Norwegian made cradle and tripod, which add 57lb (26kg). It fires 40 x 53mm grenades in a 32-round belt. Muzzle velocity is listed as 790ft/sec (241m/sec), giving a maximum range of 2,200 metres. At the time of writing, only Greece has purchased these launchers in quantity. A light-weight version, the GMW, weighs merely 57lb (25.9kg) and fits the NATO-standard tripod.

The 40AGL, made in Singapore, is another auto-loading high-velocity launcher, fed from a 50-round belt. It weighs about 33kg (41kg on the 'soft mount') and has an effective range of 200m. The 40mm South African Milkor MGL has even been copied in Croatia.

Chapter 12

Heavy Support Weapons

The classic sustained-fire guns have been the Maxim, Vickers and Browning designs, few of which have much relevance in the modern army. However, the Australian and other armies have successfully converted some 0.30in Brownings to 7.62mm NATO and, as the gun is strong and reliable, there may still be life in the design; the principal goal of all armies is efficiency, after all, and this can sometimes still be fulfilled by supposedly obsolescent guns. This is particularly true of the heavy support machine-guns, discarded by most theorists in the 1960s but subsequently found to be indispensable in Vietnam, the Arab-Israeli Wars, the South Atlantic and Iraq.

In April 1918, General Pershing, commander of the American Expeditionary Force in France, called for a machine-gun as powerful as the German 13mm-calibre M1918 anti-tank rifle. Frankford Arsenal eventually produced a 0.50in cartridge, simply by scaling-up the 0.30-06, and a water-cooled heavy machine-gun was standardised in 1921. The first air-cooled gun, developed at the request of the Cavalry Board, was adopted in 1933 as the Caliber .50 Browning Machine Gun, Heavy Barrel, M2. From 1938, the length of the barrel was increased from 36in to 45in, slowing the cyclic rate and improving accuracy.

The M2 HB remains the preferred heavy machine-gun of the US armed forces, and is likely to remain in service for some time. It seems unlikely that an ultimate replacement (XM307) will reach service for some years, and even the XM312 machine-gun is still in the experimental stage and will not reach service in numbers until 2006–7. Saco Defense is at present the only accredited US manufacturer of the M2, the current specifications being settled in 1978. The guns retain the cumbersome barrel change system, however, and the sight radius is too short to allow accurate fire. All 0.50in-calibre Brownings have convertible feed, but almost all are set to feed from the left when mounted on the standard M2 tripod. M63 anti-aircraft mounts and M31 pedestals have also been issued, together with a range of electro-optical, thermal-imaging and laser-designator sights. The XM213 was a flexible-mount version of the M2 derived from the AN-M2 aircraft gun, and the XM218 was developed specifically for the CH-47 helicopter.

Promoted by Saco Defense, the Fifty/.50 is a development of the basic M2 HB with a new all-welded receiver, a modified charging system and a detachable carrying handle attached to the barrel-support sleeve. The new cold-forged barrel, with an integral flash suppressor, can be exchanged merely by rotating the 'T'-handle and pulling it forward from the barrel-support sleeve – avoiding the headspacing problems common with standard M2 guns. The cyclic rate can be varied between 500 and 750rds/min, and the spade grips on the backplate are angled to improve control.

The Fifty/.50 weighs about 55lb (25kg), saving about 35 per cent of the weight of the standard M2 HB even though more than 70 per cent of the components are shared by the two guns.

The 0.50in-calibre Browning has also been made, most successfully, by Fabrique Nationale d'Armes de Guerre and its successor, FN Herstal; it is also currently being made in Britain by Manroy Engineering. The earliest FN-made guns were practically identical to their American prototypes, but these were replaced in the 1980s by the M2 HB-QCB, with a quick-change barrel. To achieve the quick-change, the charging handle is pulled back to its rearmost position, the carrying handle can then be rotated to disengage the locking lug, and the barrel can be pulled forward from the barrel-support sleeve. Original M2 HB machine-guns can be altered with a special upgrade kit, containing a new barrel, a barrel extension, a breech lock, a shim for the barrel-support sleeve, the barrel-support sleeve itself, and a new accelerator which effectively increases the cyclic rate.

The standard mount is the US M3 tripod – allowing 45-degree traverse, a maximum elevation of 5.6 degrees, and a depression of 14 degrees – but SG 127 pedestal and RM 127 ring mounts can be obtained for use in helicopter gunship doorways or on light warships. FN has also developed a 15mm-calibre derivative of the Browning, beginning in the 1990s, but this gun has yet to displace the venerable 0.50in guns in general service.

Mindful of the great age of the Browning, despite its outstanding qualities, the US authorities decided to seek a replacement in the form of the OCSW (Objective Company Support Weapon), the 25mm XM307. However, development of this fantastically sophisticated weapon, designed to fire high-explosive airburst ammunition under the control of a ballistic computer, has been protracted. Realising that the XM307 would not enter service until 2008 at the earliest, the 0.50in XM312 was developed as an expedient.

Similar to the XM307, but smaller and lacking the computer and special sights, the XM312 is still an extremely complicated gun. Though gas-operated, it relies on the bolt sliding within the barrel extension and the barrel extension sliding within the receiver or 'gun housing' to keep the recoil sensation to a minimum. This needlessly difficult solution to the problem of minimising dispersion of shots comes at an additional price: the cyclic rate of only 260rds/min is too low to be useful against anything other than ground targets, and it is hard to see how the XM312, which is expected to enter service in limited numbers in 2005, is an improvement over the M2 HB Browning in anything other than portability.

The Soviet Union, the Commonwealth of Independent States and now the Russians have relied in recent years on the 12.7mm NSV, not only in the heavy-support role but also as a tank and vehicle gun. However, much of the production of the NSV was undertaken in the Ukraine and has now been disrupted by the fragmentation of the Soviet Union. Consequently, the 12.7mm Kord, made in the ZID factory in Kovrov, has been accepted by the Russians as a replacement.

Though externally similar to its predecessor, the Kord relies on a displaced breech-block instead of a wedged bolt but retains the 50-round disintegrating-link belt of the NSV. The standard open sights can be supplemented by optical or electro-optical types, and a combined flash-suppressor/muzzle brake is usually fitted. The Kord is about 61in (1,550mm) long with the shoulder-stock in place, and weighs about 57lb (26kg) or 90lb (41kg) with the 6T7 tripod mount. Some guns are said to have been fitted with bipods and sent to Chechnya to serve as long-distance sniping rifles, but their performance in this role is compromised by the poor quality of the 12 x 108mm cartridges. Dispersion at 300 metres is said to be 16cm, but it is not clear whether this includes all of the rounds fired.

Chapter 13

Accessories

Sights

The earliest guns were crude, but by the fifteenth century the 'handgun' had begun to take the recognisable form of the modern long-arm. Some guns even had crude wooden half-stocks. The natural inclination of the shooter to look at the target along the barrel not only improved the precision with which shots were placed, but also inspired the search for better performance. As early as 1430, therefore, guns were being fitted with rudimentary sights. The most popular form seems to have been a blade or pointer at the muzzle (often simply filed in the flared barrel mouth) and a notch cut in the disc protecting the shooter from priming flash.

The idea of sights was soon universally established. By the sixteenth century, even the crude military matchlocks of the day were fitted with back sights in the form of a small block cut with a 'V' channel. The front sight remained a small blade, spigot or pin. The advent of rifling undoubtedly improved accuracy, though the use of patched or hammered balls slowed the rates of fire. The recruitment of clockmakers to make wheel-locks even added a craftsmanship dimension that had been absent from the crude matchlocks of earlier days. Soon, shooting competitions were being organised in central Europe and accuracy of a surprisingly high order was achieved.

However, the crudity of the coarse pin-and-notch sights soon turned thoughts to better designs. An appreciation of the curved trajectory of projectiles created multi-setting sights, often in the form of standing plates pierced with several sighting holes. 'Taking a bead' through the uppermost hole compensated for bullet-drop at extreme range, even though placing the sight-block well forward on the breech restricted the field of view. Folding-leaf sights made an early appearance, and tube-sights had become popular by the end of the sixteenth century. A sprung sight-block sliding along a stepped elevator had also been tried long before it attained great prominence in the USA in the nineteenth century.

By 1725, several attempts had been made to provide back sights which could be adjusted by screws either vertically ('elevation') or laterally ('drift' or 'windage'). These sights were generally made by instrument makers, however, and did not become common until improvements in machine-tool design were made early in the nineteenth century.

Back-sight design remained surprisingly static for many years, largely because the performance of guns remained unchanged. The first real improvement came with the adoption of the self-expanding ammunition that, virtually at a stroke, increased maximum effective range many times over.

The introduction of the rifle-musket in the middle of the nineteenth century showed that improved sights were vital to complement improved ammunition. Fixed standing-block sights were thereafter confined to short-range weapons such as hand-guns and carbines; on infantry rifles combinations of a stepped-base and a pivoting leaf or 'ladder' became customary. Though construction differed greatly in detail, sights of this pattern were popular for more than a hundred years.

An exception to the rule was the tangent sight, commonly found in Switzerland, Austria-Hungary, Italy, Germany and other parts of central Europe. The sight arm was elevated either by turning a knob or by sliding a control block horizontally along its bed. Devotees claimed that, despite excessive complication, tangent sights were stronger and more efficient than the ladder pattern.

Tangent and leaf-type back sights were comparatively delicate and expensive to make. When changes in warfare – particularly from colonial campaigns to trenchscape – suggested that refinement was superfluous, many were quick to introduce 'battle sights'. The intermediate cartridge, and an acceptance of a few hundred metres as the limit of accuracy in a military rifle, greatly helped the simplification process seen in some of today's designs. The drum sights favoured by Heckler & Koch, the US M16A2 rifle and the SIG 540/550 series, the rocking 'L' of the FNC, and the rotating multi-aperture of the AN-94 (Nikonov) are typical of the sturdiest. It is hard to see how they can be improved.

Front sights still generally consist of a simple ramp-mounted blade or barleycorn (an inverted 'V'), often protected by a sheet-steel cover. Luminous and coloured inserts or white beads have also often been in vogue. Though opinions change with equal rapidity, anything which can provide contrast against a dark background may be an asset as long as it neither distracts aim nor reflects light.

Open sights have inherent drawbacks, including coarse adjustment, poor regulation, and the relative widths of the front-sight blade/back-sight notch combination, which were often entirely inappropriate for accurate shooting at long range. These problems were exposed as maximum engagement ranges were stretched to 1,500 yards, then to 2,000 or more after the widespread distribution of small-bore cartridges loaded with smokeless propellant.

The so-called 'ghost ring' sights, often bracketed with collimators, are actually little more than large-size aperture sights – admittedly, sometimes created by image-projection – that facilitate snap-shooting by encouraging the eye to centre in the ring without unreasonably restricting the field of view.

Optical Sights

Telescopes had appeared early in the seventeenth century and become commonplace within a hundred years. Their value as a spotting aid had been established amongst artillerymen by the time of the Seven Years War (1756–63) and optically-sighted guns had proved useful during the American Civil War

(1861–5), but they were clearly unsuitable for the long arms of the day. A Briton, Major Davidson, patented an optical sight in Britain in 1862. One fitted to a 0.451in Whitworth cap-lock rifle was tested by the British Army in 1865, but not until the 1880s were trials undertaken with vigour. Mounted on Martini-Henry rifles, these sights were set far too high to be successful and had too little eye relief.

Though optical sights were used in earnest during the First World War in the hands of snipers, this was generally seen as an expedient that was not to be perpetuated in peacetime. Consequently, after the fighting had ceased, most optically-sighted rifles were either discarded or stripped of their sights and returned to ordinary service. Not until the Second World War began was interest renewed. This was largely due to the large-scale use of snipers by the Red Army, which left an indelible impression on the Germans.

However, though large numbers of Mauser rifles were issued with the 1.5x Zf. 41 – a long-eye-relief design that attached to the back sight base – the goal was little more than hitting eye-slits of tanks or fortifications at comparatively close range. Only belatedly did the Germans attempt to issue 4x sights with long-range marksmanship in mind. By this time, the quality of German small-arms had declined, and the poor inherent accuracy of the auto-loading Zf.-Kar. 43 was soon seen to be incompatible with sniping duties.

The Russians had always seen marksmanship as an integral part of training, particularly among the Communist youth organisations, and had a huge trained cadre of snipers when the Germans invaded Russia in the summer of 1941. They were customarily armed with specially selected 91/30-type Mosin-Nagant rifles, production reaching 53,195 in 1942 alone. Attempts to issue the auto-loading SNT in addition in large numbers failed – even though nearly 50,000 were made in 1941–2 – largely because of poor-quality manufacture and the complexity of the rifle compared with the old bolt-action patterns.

In the 1950s the British Army was prepared to adopt a non-magnifying optical sight with the abortive EM-2 rifle, in the hope that sighting would be facilitated and performance greatly improved. Though the rifle was abandoned, the principle of general-issue optical sights has persisted in British service, with the widespread issue of the Sight, Unit, Infantry, Trilux (SUIT, subsequently known as SUSAT) for the L1A1 and the L85 series.

Thousands of words have been written about the selection of optical sights without resolving the controversy. In the final analysis, the choice is personal – and often dictated by finance. The British Army has accepted 4x sights as the best compromise of magnification and field-of-view, as larger magnifications greatly increase vibration due to body tremors. Some large-magnification binoculars – and, indeed, tank-gun sights – have been offered with electronic stabilisation, and it seems possible that something of this type would be beneficial to snipers.

Inspired by German experience during the Second World War with the Zf. 41 sight, a low-magnification pattern with extraordinarily long eye relief, the Austrian Bundesheer has promoted a fixed-focus 1.5x sight since the 1970s. Built into the carrying handle of the Steyr AUG, this is claimed to provide a good field of view, reduce body-tremor effects, and allow the firer to keep both eyes open.

The modern optical sight is usually a seamless tube, with a diameter of 25mm or 30mm, drawn from aluminium or sheet steel. It can be anodised, blacked, nickelled, chromed, or clad in rubberised armour. The barrel of the sight contains a series of lenses, a reticle, and a method of adjusting focus. Most modern lenses consist of several individual elements even though a cursory glance may suggest them to be a single unit. The element farthest from the shooter's eye, called the objective, forms the 'primary image' – which, but for the inclusion of a separate erector lens, would be inverted.

Optical sights normally magnify the image, but the final size may vary between a modest fifty per cent gain (1.5x) and a twenty-fold increase (20x). Size and weight vary greatly, but a typical 6 x 40 sight (with a fixed 6-fold magnification and an objective lens diameter of 40mm) is 12–13in (305–330mm) long and weighs 11–12oz (310–335gm).

Superior image brightness is obtained in sights with coated lenses, identifiable by their purple-blue or strawed colour. Coating is invaluable, as 30 per cent of incidental light may otherwise be lost in the journey through the lenses of an ordinary sight – partly in the glass, but mostly by reflection at the interfaces between air and glass. The best modern sights lose less than fifteen per cent of light in this way. Matt-black internal finish minimises reflection losses, though some light still bounces around the sight-tube. In extreme cases, the image may lack colour or display ghosting.

Fields of view can be enlarged by increasing the diameter of the eye-piece lens or shortening the eye relief (the distance the eye must lie behind the ocular lens to obtain the optimum image). Moving the eye nearer the eye-piece is hazardous, however, if powerful cartridges are used and the sight can be driven back into the unwary marksman's face. A 'wide-screen' image may be obtained from rectangular objective lenses; however, unless associated with a suitably enlarged eye-piece or reduced eye-relief, the claim may be a sham.

If the reticle cross-hairs wander over the target when the head is moved up and down, or from side to side, then the sight is said to be suffering from parallax. Most ordinary telescope sights are corrected for particular distances so that the crosshairs stay motionless on the target, independently of head movement, when aim is taken at this particular range; adjustable-parallax sights work efficiently if the firer can gauge range accurately, though their value is reduced by setting the corrector for, say, 130 yards when the target proves to be 200 yards away.

Problems associated with parallax are customarily exaggerated, as the phenomenon cannot occur when the eye, the centre of the reticle and the target-image all lie on the longitudinal axis of the sight. Attempts have even been made to include 'range-finding' features in telescope sights, particularly in military designs, though an appreciable degree of skill is required to use these sights to good advantage, particularly if cartridge loads are regularly changed.

Many reticle designs are available, among the most popular being conventional crosshairs, crosshairs-and-dot, duplex (a combination of thick and thin hairs), cross-on-circle, and vertical post. Illuminated reticles are particularly useful if the levels of brightness can be varied to suit prevailing conditions. They are most useful when shooting into dark ground, especially if the colour of the battery-lit cross-hairs can be altered.

The reticle of the current Heckler & Koch G36 is an interesting combination of features. It consists of a horizontal 'anti-cant' line with a short crosshair centred in a ring. This is used for 200 metres range, the intersections of the circle and the horizontal line being the 'lead mark' for targets at 200 metres that are moving from left to right at 7.5km/hr (walking pace). Two additional crosshairs lie immediately beneath the ring, virtually in touching distance; these are aiming marks for 600m and 800 metres, the lower intersection of the centre crosshair and the circle sufficing for 400. In the lower left side of the field, a short horizontal line beneath '8642' lies above four shorter lines *en echelon* – running downward like stairs. These are used to determine range (800, 600, 400 and 200 metres) by placing a man, assumed to be 1.75m tall, between the appropriate pair.

Fixed-power sights lost ground to variable-magnification patterns in the 1990s, though the pendulum has since swung back; simplicity, particularly in a military sight that must cope with harsh operating conditions, is a most desirable goal. The 3–9x patterns are among the most popular zoom sights, though a variety of others will also be encountered. Variable-power sights are generally heavier and potentially less durable than fixed-power rivals, but such tremendous strides have been made in manufacturing techniques in recent years that this reservation is not as important as it was twenty years ago.

Most of the inherent drawbacks arise from flaws in the lens, which are summarised in *Appendix Three*. Though defective seals can also be troublesome, it is virtually impossible to grind a single-element lens to avoid distortion and problems may still be encountered when multiple elements are used.

Image-Intensifiers

The development of compact image-intensifying systems has been among the most remarkable of the advances in sighting equipment in recent years, and the reduction in price to a point where they cost little more than a good-quality camera has greatly broadened distribution.

The first attempts to improve weapon sights relied on straightforward optical means, magnifying the image so that the target could be seen more clearly. Yet targets could not be engaged in darkness, however much the image was enlarged. Some of the best-made telescope sights were capable of improving performance in poor light, it was true, but the gains were limited by the performance of the firer's own eye.

These sights give the impression of being able to see in the dark, but it is important to understand the most basic operating principle. 'Light' is little more than a label for the visible portion of the electromagnetic radiation spectrum, which ranges from gamma rays at one end (where wavelength is measured in fractions of a nanometre, 'nm') to ultra-low frequency radio waves measuring several hundred kilometres at the other extreme.

The human eye is capable only of accepting electromagnetic radiation with a wavelength of 390–750nm; though vision varies among individuals, there is comparatively little difference in wavelength response. The eye allows the wavelengths within these limits to be seen in the form of colours, ranging from red (about 700nm), orange (615nm), yellow (585nm), green (530nm), blue (470nm) and violet (about 415nm).

Animals often have excellent night vision, which sometimes merely reflects much better light-gathering abilities but can also indicate an ability to see into near-ultraviolet (short wave) and near-infrared (long wave) spectra. Infrared radiation (extending from 700nm to 10^6nm) is simply 'light' that is invisible to our eyes; it can be focused and reflected and can be polarised in the same way as visible light. The near-infrared portion, 700–1,500nm, is customarily used in television controllers and infrared film, and most video cameras will detect the presence of infrared beams even though the eye does not. Infrared wavelengths up to about 2,000–2,400nm can be used by special cameras, and even longer wavelengths – emitted by 'hot' objects – can be used to create a thermal picture of an item merely by recording the differing emissions of electromagnetic radiation from its surface.

One of the first goals was to allow vehicles to move along unlit roads without headlights to betray their presence. The German vehicle-control system known as Fahrzeug-Gerät 1229, developed by the Forchungsanstalt der Deutschen Reichspost in collusion with Leitz of Wetzlar in the late 1930s, relied on a special converter to present the human eye with an otherwise unseen image by transforming radiation with wavelengths in the near-infrared part of the spectrum.

The night sky was known to contain enough radiation in the near-infrared band to create an image, but the primitiveness of the earliest converters, which were unable significantly to magnify this radiation, resulted in very poor images. The problems were initially solved by using infrared lamps to flood the target area, which greatly improved the converted image by providing more reflected light. Now generally known as the 'active' system, this had one potentially fatal drawback, as a suitably-equipped opponent could easily detect the presence of the infrared lamp. By using a passive detector relying simply on reflected light, he could observe without being seen.

Early in the Second World War, the Germans adapted their driving aid to serve as a rifle sight, the Zielgerät 1229 Vampir. Consisting of a 13cm-diameter transmitting lamp, the converter and a magnifying eyepiece lens in a telescope-like tube, and a separate electrical supply in the form of a battery pack, the Vampir device was used in conjunction with the Kar 98k,

Gew. 43, or MP. 43/Stg. 44. It could locate targets in poor light surprisingly well, but was exceedingly cumbersome; the power pack alone weighed 33lb (15kg).

By 1945 the US Army had introduced the SniperScope. This worked on the same basic principle as the Vampir, but provided the basis for an entirely self-contained passive device; improvements in technology had discarded the infrared floodlight and the battery compartment had been made small enough to be mounted on the sight body. Though the result was still heavy, awkward and difficult to handle, it was merely a short step away from the perfection made possible by solid-state electronics.

The greatest single advance made since the Second World War concerns the converter, which was soon developed to a point where it could enhance the image electronically. This gave far better resolution and allowed targets to be engaged confidently at greater distances than the earliest active systems had done. Most modern intensifier sights follow the same general pattern, though individual details vary greatly.

Intensifiers of the first generation may be considered as a television tube inserted in a telescope sight, between the objective and eyepiece lenses. Light from the target – natural or boosted by a floodlight – entered through the objective lens and was focussed on to the front element of a converter containing a photocathode, allowing a reconstructed image to be eventually presented to the firer's eye.

However, the success of image-intensifying sights has been due entirely to the perfection of the photocathode, which is essentially the inside of a window formed as part of a vacuum tube and owes its origins to the photocell and the photo-multiplier tubes (PMTs) which were developed for medical and scientific research. The first PMT was developed by the French Atomic Energy Commission (CEA) in 1953, then improved by the Philips LEP laboratories in Paris (1956). Production began in Brive in a factory which is now owned by the Photonis company. Many types of PMT have subsequently been offered by Photonis and various rival organisations; and some units have been copied in Russia.

Light radiation from an image is focussed on to the window by conventional lenses, causing electrons to be emitted from the light-sensitive layer. The electrons are then accelerated by a current – usually applied by a small battery – to strike a luminescent screen forming the inner surface of the rear window of the tube. The phosphor converts electrons back to light radiation, forming an image corresponding to the original (but much brighter). The reconstructed image is normally inverted, but another lens, the ocular, turns it upright before entering the eye.

The key to success was the degree of amplification, releasing as many electrons as possible for each initial photon strike. Though the cascade tubes of the first-generation sights were very bulky, the inclusion of additional intermediate amplification stages gave surprisingly good performance and 60,000-fold gains were not uncommon.

Though the term 'intensifier' is customarily used for any device of this type, a distinction should rightly be drawn between *image converters*, which 'convert' an image from the invisible part of the spectrum to an image that can be viewed by the human eye, and *image intensifiers*, which effectively concentrate an image in the visible spectrum that can be only dimly seen.

Converters and intensifiers have been made in several forms, normally identified as 'generations'. This sometimes gives a clue to their age, but each of the groups possesses merits of its own and first-generation patterns are still being made for specific purposes.

Dating from the mid-1960s, first-generation diodes rely on only a single DC current to accelerate electrons, resulting in excellent image resolution but only a moderate gain in image intensity.* They can handle images in which the contrast between the light and dark portions is comparatively large, are

---

* Usually in the order of 200–500lm/lm (lm = lumen, a measure of brightness per unit area).

said to have a 'wide dynamic range' and are comparatively interference-free ('low noise'). The tubes are focussed either by reducing the distance between the photocathode and phosphor screen to a minimum ('proximity diode') or by allowing an electron lens to focus the electrons emerging from the photocathode before they reach the luminescent screen ('inverter diode'). These inverter diodes return the image to its upright form without requiring an additional optical lens, but are far more clumsy than the proximity type.

Among the advantages of proximity diodes are the absence of geometric distortion, high resolution over the entire area of the photocathode, and true 1:1 or 'same size' image transfer. They are largely immune to electrical and electromagnetic interference, and can function as ultra-fast opto-electronic shutters in camera equipment.

The Rank Pullin Individual Weapon Sight (IWS) SS20, successfully used by the British Army in Northern Ireland, the Falkland Islands and elsewhere, typifies first-generation equipment. It was 18.8in (478mm) long, 5.5in (140mm) wide and weighs 6.1lb (2.8kg). Performance included the ability to identify a man-size target at 300m under starlight conditions and to act as a passive infrared detector at 500–600m. However, the great weight of the SS20 – and comparable equipment used elsewhere – added a considerable burden to soldiers armed with the 7.62mm L1A1 rifle; consequently, the SS20/AR-15 or SS20/M16 combination was customarily preferred.

The major drawbacks of these first-generation intensifier sights were expense, excessive size and the delicacy of the converter unit. Improvements in converters, which have now generally changed from cascade-type photocathodes to include fibre-optic micro-channel plates, have allowed intensifier sights to be reduced to surprisingly compact dimensions. Their performance remains much the same as that of their predecessors (perhaps limited by maximum attainable image gain) and the optical components remain largely unchanged, but a considerable reduction in manufacturing costs has been reflected in price.

Second-generation systems may also take proximity- or inverter-diode form. The major change lies in the interposition of a micro-channel plate (MCP), introduced in 1973, between the photocathode and the luminescent screen, enhancing not only the energy of individual electrons but also allowing them to multiply. Electrons from the photocathode pass through tiny holes in a conductive glass plate, rarely more than 10^{-7} mm in diameter. Secondary emissions occur as each electron strikes the sides of the hole; for each electron that enters, ten thousand may emerge. Image resolution and dynamic range suffer by comparison with the first-generation diodes, but luminous gain is far greater: 10,000lm/lm for a single MCP and as much as 10 million (10^7) for two MCPs in stacked configuration.

Typical of second-generation equipment is the Rank Pullin SS86 Crew-served Weapons Sight (CWS), used in conjunction with heavy machine-guns, recoilless guns and some types of vehicle armament. This is capable of 6x magnification, can focus down to 30m and has a view-field of about 6 degrees. The sight measures 14.4in (365mm) overall, has an objective lens diameter of 4.3in (110mm), and weighs about 5.1lb (2.3kg). Power is derived from batteries and the brightness of the illuminated reticle is varied automatically by scene luminescence; the presence of a main battle tank (MBT) can be detected under starlight conditions at 1,000m.

Third-generation diodes are proximity-focus patterns with micro-channel plates and special gallium arsenide photo-cathodes. These give a better luminous sensitivity (1,200µA/lm instead of 300µA/lm) than the bi-, tri- and multi-alkali photo-cathodes used in earlier generations. They are specifically intended for use in infrared and near-infrared spectra, and are unsuited to ultraviolet. Their sensitivity makes them susceptible to interference from heat ('thermal noise').

New fourth-generation converters, introduced in the USA by ITT Industries, embody improved manufacturing techniques in a search for more gain and greater resolution. The ITT MX10160B has a 18mm-diameter inversion cathode with a gallium arsenide 'filmless' photocathode bonded to glass; MCP current amplification; and an inverting fibre-optic phosphor screen. The converter is 1.45in (37mm) long, with an external diameter of 1.23in (31mm), and weighs about 4.5oz (128gm). The MX-10160B can be retro-fitted to AN/AVS-6 and AN/AVS-9 helmet sights, to Mini-N/SEAS observation sights, F7001A gunsights and many other intensifiers fitted with second- and third-generation converters.

A basic unit of measurement, the lux, is defined as the amount of illumination produced when 1 lumen is distributed evenly over an area of 1 square metre; or, alternatively, the illuminance on any point of a surface 1 metre from a point light source of 1 candela (1 international candle power). In practical terms, this is generally explained as the level of illumination achieved by good street lighting, or by a full moon on snow or desert sand. By comparison, dusk, with the true colours still largely visible, will increase illuminance by a factor of ten; full sunlight will increase it by 100,000 times or even a million-fold.

Most intensifier sights will black out under even 1-lux conditions unless suitable filters are used, as they are designed to perform under much less favourable conditions. Filtering needs to be excessive if the sights are to remain serviceable in sunlight, otherwise conventional optical equipment must be substituted. Some of the more sophisticated sights can vary the filtering level simply by adjusting the operating voltage, but others require filters to be adjusted manually.

Attempts have been made on night-vision goggles (for example the Oldelft HNV-1) to provide a satisfactory way of handling low-light and flash-light conditions simultaneously, often with the aid of holographic optical elements (HOEs). This is an area in which rapid advances seem certain to be made.

Intensifiers are at their best in conditions ranging from overcast starlight to full moonlight with light cloud cover. Full moonlight may bring excessive brightness and the beginning of black-out, whereas overcast starlight or unbroken cloud cover may reduce even a third-generation intensifier to impotence in shadowy woodland.

Once restricted to military service and government-funded security organisations, equipment of this type now lies within the grasp of much smaller clients. The Kite Night Sight, made by Pilkington Optronics for service in more than forty countries, is typical of the 1990s output. Equipped with second- or third-generation intensifier tubes, it offers 4x magnification, a view-field of 8° 30' and configurations suited to differing weapons. Two 1.5-volt AA batteries allow continuous use for up to 70 hours.

Kite is 10in (254mm) long, has a 2.9in (73mm) diameter objective lens and weighs about 2.65lb (1.2kg) with its batteries. It has a fixed or adjustable-diopter eyepiece with an eye relief of 1.2in (30mm) and can be focussed from 15m to infinity. The standard second-generation intensifier tube permits a standing-man target to be distinguished under starlight (0.001 lux) conditions out to 300 metres.

Diodes are made only by a handful of companies, including ITT in the USA, NEC in Japan, Photonis in France and Proxitronic (formerly Bosch-Fernseh) in Germany. Consequently, though there is a surprising variety of branded sighting equipment, the essence of their operation – the converter tube – is simply bought-in when required. In 2000, for example, Photonis was exporting to more than twenty-five countries. Products included the XX1080 first-generation converter, still preferred for vehicle-driver night-vision aids, alongside a variety of second-generation image-intensifier tubes (IITs), including the 50mm diameter XX1300 and the 25mm diameter XX2050. The latter was only 25mm long, or 40mm if the optional fibre-optic expander was requested. XX2050 converters of this type have been used in vehicle telescopes such as the AN/PVS-4, ANITVS-5 and ANNVS. They offer simple optics in a small and inexpensive package, which makes them attractive for large-scale use where ultimate sophistication is unnecessary.

Photonis also makes a variety of 18mm-diameter double

proximity tubes, which are commonly substituted in AN/AVS-6, AN/AVS-9, AN/PVS-5, -7A, -7B, -7C and -14 (AN/ANVIS) night-vision goggles. The original second-generation designs, introduced in 1974, have been replaced by the SuperGen (1985) and HyperGen (1997) versions. Image-intensifier tubes have also proved their value in cameras (still or video), allowing photography in otherwise hostile conditions.

Thermal-Imaging Systems

Similar to intensifiers in many respects, these rely on a different operating system – reconstructing images from tiny differences in thermal emissions. Even over the distances relevant to surveillance or military engagement, however, thermal emissions from potential targets are customarily absorbed or scattered by the atmosphere by the time they reach the firer. Fortunately, there are two principal wavelength windows, 3,000–5,000nm and 8,000–13,000nm, where thermal emissions penetrate the atmosphere efficiently. The sights can perform much better than those relying on infra-red spectra, but need to be cooled continuously (often relying on liquid nitrogen) and are usually bulky.

A typical device of this class, the Lasergage Hand Held Thermal Imaging System, can resolve temperature differentials as small as 1° C. Designed to operate in the 3–5 micron spectral band, it has a 0.75x magnification, a 21-degree viewfield, and measures approximately 27cm x 17cm x 17cm. A night-sight variant, the Lasergage LWS 1060, was claimed to be able to identify man-size targets in low light at ranges as great as 300m. Minimum focus was 25m, magnification was 3.5x, and field of view was about 8°. The sight could be adapted to fit a range of firearms; 10.4in (265mm) long, it had a 3in (75mm) diameter objective lens and weighed just 31.6oz (895gm).

Attempts have also been made to combine thermal-imaging and image intensification in the same sight, giving the ability to superimpose the infra-red and thermal-emission images to improve performance. Though work has now reportedly ceased, there may yet be development potential in multi-system sights of this type.

Designators

The basis of many modern targeting systems is a laser beam, though the details vary greatly from manufacturer to manufacturer. The principle of the laser has been known for many years, but the first commercially practicable system – based on rods of ruby – was not perfected until the early 1960s.

The name Laser is an acronym of *Light Amplified* by *Stimulated Emission* of *Radiation*. The basic principles involve exciting individual atoms with a beam of light to generate additional radiation in phase with the light beam, which is thus reinforced. The results can be magnified to produce a beam of coherent (single frequency) light of great power.

This system has been widely touted as the 'death ray' beloved by science fiction, though this technology has yet to be perfected. A more accessible benefit has been the development of continuous-line projectors used for alignment and surveying tasks. Lasers of this type, usually gas-discharge patterns, inspired the development of aiming projectors.

Some laser-designators operate in the visible spectrum – projecting a mark that can be seen by the firer and the target at all times – while others operate in the infra-red bands and require an additional detector in the form of a head-set. The visible lasers customarily rely on discharges from an excited helium-neon mixture, whereas infra-red designs may use carbon monoxide or even hydrogen cyanide.

A typical laser target indicator, made by Pilkington in the early 1990s, operated on 820nm wavelength. Powered by two small batteries and weighing just 12oz (340gm), it projected an infra-red dot to a maximum range of 500m, which, in conjunction with an image intensifier, greatly accelerated target acquisition.

The SIG LAS/TAC (Laser and Tactical Light) system, introduced in 1997, can be obtained for the P220, P226, P228 and P229 pistols in two light-projecting and three laser-projecting configurations. The impact-resistant modules are made of Teflon-coated aluminium alloy and sealed against water to a depth of 10 metres. The lights can use xenon bulbs of 24 and 45 lumens with 1.3in (33mm) reflectors, powered by lithium batteries (3V and 6V respectively), the larger version being about 5.1in (13cm) long with a weight of 6.8oz (193gm). Battery life is about one hour of continuous operation.

The intensity of the laser can be Super Power Point (635nm), Magnum Power Point (650nm) or Standard Point (675nm). An infra-red option (835nm) can be supplied for use in conjunction with night-vision goggles. The lasers have an emission rating of 5mW, a beam diameter of 0.2in (5.2mm) at 23m, and are powered by 3-volt lithium batteries giving a life of eighteen hours. The modules are 3.6in (91mm) long and weigh about 5.6oz (160gm).

The head-sets used with infra-red lasers are usually equipped with monocular intensifier-type detector tubes, often disguised with binocular eyepieces. These allow the firer to look away from the target whenever necessary, instead of demanding continuous observation of the target. When a target is selected, relying on the head-set to create the illusion of daylight under starlit conditions, the designator is activated and an aiming mark appears on the target. Assuming the sights are properly adjusted for range, the shot will strike the aiming mark without requiring undue concentration on the part of the firer.

Designator systems undoubtedly improve shooting skills, particularly snap-shooting, but the designator unit must be activated to obtain a sighting mark and proceeding in too leisurely a fashion can encourage counter-sniping. Restrictions are also placed on peripheral vision by head-set construction.

Collimators and Associated Sights

Though image-intensifying sights have made tremendous progress in recent years, they are still expensive compared with optical sights. Beginning with the late, lamented Singlepoint, introduced in 1968, attempts have been made to enhance snap-shooting with sighting equipment which relies on an optical illusion. These collimator sights combine an aiming mark within the sight body, illuminated either by ambient light or by electrical batteries, with the ability of the firer's binocular eyesight to accommodate the reflected aiming mark and a view of the target simultaneously.

Singlepoint appeared to be projecting a red dot onto the target and undoubtedly facilitated rapid fire, but few of these sights, even those with powered reticles, have proved to be of much use in darkness. Ambient-light reflectors are also generally ineffective under dark-to-light conditions.

The collimator sights lost favour for much of the early 1990s, even though the South African Armson OES (Occluded Eye Sight), with a tritium-illuminated reticle, had been touted with surprising vigour since its introduction in 1981. However, FN Herstal is currently promoting a powered sight of this general class on its P-90 Individual Weapon and the Trijicon Advanced Combat Optical Gunsight (ACOG) Reflex Sight is being tested by the US Army for compatibility with the Close Combat Soldier Enhancement Program. The intensity of the amber aiming dot of the ACOG Reflex unit adjusts automatically to surrounding light levels, being powered by a combination of ambient light and a tritium lamp.

Another major advance is the Bushnell HOLOsight, which makes use of the ability of a laser-generated hologram to produce virtually any type of two- or three-dimensional reticle. The HOLOsight uses a microprocessor to control auto shut-down mode and the user-selectable brightness/start-up settings. One of the most interesting features is the three-dimensional 'Rising Dot', which gives the illusion of projecting a line from the gun-barrel to end in a dot beneath a half-circle reticle.

Silencers

The first effective silencer was the work of Hiram Percy Maxim, son of the inventor of the machine-gun. After an abortive 1908 pattern, with a odd-looking silencer housing that was orientated vertically, Maxim progressed to the familiar axial-cylinder design in 1910. The silencers made for the Maxim Silent Firearms Company by Colt were not only successful – thousands were sold prior to the implementation of the 1934 US Gun Control Act – but also surprisingly efficient, even in tests against some of the leading designs of the modern era.

Maxim relied on a bank of serpentine spring-steel baffles with an axial hole, slightly larger than the bore diameter. His intention was to trap the propellant gas following the projectile, allow it to expand within the closed cylindrical silencer body, and then vent it harmlessly (and silently) to the atmosphere. This was not only the first of many essentially similar designs, but also the inspiration for countless inventors, seeking to avoid patent litigation, to search for other methods of reducing the unmistakable noise of a cartridge being fired.

The American Expeditionary Force took Maxim silencers to Europe in 1917, intending to issue them with sniping rifles, but the trenches of the Western Front proved to be unsuitable for them. However, huge numbers of silencers (more accurately called 'sound suppressors') were sold commercially after the war had ended, often for use on 0.22in-calibre sporting guns being used for practice or recreational purposes in urban environments. The 1934 Gun Control Act, passed in the middle of the Great Depression, not only placed severe restrictions on the private ownership of machine-guns in the USA – a result of the mobsters' indiscriminate use of Thompson submachine-guns – but also, paradoxically, placed restrictions of almost equal severity on the silencers. This is said to have been intended to reduce the numbers of domestic animals that would be shot for food by the sharecroppers and others who were effectively starving to death in the dustbowl heart of America.

Like so much gun-related legislation, there is no real evidence that the licensing of silencers had any effect at all. Ironically, though the use of silencers is still strictly controlled in countries such as Britain and the USA, where they are often seen largely as assassins' tools, there are no such restrictions in France; consequently, inexpensive silencers, particularly the Silencieux Unique, are still being marketed in large numbers.

The ease with which silencers can be made has tempted many manufacturers to offer them with anything from submachine-guns to full-power rifles – including 0.50in-calibre sniping rifles! The 0.50in designs are very large, the SIOPTS SO-50 fitted to the Barrett M50 rifle, for example, is 20in (51cm) long, has a diameter of 2in (5cm), and weighs about 4.5lb (2.05kg).

However, the comparative ineffectiveness of silencers when used with supersonic ammunition – though 'noise suppressors' have appeared on guns such as the M16A1, they are not always entirely successful – has persuaded some special forces to turn to silenced submachine-guns (*see below*), where the penalties of weight and size are not as severe as they can be with a pistol.

Though the reduction in noise levels can vary, silencers also often double as effective flash-suppressors and recoil reducers. This can be a great asset in some environments, such as oil refineries or chemical plants, where the flash of propellant burning at the muzzle could have catastrophic consequences. These situations also benefit from ammunition loaded with flashless propellant and an appreciation that some guns may experience flashes at the ejection port as well as the muzzle.

Fitting a silencer to a gun-muzzle can also affect the aim-point, and thus the adjustment of the sights. This phenomenon has been known for many years, owing to the comparable effects of adding a bayonet. Trials undertaken in Britain in the early twentieth century showed that the Russian 1891-pattern socket bayonet moved the point of impact nearly two feet downwards at 200 yards. Trials undertaken in Finland ninety years later, with a 7.62mm Valmet m/62 assault rifle, confirmed that, unless they were an integral part of the structure of the gun, silencers also altered the mean point of impact. Even the standard flash eliminator/bayonet mount of the m/62, which weighed 100gm, moved the point of impact 65mm downward and to the right. When multi-baffle silencers were substituted, the effect was to move the impact point first almost directly to the right, and then up and to the right until, with the TX-8 silencer (370gm), it was 266mm away from the 'clean barrel' mark.

The changes are presumed to arise from the effect on barrel harmonics of variable muzzle weights. They also seemed to have a beneficial effect on accuracy, as the diameter of the 'no weight' control group, 2.94in at 98 yards (90m), was steadily reduced by the addition of extra mass at the muzzle. However, relative accuracy is impossible to analyse satisfactorily on the basis of a single five-shot group fired at each stage.

Among the greatest advances in silencer technology in recent years has been the introduction of the 'wet' or lubricated silencer, which has greatly reduced the size of the expansion chamber without compromising the reduction in noise levels. The drawback to these units is the need for constant re-lubrication, which, however, can be obtained with a variety of liquids.*

Military-type silencers are now being made in the USA by a group of specialist engineering companies, including Arms Tech of Phoenix, Arizona; Ciener of Cape Canaveral, Florida; Knight's Armament Company of Vero Beach, Florida; LaFrance Specialties of San Diego, California; and SIOPTS of Newport News, Virginia. In Europe, Brüggen & Thomet of Spiez, Switzerland, and Asesepänliike Br-Tuote Ky of Joensuu, Finland, both make silencers that are suitable for CTW use.

Silent Pistols

When the Second World War began, the question of how best to kill silently arose. Silencers were seen as an obvious answer, particularly when used in conjunction with ammunition that

* A drawback of the 'wet' system is that a lubricant mist is customarily ejected from the silencing chamber, and there is also the potential for leaks backward through the joint between the muzzle and the silencer itself. This presents comparatively little problem with water, but could be less acceptable with any perfumed lubricant . . . or urine. See Alan C. Paulson, *Silencer History and Performance*, Vol. 1 (1996), pp. 192–3, for a humorous (if authoritative) treatment of a test.

had been loaded to give subsonic velocity. This avoided the supersonic crack as the projectile transcends the sound barrier (about 1,100ft/sec at sea level), which is reasonably easy to trace. A subsonic report has no such signature, and is notoriously difficult to pinpoint. Though attempts were made to silence infantry rifles, these were rarely used for clandestine purposes; much more successful, numerically and in terms of results, were the silenced pistols and submachine-guns.

Probably the best known of the Allied guns was the 0.22in LR rimfire High Standard HD-MS pistol, which relied on a ported barrel inside a large cylindrical expansion chamber filled with mesh-like baffles made of tinned bronze. The High Standard was introduced during the Second World War, but remained in service for many years. One was retrieved from the wreck of the U-2 spy plane flown by Gary Powers, which was downed over the USSR in 1960; others were used by the CIA, Navy SEALs and US Special Forces in Vietnam. High Standards were carried by Delta Force personnel on the disastrous mission to rescue US hostages in Iran, and are still being held in reserve. Though their silencer technology is primitive, tests have shown that the noise reduction is surprisingly effectual.

However, the most successful (if unsung) 'eliminator' was probably the British Welrod pistol. Designed specifically as a silent pistol, made in 9mm (Mark 1) and 0.32in Auto/7.65mm ACP (Mark 2), this manually-operated gun was large, cumbersome, and difficult to handle. The 9mm gun was about 14.4in long and weighed about 2lb 10oz; it had a 6-round magazine and was designed to fire specially loaded subsonic cartridges that generated a muzzle velocity of about 1,000ft/sec. The silencer consisted of a perforated barrel, a cylindrical expansion chamber, and two (9mm guns) or three (0.32in version) sub-bore diameter baffles. The projectile 'wiped' through the baffles before emerging from the muzzle, leaving the expanded gases to leak to the atmosphere. Firers described the noise as a short muffled crack followed by a short hissing noise as residual gas left the muzzle. Tests have shown that the silencer, at least when the baffles were new, reduced the 9mm firing-signature from about 150 dB to 115 dB.

The Welrod was designed by the SOE staff stationed in Welwyn, Hertfordshire, and made by BSA Guns in Birmingham. At least a thousand were ordered, but the actual quantity made during the Second World War has never been satisfactorily determined. However, it was large enough to have had a perceptible influence on the secret war. Used by the SOE, the OSS and resistors in occupied Europe, the Welrod survived to be used in Korea, Northern Ireland and Vietnam. One 9mm Mk 2 gun displayed in the national museum of Denmark, in Copenhagen, belonged to Captain Ole Geisler of the Holger Danske resistance group. Trained by SOE in Britain, Geisler is credited with killing more than twenty German military and administrative personnel in 1944–5. Writing in *The Small Arms Review* in 1999, David Truby reported the reminiscences of British Army officer and SOE operative officer Len Jameson:

> We'd given a Welrod to one of our most loyal boys and he smuggled it into the inn [in German-occupied France] at great risk to himself . . . A bunch of his mates crowded around talking, then bellied up to the bar, surrounding the mouthy mark we were hitting. The lad stuck the Welrod right into the collaborator's chest and put a round through his heart . . . nobody heard a sound. They propped the body into a chair and left by ones and twos during the next ten minutes . . . [the Germans] didn't notice anything was wrong for hours.*

The chilling feature of the Welrod was that it was specifically designed to be used at close range. The operating manual laconically recorded the recommended range as '5–7 yards', and suggested that the ideal situation was to touch the target with the tip of the silencer.

The small size and relatively low power of service handguns

* J. David Truby, 'The UGLIEST 60 Year Old Gun I Ever Saw', in *The Small Arms Review*, Vol. 2, No. 4 (January 1999), p. 38.

generally prevent them being used in conjunction with special equipment, and comparatively little development of silencers was undertaken immediately after the end of the Second World War. However, work did commence in the later 1950s, and Walther, to name one gunmaker, developed a successful multi-baffle design intended for use on the P. 38, PP/PPK series and similar pistols.

When the US armed forces became embroiled in the fighting in Vietnam, they began to encounter 'assassination pistols', produced by the Chinese, with their expansion chambers integral with the barrel/receiver group. The Type 64 could operate as a conventional semi-automatic or fire single shots, with the slide locked shut to reduce the amount of mechanical noise generated in the normal auto-loading action. The gun fired a 7.65 x 17mm cartridge similar to the 7.65mm Browning, and had a large-diameter barrel casing containing a perforated baffle-type silencer.

The Type 67 was similar, but had an improved tubular silencer extending from the muzzle. The North Koreans also made a silenced pistol, a variant of the standard Type 64 (a copy of the 1900-model Browning blowback!), but this was much more conventional than the Chinese weapons and could only fire semi-automatically.

Impressed by the performance of the Chinese pistols, the US Special Forces demanded silenced weapons of their own, the Navy – particularly vocal – promoting development of a silenced 9mm automatic pistol for its SEAL teams. A representative Walther silencer was purchased, and the Naval Ordnance Laboratory began work on a modified version that would suit US needs. The result was the WOX-1A, subsequently known (after modification) as the Silencer, Mark 3 Model 0, or 'Hush Puppy'.

The new silencer was intended to be used with a specially-modified Smith & Wesson M39 pistol, known during development as the WOX-13A, with a steel frame and a slide lock that could be engaged to prevent the slide recoiling when the gun fired and betraying the position of the firer by the mechanical noise of the reloading cycle. It is said that about 120 guns of this type were made, to be used with special low-velocity 9mm Mark 144 Model 0 cartridges. These were loaded with green-tipped bullets weighing 158 grains. However, the ammunition developed chamber pressures that were too high for the slide-lock system, and the guns began to fail after only a few hundred rounds had been fired. Smith & Wesson then supplied a modified gun with a 13-round magazine, which became the commercial Model 39 but was known to the US Navy as the 9mm Pistol, Mark 22 Model 0. Caps, plugs and special accessories allowed the assembly to be carried safely under water.

The silencer insert could fire thirty subsonic rounds or merely six standard supersonic rounds before needing replacement, largely because the polypropylene 'wipe'-type baffles began to wear out. The accessory kit issued with the pistol contained twenty-four special cartridges and a replacement silencer insert. The empty weight of the entire assembly was only 34oz, overall length being 12.8in.

The Hush Puppy was well-liked by the Navy SEALs and the other special forces who used it, but extraction problems persisted. Eventually, Reed Knight of Knight's Armament Company substituted a strengthened Beretta M9 pistol with a special slide-lock that pivoted beneath the frame ahead of the trigger. This proved to be much more durable than the Smith & Wesson. However, the introduction of heavyweight bullets in the 1980s strained even the modified Beretta to its limits. The 'Hush Puppy' eventually became the 'Snap-On', which has been used by the US Army and the USAF.

Very few purpose-built silenced pistols have been built in the West in recent years, reliance being placed instead on minor modifications of standard designs to accept 'add-on' suppressor units. This has not been true of the Soviet Union, where integrally silenced versions of the Stechkin and Makarov have been made in small numbers.

The PB, or silenced Makarov, was designed by technicians in the Tula small-arms factory. A large-diameter silencing chamber attached to the frame, the slide being adapted appropriately, and ports were drilled through the barrel into the bore. When the gun was fired, gas leaked through the ports into the silencer chamber, where its passage was interrupted by six annular layers of fine steel mesh. It then passed out into an auxiliary expansion chamber, filled with disc-like baffles, and then out through the end cap. Owing to the position of the shroud around the barrel, the return spring was moved into the grip behind the magazine well. The PB was about 12.2in (310mm) long and weighed about 32.5oz (920gm) without its magazine.

The APB, a different proposition, was a comparatively minor adaptation of the standard selective-fire Stechkin pistol (APS). This had been adjudged a failure in its intended role of sub-submachine-gun, but was large enough to be converted. The mechanism relied on a narrow annular chamber around the barrel, which received gas from the bleed-ports; when the bullet had passed out of the barrel, the gas flowed back into the bore and out through the baffle-type silencer attached to the muzzle. The barrel protruded from the slide to accept the 1.4in (36mm) diameter silencer unit, which was about 9.1in (230mm) long, and a rod-type shoulder-stock could be attached to the heel of the butt when needed.

A typical modern 'add-on' silencer, screwed to the muzzle of the FN Five-seveN pistol, is 8.5in (216mm) long with a diameter of 1.2in (31mm) and weighs about 5.9oz (168gm). It is claimed to reduce the signature of firing by 30dB with Sb193 ammunition.

Submachine-Guns

Silenced submachine-guns have been popular since the Second World War, when they were used by Commandos, SAS, OSS and SOE. In 1942, the OSS ordered a thousand 0.45in ACP M3 submachine-guns from High Standard, fitted with Bell Laboratories silencers. Surviving guns were issued to selected US airborne personnel on D-Day in June 1944. Ironically, a copy of the OSS silenced M3 in 9mm Parabellum (the Chinese Type 37) was used by North Vietnamese regular troops in night raids, intent on silencing US and ARVN guards before attacks began.

The silenced M3 was not particularly popular, the men preferring the British Sten Mk 2S which had been proven on commando and special forces missions.

The Sten Gun, crude but effective, was introduced in the early part of the Second World War when the situation in Britain was at its most hopeless. Consequently, the Sten was intended to be made by a broad range of subcontractors with no previous experience of small-arms components, and the quality was often very poor. However, the design was sound and performance proved to be better than expected. The construction of the barrel and barrel casing on the Mk 2 Sten (though not the simplified Mk 3) favoured the attachment of a silencer. Two regulation-issue units were provided, the earlier with six barrel ports, thirty flat baffles, and nine mesh disks between the first and last pair of baffles; and a second, later, pattern with two groups of barrel ports, eighteen conical baffles, and felt 'wipes' inside the muzzle cap. The Special Operations Executive developed its own form of silencer, which was effectively a tube-in-tube design filled with baffles.

The performance of the Sten silencers was surprisingly good, reducing the noise levels from about 160 dB to 135 dB in semi-automatic fire. They added considerably to the weight of the gun, and had a limited life, but they were among the best issued during the war. The biggest problem with the use of silencers and subsonic ammunition concerned the design of the Sten bolt, which was too heavy to operate satisfactorily with the reduced impulse. A lightweight bronze bolt was tried with some success, but the integral firing pins broke too easily and a steel bolt was substituted.

The silenced Sten gun was replaced by the silenced Sterling, which is still in British service. However, the L34A1 is appreciable longer than the silenced MP5 and is generally restricted to regular personnel. The CIA reputedly used a silenced version of the Swedish-made Carl Gustav (KP m/45B) in the 1960s, when efficient silenced submachine-guns were in short supply. This, too, was a conventional and comparatively clumsy gun.

The design of the Heckler & Koch MP5 SD1, however, benefits from the compact bolt system and also from the integral fore-end/silencer casing. The Ingram Model 10 may also be encountered with a 'noise suppressor' attached to the muzzle, but this adds about 545 grams to the laden weight as well as almost doubling overall length. The Ingram also customarily suffered from the shortness of the threaded portion of the muzzle, and the silencers were apt to work loose. If they drooped so that the central port in the baffles no longer aligned with the axis of the bore, the bullet struck the baffles (or even the end cap) and the silencer ceased to function effectively.

Rifles

The standard Soviet/Russian AK-74 can be fitted with a PBS-1 plug-and-baffle silencer, suitable for use with special subsonic heavy-bullet ammunition. Special sights must be also attached. More innovative is the AKS-74Y, a derivative of the basic rifle with an integral silencer casing around the barrel. The gas-tube has been shortened to account for lower power – the subsonic cartridge is used – and the front sight has been moved back to abut the shortened fore-end, accommodating the multi-diameter silencer casing. The AK-74UB is another shortened version, but chambers the special 7.62mm piston cartridges and lacks the bulky silencing attachments that characterise the other guns; its biggest failing is simply that it cannot accept standard 5.45 x 39mm rounds in an emergency. The AKS-74Y and AK-74UB may be encountered with a special single-shot bolt-action BS-1 silenced grenade launcher (*q.v.*) attached to an auxiliary pistol grip offset to the left beneath the fore-end. A magazine for the 7.62mm grenade-launcher blanks lies inside this pistol grip.

The Soviet Union introduced two essentially similar guns in the 1980s, chambered for a special 9 x 39mm round made by enlarging the neck of the standard 7.62mm M43 design to accept heavy bullets that promised an acceptable combination of effective range and stopping power at subsonic velocity. Designed by Serdyukov and Kraskov, working in TsNIITochmash in Klimovsk, the Silent Sniper Rifle (VSS) and the Silent Assault Rifle (ASS) have been used extensively by the Soviet and Russian Special Forces, and are said to be exceptionally effective.

They shared the same action, which was effectively a reduced-scale version of the Dragunov (SVD) sniper rifle with the additional ability to fire automatically. The guns weighed only 5.7–6.6lb (2.6–3kg) apiece with 10- or 20-round magazines, and had a maximum effective range of 400 metres. They had full-length silencer casings running from the breech to the muzzle; the VSS also had a fixed combination butt/pistol grip unit, whereas the ASS – usually fitted with the 20-round magazine – had a conventional pistol grip and a folding butt. A tangent-leaf back sight was fitted to the rear silencer casing, but the guns were usually encountered with either the PSO-1 optical or 1PN51 intensifier sight attached to a bracket on the left side of the receiver.

Piston Cartridges

An alternative method of suppressing the noise of firing was perfected in the USSR, where the first successful piston-cartridge was introduced with compact silenced pistols. The idea appears to have been patented in Britain as early as 1906, when S. Rogozea received protection for a muzzle-trap-and-sabot system specifically intended to reduce the noise of firing; it was resurrected in the USA in the 1960s as the 'Whisper' round, when an internal piston was used, but only the Soviet designers have succeeded in bridging the gap between theory and practice. When the guns are fired, a short cylindrical piston within the elongated cartridge case thrusts the projectile forward, but then locks into the neck to seal residual propellant gas inside the special thick-wall cartridge case.

The first gun to be introduced, in 1972, was the MSP. This was a break-open or 'tip barrel' pattern, operated by a lever on the rear left side of the breech, which held two long-bullet SP-3 rounds in a special clip. The MSP (which was apparently made only in small quantities) was an ultra-compact design, with a sequential firing system and a winter trigger that could be folded down beneath the trigger guard.

More impressive was the PSS, designed by Viktor Levcheno, which appeared in the late 1970s. This was a traditional blowback self-loading pistol in most respects, weighing 31oz (880gm), but was betrayed by an exceptionally broad grip to receive the detachable 6-round box magazine. Even though the flat-nosed bullet of the SP-4 piston cartridge was recessed, in the same way that ammunition for the 7.62mm 'gas-seal' Nagant revolver had been, the case was still 1.6in (41mm) long – much longer than conventional patterns such as the 9mm Parabellum (0.75in/19mm long). The PSS is claimed to have an effective range of fifty metres, and the bullet can pierce body armour or steel helmets at twenty metres.

The PSS has been used by Spetsnaz and other Soviet/Russian Special Forces alongside the NRS-2, which was originally developed in Klimovsk for paratroops. This combination knife-pistol has a simple rotating-bolt action built into the pommel and a barrel chambered for the 7.62mm SP-4 cartridge running the length of the hilt. The sheath has a variety of tools, including an efficient wire-cutter, and the whole unit can be attached to a special two-strap leg harness.

The ammunition presumably has a short effective range, but performance details are lacking. A similar 6mm 'Hazmat' round has been developed in the USA by Arms Tech, but is currently restricted to military and government-agency sales.

Appendix 1

Ammunition

The efficiency of small-arms ammunition has been the subject of many reports, opinions and claims. It is probably true to say that it has excited greater controversy than practically any other single facet of small-arms technology, and also that few of the rules have yet been agreed.

The principal problem is that few authorities, owing largely to use of differing criteria, have been able to agree basic parameters. Even within the confines of NATO, national preference and national prejudice have often played their parts to the full. Thus the British Army initially refused to accept the 7.62 x 51mm and 5.56 x 45mm rounds, both of which were designed in the USA.* Some commentators have even seen in this the root of the problems with the current service rifle, the L85A2, which was originally designed for a short-lived 4.85mm round.

The search for the optimum military cartridge has been under way since the invention of smokeless powder more than a century ago. Many authorities in the early 1900s championed 6.5mm or 7mm (the 7 x 57mm Mauser being a particular favourite), but decisions taken by those who were concerned only with long-range striking power ensured that rifle cartridges issued in the armies of the Big Five – the USA, Russia, Britain, France and Germany – did not drop under 0.300in-calibre until recent times. The lessons of the First World War, and many subsequent studies suggesting that combat range rarely exceeded

---

* The root of this controversy is sometimes seen in the US rejection of the British 0.280in round in the late 1940s, at a time when the US Army was unwilling to accept any cartridge that offered substantially less power than the 0.30in M1906

400 metres, were simply ignored by high-rankers with the power to ensure that they had no effect on tactical doctrines.

This the Germans changed in the Second World War, with the introduction of the short 7.9mm assault-rifle cartridge. The Soviets followed almost immediately, but the US Army stead-fastly refused to compromise when the British produced an 0.280in round in the 1940s. Ironically, the ballistic properties of the 0.280in were not dissimilar to those of the 7 x 57mm Mauser. It was a surprise, therefore, particularly after forcing the 0.30in T65E3 cartridge on NATO, when the US Army suddenly backed the 0.223in/5.56mm round and the lightweight AR-15.

The earliest rifles, soon reclassified as XM-16, were tested extensively in Vietnam in the early 1960s. There, the slow 1-in-14 rifling twist promoted horrible wounds that sometimes shocked even the firers. Though still satisfying the Geneva Convention, which accepted nothing less than a fully metal-jacketed projectile, the bullet from the 5.56mm cartridge operated on the limits of stability and was found to cartwheel when it struck the target, inflicting an inordinate amount of tissue damage.

Once the rifles were tested in arctic conditions, however, accuracy deteriorated to unacceptable levels. This forced a change to 1-in-12 rifling and, ultimately, the acceptance of a Belgian-designed cartridge. This was undoubtedly a better compromise, but the extraordinary wounding capacity of the original US cartridge was lost. The eventual adoption of 1-in-7 rifling subsequently restored much of the hitting efficiency, apparently by increasing the rotational velocity of the bullet to a point where it begins to fly apart on striking the target.

This story simply highlights the fact that cartridge design is inevitably a compromise, and that no single cartridge can possibly satisfy all the roles in which it is used. The needs of each class of weapon are different – for example a handgun, which is used only at very short range, must drop an assailant as rapidly as possible whilst a rifle bullet must retain sufficient striking power at long range.

Theoretically, military ammunition must conform to the Geneva Convention; in practice, terrorists and fanatics cannot (and, indeed, do not) subscribe to such restrictions, and most soldiers know that soft- or hollow-point bullets create far greater wound cavities. They also give much greater kinetic shock than standard jacketed patterns, which often simply pass through tissue to continue on their journey with energy only slightly diminished.

There is little doubt that commercial hollow-point ammunition has been used in the former Yugoslavia, as many wounds have borne silent witness. There is also no doubt that men of the special forces – faced with the need to make rapid kills with the least possible commotion – will also use non-standard bullets if necessary.

A favourite method used in the past has been to load revolver cartridges with wadcutter projectiles, or simply to reverse conventional bullets in their cases. Though these expedients greatly reduce effective range, the projectiles have a tremendous stopping effect in relation to comparatively low penetration.

Many studies have shown that, to give sufficiently high levels of hydrostatic or kinetic shock,* a projectile has to be travelling at 2,000ft/sec or more. This is regularly achieved in the modern assault-rifle cartridges, but eludes virtually all standard pistols. Attempts have been made to rectify this deficiency with special designs such as the Glaser Safety Slug, whose bullet contains metal shot set in a polymer matrix. The projectile case supposedly ruptures on striking the target, allowing the shot to scatter. Alternatively, cartridges such as the French Très Haute

---

* Descriptions of hydrostatic shock are based on the theory that a vessel containing liquid will rupture at the weakest point when an attempt to compress the liquid is made As the human body is largely liquid, so the argument goes, damage arising from hydrostatic shock may occur when it is struck by a high-velocity bullet. Kinetic or sonic shock occurs when a rapidly moving bullet imparts energy to tissue, causing the wound cavity to expand momentarily to many times the volume of the final wound channel and create a temporary vacuum into which air flows rapidly. Though the effects are very short-lived, the pressure is so great that organs may rupture some distance away from the point of strike.

Velocité (THV), loaded with lightweight projectiles moving at very high speed, are designed to penetrate the body armour from which a Glaser Slug may simply bounce.

Attention has regularly been drawn to the unsuitability of many conventional tests conducted on ballistic gelatine chosen because of its supposed similarity to flesh. Assessments of permanent and temporary wound cavities mean very little if, as can often happen, a slow-moving handgun bullet is prevented from expanding by a layer or two of clothing plugging its nose cavity.

The arguments will doubtless continue to rage; some US Army experts argued for many years that the 0.45in pistol cartridge was too powerful to use to train inexperienced recruits, and others averred that 0.45in was the minimum calibre permissible in a military handgun, Now that the 9mm Parabellum cartridge has been substituted, the FBI and others are realising that the efficiency of full metal-jacket projectiles declines in direct relation to reduction in calibre, and that excessive penetration is no substitute for stopping power. The most important contributor to the latter is bullet design, not calibre or velocity. The theoretically feeble lead-bulletted 0.22in rimfire is a much more effective hitter than the 0.25in ACP loaded with a jacketed bullet, whereas a jacketed 0.45in ACP is far inferior to a 9mm Parabellum hollow-point.

Boat-tailed, or streamlined bullets offer considerably better performance at long range (compare the flat-base 0.30in M2 bullet in the Garand and the boat-tail sS pattern in the FG. 42). The heavier boat-tailed US 0.30in M1 bullet will carry up to 2,000 yards farther than the M2. In the 1920s, British trials showed the maximum range of the Swiss M11 cartridge – with a boat-tail bullet weighing 174 grains – to be 4,457m at an elevation of 34° 42'.

Other maximum ranges include 1,600yd for the 9mm Parabellum and 1,640yd for the 0.45in ACP (when fired in short-barrel pistols), 2,200yd for the US 0.30in M1 Carbine cartridge, and 7,275yd for the 0.50in AP M2 in the Browning machine-gun.

If the performance of the 7.62 x 51mm bullet at 1,000 metres is taken as an example, the muzzle velocity of 840m/sec has dropped to only 310m/sec when the striking point is reached. To hit the target requires that the gun barrel must be elevated to a little under one degree; however, as the maximum height of the trajectory is no less than 5.46m above the line of sight, there is a considerable 'safe distance' in which a man will not be struck – permitting covering or 'overhead' fire when required.

Owing to the effects of air resistance, the trajectory is asymmetrical and the bullet drops at an appreciably sharper angle (1° 40') than it rises. As a result, the vertex or 'high point' of the trajectory lies at 583m rather than the 500-metre midway point. The difficulties of hitting moving targets at long range are implicit in the flight-time, as a little over two seconds elapse before the bullet strikes the target. If the range is doubled, to 2,000 metres, the flight-time is almost 6½ seconds. For the smaller 5.56mm bullet, the time to 1,000 metres is comparable with that of the 7.62mm pattern; at 2,000 metres, however, the 5.56mm takes 2 seconds longer than the latter to reach the target.

Very few non-shooters can visualise what can be expected of a modern submachine-gun or assault rifle. For the purposes of *Guns of the Elite*, therefore, shooting results were obtained from a number of guns. These show that most modern rifles will place approximately half the shots inside a 2-inch diameter circle at 100 yards; at 200 yards, the average is nearer 6 inches; and, at 500, somewhere between 12 and 20 inches. Though these sound quite impressive, it must be remembered that many shots lie outside the mean diameter – in some cases, surprisingly far away. This means that, at 500 yards, a few stray individual shots may lie *4 feet* away from the group-centre.

The inherent inaccuracy of the gun/cartridge combination is also affected by the efficiency of sights that may be sturdy rather than sophisticated. Many modern rifles have fixed aperture-type battle sights in which the aperture has to be large enough to accommodate a variety of users. This, however, may allow any one user's eye to wander and the aim to vary. Generally, few concessions are made to range apart from providing a rocking-'L' with two or more settings. The open tangent-leaf AK and AKM back sights are notably coarse, particularly compared with the adjustable rotary pattern on the Heckler & Koch rifles or the adjustable aperture of the M16A2. Thus, it is easier to shoot the H&K G41 accurately than the AKM, even though there could be little to choose between the rifles if they were to be fired from a fixed rest.

Although the 5.56mm rifles do not appear to show much advantage over the 7.62 x 39mm Warsaw Pact rivals as far as accuracy is concerned, the looping trajectory associated with the AKM and the vz/58 hinder range-gauging. At 400 yards, with the sights set for 250, the 5.56mm M193 bullet strikes about 18 inches below the aim-point, the muzzle velocity of 3,100ft/sec having declined to 1,550ft/sec. For the standard M43 Russian cartridge, the figures are about 36in, 2,325ft/sec and 1,050ft/sec respectively. The full-power 7.62mm NATO cartridge returns about 20in, 2,820ft/sec and 2,035ft/sec, showing no real trajectory advantage over the lightweight faster-moving 5.56mm bullet, but retaining much more striking energy – 980ft-lb compared with about 145ft-lb at 600 yards.

The sniper rifles, of course, shoot appreciably better than assault rifles. To illustrate the performance of the modern semi-automatic rifle in greater detail, Heckler & Koch very kindly supplied three series of 3 x 10 shots fired with a 5.56mm G41, a 7.62mm G3 and a 7.62mm PSG-1 sniper rifle. Each rifle used in the tests was fitted with an optical sight, and was fired from a wrist-rest.*

> *5.56mm Gewehr 41 Zf:* mean radius 10.3mm (0.406in) at 100m. The farthest shot lay 30.3mm (1.19in) from the centre. Thus, all thirty shots would have been contained in a 61mm circle.

---

* The targets were analysed on the statistically-acceptable principles expounded by the author in *The Pistol Book* (Arms & Armour Press, 1983).

7.62mm Gewehr 3 Zf: mean radius 13.2mm (0.520in) at 100m. The farthest shot lay 28.8mm (1.13in) from the centre. All thirty shots would have lain inside a 57mm circle, though fewer struck near the centre than in the G41 trial.

7.62mm Präzisions Scharfschutzen-Gewehr 1 (PSG-1): mean radius 6.9mm (0.271in) at 100m. The farthest shot lay 15.4mm from the centre, and all thirty would have struck within a circle measuring 31mm – an impressive performance.

Although the chances of hitting a static target may seem reasonable enough, particularly when the rifle is fitted with optical sights, movement introduces another dimension. The 7.62 x 51mm NATO SS77 bullet takes 0.77 seconds to cover 500 metres; at this range, a man walking at 5km/hr will have moved 1.08 metres (a little over 40 inches); a running man will have moved more than twice this distance, and a calculation must be made mentally to 'lead' the target with the sights. And, if the man is also zigzagging, the chances of a hit reduce still more.

Consequently, having approached as near to the target as they dare, snipers wait until they have a static shot; the special CTW forces, by and large, attempt to get to close quarters, where the first shots can be made to count by minimising the firer/target distance.

Appendix 2

Optical Sight Lens Problems

Astigmatism is simply an inability to focus lines that cross each other at widely diverging angles. Focusing on chicken-wire or similar diagonal-link fences will often reveal if the strands running in one direction are as clear as those running in another. If no difference can be detected, then there is minimal astigmatism in the lens system. Sights of this type may be labelled 'anastigmatic'.

Chromatic aberration arises from the inability of a lens to focus light rays at a single point. Ordinary 'white' light is composed of a rainbow in which the wavelength (and hence focal length) of each component differs; if the lens is badly corrected, a blurred image with a coloured corona or 'halo' may be visible. Sandwiches of thin glass are used to unify focus, each diffracting or 'bending' a portion of the light at a different angle. If the image is properly focused and no obvious coloured halo or corona effects are visible around small objects, the lens system has been corrected satisfactorily for chromatic aberration. It will usually be marked 'achromatic'.

Coma occurs when a lens, unable to focus light passing through it obliquely, 'smears' an image outward towards the edges.

Field curvature arises when elements in the lens system, particularly the erector components, produce an image with blurred edges and a pin-sharp centre – or, conversely, a blurred centre with crystal clear margins.

Field of view results solely from dividing the angle of view by magnification. An enormous objective lens contributes little to performance unless the eye-piece lens is also enlarged. Too restricted a view makes target acquisition difficult; this has little importance in shooting at static targets, but the same cannot be said of combat and it is vital to find a compromise. Variable-magnification or 'zoom' sights are greatly favoured, as they allow a single sight to be used under a variety of conditions, but it must be remembered that the field of view declines as magnification rises. At 100 yards, the field of a sight of this type drops from 41ft at 3x to only 15ft at 9x; the field of view of an 8–40 x 56 sight is merely 2.6ft at the highest power.

Image distortion occurs when the lenses have been ground so poorly that parts of the image may seem twisted or bent. Focusing on a brick wall or similar grid-like pattern in the middle distance will show whether horizontal and vertical lines are straight, and whether they focus sharply across the entire field of view simultaneously. If the sight passes this examination, the chances are that its lenses have been adequately corrected for coma, field-curvature and image distortion. Sights of this type are often termed 'orthoscopic'.

Magnification is simply the relationship between the size of the object seen through the sight compared with that seen with the naked eye. The true magnification can sometimes be gauged by keeping the second eye open and comparing the two images, but this is an unsatisfactory method. Alternatively, a piece of thin paper can be placed over the eyepiece of a sight pointed at a bright light. As the paper is drawn backwards, the circle of light diminishes until it reaches a minimum and then begins to grow. This establishes the eye-point – the optimum distance at which the eye should be placed – and the sight aperture, which is the diameter of the circle of light at its smallest point. Magnification can be calculated by dividing the sight aperture into the diameter of the objective lens, though this can give a slightly false figure.

Relative Brightness. The limited ability of the human eye ensures that all sights will perform adequately as long as the diameter of the objective lens exceeds 12mm. Large-diameter objectives make no different to resolution of detail, assuming magnification remains unchanged, though they do offer greatly improved transmission of light. To determine the relative brightness of a particular sight, the result of dividing the effective diameter of the objective lens by the sight aperture is simply squared. If a 6x telescope sight has an objective lens diameter of 40mm and a sight aperture of 5mm (see *Magnification*), then its relative brightness is 64. Transmission of light is limited by the iris in the human eye, which adjusts automatically to ambient light. But iris diameter rarely exceeds 3mm in daylight and, therefore, any relative brightness greater than 9–10 is wasted: at dusk, conversely, the iris can expand to a little over 5mm for an optimal relative brightness of 25–30. Some large-objective sights may provide relative brightnesses as great as 100, allowing the eye to see detail in conditions where ambient light is insufficient to satisfy even the fully-opened iris.

Resolution of any lens in a small-diameter telescope is limited by the performance of the human eye. A normal eye can resolve detail as fine as a minute of arc, one sixtieth of one degree. To find the potential acuity of the eye when presented with a magnified image, therefore, the minute of arc is simply divided by the true magnification: a 4x sight would improve the resolution to a quarter of a minute of arc (15 seconds of arc).

Spherical aberration is caused by light rays from the outer margins of the lens focusing ahead of those from the centre, blurring the image. Though this can be minimised by accurate grinding, the work must not disturb essential colour correction. Lenses have been corrected for spherical aberration if all the differing parts of the image focus simultaneously when adjustments are made. Sights of this type are generally known as 'aplanatic'.

Bibliography

Anon.: *Report of the Special Subcommittee of the M-16 Rifle Program*, Deutschland Ordnance, Santa Clara, California, 1968 (reprint of US government documents)

Baer, Ludwig: *Die leichten Waffen der deutschen Armeen, 1841–1945*, Journal-Verlag Schwend GmbH, Schwäbisch Hall, 1976

Bolotin, David N.: *Sovetskoe Strelkovoe Oruzhiye*, Voennoe Izdatelstvo, Moscow, 1988

—— *Soviet Small-Arms and Ammunition*, Finnish Arms Museum Foundation, Hyvinkää, 1995

Cook, Chris, and Stevenson, John: *The Atlas of Modern Warfare*, Weidenfeld & Nicholson, London, 1978

Craig, William: *Enemy at the Gates: The Battle for Stalingrad*, Hodder & Stoughton, London, 1973

Datig, Fred A.: *Soviet Russian Postwar Military Pistols & Cartridges, 1945–1986*, Handgun Press, Glenview, Illinois, 1988

Dewar, [Colonel] Michael: *The British Army in Northern Ireland*, Arms & Armour Press, London, 1985

—— *War in the Streets*, David & Charles, Newton Abbot, 1992

—— *Weapons & Equipment of Counter-Terrorism*, Arms & Armour Press, London, 1987

Dobson, C., and Payne, R.: *The Weapons of Terror: International Terrorism at Work*, Macmillan, London, 1979

Dugelby, Thomas B.: *EM-2 Concept & Design: A Rifle Ahead of Its Time*, Collector Grade Publications, Toronto, 1980

—— *Modern Military Bullpup Rifles*, Collector Grade Publications, Toronto, 1984

Eshel, David: *Elite Fighting Units*, Arco Publishing, New York, 1984

Ezell, Edward C.: *The Great Rifle Controversy*, Stackpole Books, Harrisburg, Pennsylvania, 1985

—— *The AK-47 Story*, Stackpole Books, Harrisburg, Pennsylvania, 1985

—— *Small Arms Today: Latest Reports on the World's Weapons and Ammunition*, Stackpole Books, Harrisburg, Pennsylvania; 2nd edition, 1988

—— (ed.) *Small Arms of the World*, Stackpole Books, Harrisburg, Pennsylvania; 12th edition, 1984

Ferguson, Tom (Jack Lewis, ed.): *Modern Law Enforcement Weapons & Tactics*, DBI Books, Inc., Northbrook, Illinois; 2nd edition, 1991

Fowler, Will: *The World's Elite Forces: Arms and Equipment* (Greenhill Military Manuals), Greenhill Books, London, 2001

Geraghty, Tony: *Who Dares Wins*, Arms & Armour Press, London, 1980

—— *This is the SAS*, Arms & Armour Press, London, 1982

Götz, Hans-Dieter: *Die deutschen Militargewehre und Maschinenpistolen 1871–1945*, Motor-Buch Verlag, Stuttgart, 1974

Hatcher, [Major General] Julian S.: *The Book of the Garand*, The Gun Room Press, Highland Park, New Jersey, 1977

Hogg, Ian V.: *Ammunition* (Greenhill Military Manuals), Greenhill Books, London, 1998

—— *Counter-Terrorism Equipment* (Greenhill Military Manuals), Greenhill Books, London; reprinted edition, 2001

—— (ed.): *Jane's Infantry Weapons*, Macdonald & Jane's, London, published annually

—— *Military Pistols & Revolvers*, Arms & Armour Press, London, 1987

—— (John Walter, ed.) *Small Arms: Pistols and Rifles* (Greenhill Military Manuals), Greenhill Books, London; revised edition, 2003

—— *Submachine Guns* (Greenhill Military Manuals), Greenhill Books, London, 2001

—— *The World's Sniping Rifles* (Greenhill Military Manuals), Greenhill Books, London, 1998

—— and John S. Weeks: *Military Small Arms of the 20th Century*, Krause Publications, Iola, Wisconsin; 7th edition, 2000

—— and John S. Weeks (John Walter, ed.): *Pistols of the World*, Krause Publications, Iola, Wisconsin; 4th edition, 2004

Johnson, Melvin M., and Haven, Charles T.: *Automatic Arms: Their History, Development and Use*, William Morrow, New York, 1941

Labbett, Peter: *Military Small Arms Ammunition of the World, 1945–1980*, Arms & Armour Press, London, 1980

Ladd, James D.: *Inside the Commandos*, Arms & Armour Press, London, 1984

Leasor, James: *Green Beach*, William Heinemann, London, 1975

Lewis, Jack (ed.): *Handguns '92*, DBI Books, Northbrook, Illinois, 1991

Long, Duncan: *Assault Pistols, Rifles and Submachine Guns*, Paladin Press, Boulder, Colorado, 1986

—— *Combat Ammunition*, Paladin Press, Boulder, Colorado, 1986

Macdonald, Peter: *The SAS in Action*, Sidgwick & Jackson, London, 1990

Markham, George [John Walter]: *Guns of the Elite* ('Special Forces Firearms, 1940 to the Present'), Arms & Armour Press, London; 2nd edition, 1995

—— *Guns of the Empire: Firearms of the British Soldier, 1837–1987*, Arms & Armour Press, London, 1990

Millar, George: *The Bruneval Raid*, The Bodley Head, London, 1974

Mullin, T. J.: *Special Operations Weapons and Tactics*, Greenhill Books, London, 2003

Musgrave, Daniel D., and Nelson, Thomas B.: *The World's Assault Rifles & Automatic Carbines*, TBN Enterprises, Alexandria, Virginia, *c.* 1969

Nelson, Thomas B., and Lockhoven, Hans-Bert: *The World's Submachine Guns (Machine Pistols)*, Vol. I, TBN Enterprises, Alexandria, Virginia, *c.* 1964

Parrish, Thomas (ed.): *The Encyclopedia of World War II*, Secker & Warburg, London, 1978

Paxton, John (ed.): *The Statesman's Year Book*, various editions, Macmillan, London; published annually

Rivers, Gayle: *The Specialist: The Personal Story of an Elite Specialist in Covert Operations*, Sidgwick & Jackson, London, 1985

Ryan, Cornelius: A *Bridge Too Far*, Hamish Hamilton, London, 1974

Robinson, Mike: *Fighting Skills of the SAS*, Sidgwick & Jackson, 1991

Smith, Graham (ed.): *Weapons of the Gulf War*, Salamander Books, London, 1991

Stevens, R. Blake: *North American FALs: NATO's Search for a Standard Rifle*, Collector Grade Publications, Toronto, Canada, 1981

—— *UK and Commonwealth FALs*, Collector Grade Publications, Toronto, Canada, 1983,

—— and Ezell, Edward C.: *The Black Rifle: M16 Retrospective*, Collector Grade Publications, Toronto, Canada, 1987

—— and van Rutten, Jean E.: *The Metric FAL: The Free World's Right Arm*, Collector Grade Publications, Toronto, Canada, 1985

Skennerton, Ian: *The British Service Lee*, Arms & Armour Press, London; 2nd edition, 1990

Swearengen, Thomas F.: *The World's Fighting Shotguns*, TBN Enterprises, Alexandria, Virginia, 1978

Thompson, Julian: *No Picnic: 3 Commando Bridge In the South Atlantic, 1982*, Leo Cooper/Secker & Warburg, London, 1985

Thompson, Leroy: *Combat Handguns* (Greenhill Military Manuals), Greenhill Books, London, 2004

—— *Combat Shotguns* (Greenhill Military Manuals), Greenhill Books, London, 2002

—— and Chappell, Michael: *Uniforms of the Elite Forces*, Blandford Press, Poole, 1982

—— and René Smeets: *Great Combat Handguns*, Arms & Armour Press, London; 2nd edition, 1993

Wahl, Paul: *Carbine Handbook: The Complete Manual and Guide to the US Carbine, Cal. .30, M1*, Arco Publishing, New York, 1974

Walter, John D.: *Kalashnikov* (Greenhill Military Manuals), Greenhill Books, London; reprinted edition, 2002

—— *Modern Machine-guns* (Greenhill Military Manuals), Greenhill Books, London, 2000

—— *Modern Military Rifles* (Greenhill Military Manuals), Greenhill Books, London, 2001

—— *Rifles of the World*, Krause Publications, Iola, Wisconsin; 2nd edition, 1998

—— *The Pistol Book*, Arms & Armour Press, London; second edition, 1988

—— *The Rifle Book*, Arms & Armour Press, London, 1990

—— *The World's Elite Forces: Small Arms & Accessories* (Greenhill Military Manuals), Greenhill Books, London, 2002

Zhuk, Aleksandr B.: *Strelkovoe Oruzhie*, Voenno Izdatelstvo, Moscow; revised edition, 1992

—— (John Walter. ed.): *The Illustrated Encyclopedia of Handguns*, Greenhill Books, London, 1995

Index

Page numbers in italic refer to illustrations